Advance Praise

It's a fabulous journey through geographical spaces in Durban, in Africa, England, Europe, Asia and Australia. A wonderfully rich if somewhat difficult life.
Uma Dhupelia-Mesthrie, author & editor of *From Cane Fields to Freedom*.

Alongside the unprecedented state of the world, what better time to read this rolling and inspiring life story. I found it detailed and open hearted.
Hazel Carey, author of *Ubuntu: My Life in Other People*

This is an honest and riveting biography of Bala Mudaly, a Durban born son of a working-class family, growing up under apartheid. This book is a valuable addition to the growing body of literature on the experiences of second generation descended of Indian indentured workers.
Omar Badsha, *Founder & CEO of South African History Online*

'This is a remarkable memoir pulling the reader into Mudaly's recollections while reliving with him the harsh reality of segregation in South Africa, reminding us all of the constant struggles between races, past and present. It's as thoughtful as it is thought-provoking, full of insight, resilience and reflection.'
SC Karakaltsas, author of *A Perfect Stone*

Colour-Coated Identity:
A Journey Beyond Racial Divides

Bala Mudaly

A Memoir

Tale

Some names and identifying details have been omitted or changed to protect the privacy of individuals.

Names of population groups and places in South Africa are used consistent with historical periods. So too are slangs and local references.

Copyright: Every effort has been made to trace copyright holders or use works in the public domain

First Published 2021
Copyright © 2021 Bala Mudaly
All rights reserved.

National Library of Australia Cataloguing-in-Publication entry:
Creator: Mudaly, Bala, author.
Title: Colour-Coated Identity: A Journey Beyond Racial Divides
ISBN: 978-0-6480386-9-6
Subjects: Memoir

Tale Publishing
Melbourne Victoria

Contents

Foreword i

Introduction 1

Part 1: Under a South African Sky (1938 – 1963)
A Recollection of Childhood 5
Primary School Years 13
High school years 40
University Life and Challenges 50

Part 2: Breaking Through the Apartheid Barrier
Zambia (January 1964 – December 1967) 74
Britain (February 1968 – 1 June 1969) 102
Stratheden Hospital 106
Overland to Ancestral India 125

Part 3: Back in Apartheid South Africa (1969 – 1988)
167

Part 4: Becoming Australian
First Hurdles 221
First and Only Empoyment 223
First and only Home 225
Orientation to Indigenous Peoples 228
Australian Red Cross Volunteer 240
ANC Support Group 244
Amnesty International Australia 249
Feeling Australian 253

Part 5: Visits to South Africa as an Outsider   256

Concluding Thoughts   264
Family Photo 1953   270

References   271
Acronyms   274
Chronology   275
Acknowledgements   276

Appendix: The Shaping of Identity – Other Influences
Landscapes, Memory and Me   280
A Life Lived in South African Books and Writings   293

'Not everything that is faced can be changed, but nothing can be changed until it is faced.' **James Baldwin**.

'Let us unite, not in spite of our differences, but through them. For differences can never be wiped away, and life would be so much poorer without them. Let all human races keep their own personalities, and yet come together, not in a uniformity that is dead, but in a unity that is living.' **Rabindranath Tagore, China 1924.**

Dedication

To the many good people who populate
my lifetime of memories

Foreword

There are too many memoirs of the 'then this happened, then that happened' variety without the elements of subtlety and surprise in the telling and with insights that stretch beyond the details of the case of one life. This stunning life story by Bala Mudaly, *Colour-Coated Identity*, offers exactly that which is so often missing in the post-apartheid memoir---novelty, nuance and the bigger story about coming to terms with identity, history, politics and place. What a thoroughly enjoyable read.

How should one understand the place of the Indian South African in an African country settled by Europeans and which for more than three centuries was governed by an ideology of white supremacy? It is not as if prominent intellectuals such as Betty Govinden or Ronnie Govender have not taken on this question in literature or Goolam Vahed and Ashwin Desai in the social sciences. What Mudaly does, however, is to account for that intriguing question through the literal and metaphorical journey of his own life as a South African of Indian ancestry.

That journey starts with a vivid description of the entangled life of a Tamil family in the coastal city of Durban. The devastating impact of the family's upheaval from Cato Manor to make place for whites is held in tension with the striking beauty of the Bluff that remains etched into the author's memory. The Tamil literature and language in the home co-exists with childhood literatures of the English world (Fitzpatrick's *Jock of the Bushveld*) in his education. The awkward interaction with whites at Indian weddings happens in the context of the unrelenting segregation of the races. The bussing of Indian school children to welcome English royalty with flags and song (God save our gracious King) unfolds against the backdrop of a growing black nationalism (including the Natal Indian Congress) in the city. The anti-Indian riots of 1949 by Zulu factions find the family home protected by a Zulu compatriot. All of these events shape the consciousness of a young Bala Mudaly—and sets the stage for the next step in his journey.

After training at the University College of Fort Hare and the University of Natal, the author decides to find work as a teacher in rural Zambia and later in Lusaka, the capital city. It is a difficult journey and one that scars him physically as the result of a car accident. Yet it is also a time of learning about politics and the frontline states, including a memorable meeting with the impressive ANC leader, Oliver Tambo. As will happen often in his long journey, Mudaly returns home to touch base with family and friends before the next departure. Each return opens his eyes to what South Africa is and what it has become.

It is time again to leave and he finds himself in a dreary London waiting for the papers that allow for travel and employment. The loneliness eats away at the young psychologist but eventually an opportunity comes his way to work at a hospital in an isolated area of Scotland in less than glamorous circumstances. From there his journey continues through Europe on his way to the family's ancestral land of India. Like all South Africans of Indian ancestry who make the journey, there are emotions of belonging and not belonging as the reality of an African identity kicks in. In Chennai, the story about the competing loves of two sisters is sad and funny as the young psychologist wonders openly about the possibilities. It is time to once again make the journey back home. From the vantage point of the docking ship, there is a new perspective on Durban.

As in every leg of his transcontinental journey, there is a narrative thread of hardship as an outsider in a foreign country and as an outsider in his own country. A prized (if delayed) registration with the South African Medical and Dental Council (SAMDC) is no guarantee of a job as the country's first "non-white" psychologist. The struggle and frustration are felt on every level but eventually some work opportunity opens up. After a while, it is time to travel again, this time to Australia where the intense loneliness and sense of dislocation bite again. Eventually, a comfortable job is found, and the author settles in Australia for more than 30 years through retirement. There is, of course, the return trips to a changing South Africa. The country has changed but so has Bala Mudaly.

It is the searing honesty of the writing that first gripped me. The *kaffir boom* is called by its disturbing name. The racial nicknames of apartheid are used without flinching

(African, Coloured, Indian, White) and with some unsettling descriptions of some of the characters so named. The traumatic account of Black apartheid constables chasing another Black man towards a drowning death in a Durban lake is relayed as fact.

Without preaching, Mudaly demonstrates how he changes and how his life is enriched through a long and difficult journey in which nothing could be taken for granted and everything was a struggle. With each step in his journey, he grows. Moments of ethnic chauvinism give way to enduring commitments of interracial solidarity in the broader struggle for human liberation. At the end of a moving and compelling story, the author arrives at his desired destination as captured in the apt subtitle of the book: *A journey beyond racial divides*.

More than 25 years since the end of legal apartheid, and in the middle of a pandemic, *Colour-Coated Identity*, is a story South Africa so desperately needs right now.

Jonathan D Jansen
Stellenbosch University
August 2020

Introduction

He's on his last lap. The euphemism favoured by my father when referring to someone he believed would soon *kick the bucket* (another favoured expression). He is now long gone, and I am in my eighties. As a migrant to Australia, I have been away from South Africa, the land of my birth, for more than thirty years. For a while now I have been preoccupied with mining my memories - recalling, reflecting, and writing. The consequent outcome is a testimony to my life and times, making sense of who I truly am. '*Understanding memory,*' says Patti Miller, an authority on the genre of life-writings, '*goes to the heart of who we are as human beings – uncertain and changing in form as clouds in motion*' (The Memoir Book, 2007)

This memoir is a composite structure, a myriad of personal vignettes, a set of extended themes reflecting and reminiscing on my life's journey as I learnt to negotiate the thorny path of a vexed and racialized world. I suggest that the person I am today, my largely cosmopolitan and egalitarian identity, was influenced and shaped, cumulatively, by many complex currents I encountered on the way. I have now a more realistic sense of who I am within the broader context of my contemporary world.

Undertaking this memoir has given me a rare opportunity to explore how the personal, political, and professional aspects converged to make a composite 'me'. In so doing, I have attempted to be fully present in the narration of my life story.

Part 1
Under a South African Sky (1938 – 1963)

We grew up knowing no other life and, later, accepting that we were powerless to change our lived world of segregation. Black muted protest from the fringes accounted for nothing-
Maya Angelou

A Recollection of Childhood

Come with me as I go exploring the uncertain and elusive landscape of my mind. I begin this journey in search of my earliest recollection in a world tainted by race and colour.

My sister, Kamla, and I are playing in the veranda of a two-roomed *outhouse* which my parents have rented. I'm about three years old - a few years younger than my sister. We are startled by a large man in an oversized coat who bolts past the house and across the rock-strewn vacant lot opposite. He keeps looking this way and that as he runs, crying 'Haibo! Haibo! (Oh no! Oh no!).' There is a lot of shouting from men in khaki uniforms rushing after him, wielding batons. The big man runs straight into the quarry lake. His head bobs up a few times, his hand reaching out. Then he disappears.

I collapse onto my knees screaming. Kamla calls out to my mother and drags me into the kitchen. 'Kaapi Thana Thay-hi,' I cry. 'Kaapi Thana Thay-hi.' I was a little slow in learning to speak, but my mother understands my garbled Tamil. She squats and hugs me, wiping away my tears with the end of her sari. 'So, you saw natives (black Africans) fighting, eh?' she says. 'You got frightened? My little baby.'

I feel consoled. But my sister is not that lucky as my mother scolds her for not getting me indoors straight away when the commotion happened.

'Come, come Amma, see many police at the water,' says Kamla undeterred. She is the curious one and rather eager not to miss any of the action. My mother (with me at her hip) steps onto the veranda, just as a body is lifted out of the lake, dangling like a large fish at the end of a line, dripping. My mother groans and turns away. My sister, frightened at the sight, sniffles and clings to my mother's side. But, fortunately, I cannot work out what I've seen.

Years later, when I spoke to my mother about this dreamlike recollection, she confirmed that a black man had drowned that day - pursued by black constables. 'I think he did something wrong,' she said. 'That's why the police chased after him.' I was not so sure. Even at the tender age of three, it seems, I had some awareness that my immediate world was also populated with people unlike us - black people who appeared much poorer than us, always seeking casual work or begging for food. Their presence would loom large in my consciousness over the years to come.

This shocking event had happened in 1941 in Cato Manor, a thirty-minute bus ride from the town centre, Durban. My family had relocated from Malvern in the rural outer fringes, to semi-developed Cato Manor a year earlier to be closer to my mother's family. The outbuilding they rented belonged to an uncle of my mother, Mr KM Gounden. He was a school principal. The outbuilding was at the rear of the main house in Booth Road, at the intersection with Bellair Road.

I remember Malvern as lush and hilly. The trains from Berea station to Malvern would take the bends carefully, and we would sway to the clickety-clacks. *Bundu*. That is what people called such relatively remote places. Indians who had completed their *indenture* acquired modest plots of land. They slogged long hours to clear the virgin bush and build sturdy houses with timber and iron sheets. They grew vegetables and planted fruit trees such as mango, pawpaw, banana, and avocado.

I was the second born, and my father was thrilled it was a son. My sister had come two years earlier in 1936. Consistent with tradition, my father, also being the eldest son, was expected to remain in his parental home after marriage. His mother had died years earlier. In my collection of forgotten archives of photos, there is a remarkable one of her in death. Dignified and in deep repose. I wonder what would have prompted someone to take this photo. Remarkable, considering that a box camera would have been a rare and expensive item in those early days for people of limited means.

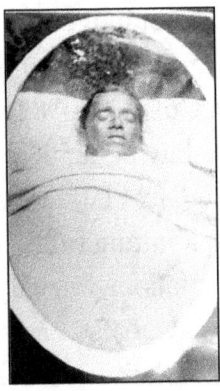

Grandmother

My grandfather's house was a flat-roofed wood and iron building – almost as if it were knocked together over a weekend with a few helping hands. It is a mystery, however, how my grandfather (enticed from India by the British under its questionable indentured labour scheme) had come by this piece of real estate, having been, in his later working life, a mere clerical hand in the railways. According to my mother's narrative it was a challenge for her to move there as a naïve newlywed bride of nineteen. There was no piped water and no electricity. And the pit toilet among mango trees was a nightmare. Spiders and crazed bottle-green flies claimed it as their special haunt.

My father smiled sheepishly when she told us in Cato Manor, years later, about kneeling on the floor to cook over an improvised wood fire:

'My eyes and nose running and burning very bad. I'm coughing and coughing. Just then your father comes rushing from work and sees me like this. He's very ashamed and worried for me.'

'But I took you away from there, didn't I? Didn't I?' he'd plead so that we'd not judge him too harshly.

Durban, (named after Sir Benjamin D'Urban, a British Governor of the Cape Colony in 1836) was in the 1930s an impressive little town, having achieved city status in 1931. It had a Victorian style City Hall and a natural harbour well protected by the Bluff, a jutting ridge of land. It also boasted a whaling station and a labour-intensive sugar industry. My father told us that one day he had crossed the bay by ferry to the whaling station at the foot of the Bluff and bought a small parcel of whale meat. 'Because why?' Kamla asked. 'Wait I tell you. You see my friend, Ramdas, he gave whale meat to his wife for bad chest.' Hence, my father was convinced that whale meat would cure my younger brother's troublesome asthma. I am not sure if it ever did. But my mother had the unenviable task of making it palatable.

The largely impoverished indigenous black population lived in shack settlements on the fringes of the city, while hundreds of Indians employed by the municipality and in the railways were housed in congested sub-standard cluster units called barracks - Railway Barracks and Magazine Barracks. The merchant-class Indians provided for themselves. Racial segregation was still very much in place being the established practice of the British at the level of state and local governments. It was the standard policy of the Union of South Africa, a merger in 1910 of two British colonies and two Boer Republics. Segregation was entrenched in legislations.

From memory as a primary school kid, I recall going often into town with my father. Durban (known as *eThekwini* in indigenous Zulu, or *Durbs* by upcountry visitors) was clean and posh, especially the financial and commercial hub which included West, Smith and Field Streets, with the key landmarks being the impressive colonial style post office with a clock tower, the city hall and the central train station. Whites had a monopoly over this complex both as customers, employees, and business owners. However, prosperous Indians (mostly economic migrants from Indian states such as Gujarat had established thriving shops and market stalls a little away from the white section. This part was called the *Grey Street complex*, dominated by Grey, Victoria, and Prince Edward Streets, but also spreading towards the Grayville Racecourse. This area became as familiar to me as the back of my hand. Some called this part of Durban *the casbah*.

I am not aware of Blacks or Coloureds (descendants of Whites cohabiting with both imported slaves and indigenous peoples such as the San, Koi-San, Xhosa, Zulu) owning businesses at the time. The thriving success of many small Indian businesses was a direct result of impoverished working-class Blacks, Coloureds and Indians compelled to shop here with no other cheaper options. Poorer Indians were employed as shop assistants while Blacks had more menial jobs such as cleaners and barrow boys – loading and off-loading goods and provisions from vehicles.

My grandfather (my mother's father) once leased a kiosk at the municipal market in Victoria Street. One busy Christmas, my mother sent me to help him. The kiosk was cramped, with room for one person only – standing! My grandfather mostly sold standard-sized loaves of bread, tobacco and cheap sweets which were displayed on a long white enamel counter-tray, accessible to customers from the outside. This metal tray, when drawn up like a draw bridge (at closing time), served as a shutter which sealed off the kiosk.

The customers were almost all black people. At Christmas they would be rushing back to their traditional rural villages to be with family. My grandfather in his late 60s, was a fierce and impatient man. He got me standing on the pavement just outside the kiosk and under his watchful eye. I was instructed to keep calling out to passing Blacks (spruiking) to buy our stuff. 'Woza, woza. Ukuthenga isinkwa, nogway. Ushibhile kakhulu.' (Come, come. Buy our bread and tobacco. Very cheap). I found the task frighteningly hard and exhausting. And I got the Zulu (local black language) words all muddled as my tongue would not cooperate. My grandfather simply glared at me. When lunchtime came, he dismissed me with bus fare to go home.

Central Durban is now a totally different place. It has become a congested, garbage-strewn, and run-down city. Vacant and shuttered shops are to be seen. Others are now run by recent migrants and refugees (labelled as *foreigners*) from such places as Pakistan, China, Nigeria, Sudan, and from countries closer to South Africa like Zimbabwe, Malawi, Zambia, and Mozambique. The pavements are taken over by impoverished black informal street traders eking out a living. Mothers and grandmothers are mostly the ones who persist as informal traders – always stoic and dignified. Young black men, mostly unemployed and disaffected, take to crime. A much easier way to make a quick buck!

Coloured, Indian and Whites are wary of shopping in the city centre. Almost all the Indian families, who had once occupied flats above the shops they owned, have fled to the relative safety of suburbs on the fringes of the greater-metro region. Many large financial and commercial houses, once the economic anchors of the CBD, have relocated. Squatters have moved in occupying and trashing several flats and multi-storey buildings especially along streets near Albert Park. There is talk of urban renewal. But this requires massive financial investment and enormous political will – both in rather short supply at present perhaps because of rampant corruption and financial mismanagement at all tiers of government.

Nothing particularly earth-shattering seems to have

happened in 1938, the year I was born, either in South Africa or overseas.

In the 1930s, most ordinary folks like my parents, contending with more immediate everyday worries would, perhaps, have felt glad that the larger world in which they lived appeared reasonably settled. Memories of hardships endured during the catastrophic Great War of 1914-18 would be etched in their memories. So too the terror of the Spanish Flu, which seemed more deadly than the prevalent measles and tuberculosis.

Of course, the impression that the world had returned to peaceful ways was simply an illusion or so much wishful thinking. Now we know that, in fact, it was a period of ominous undercurrents which surfaced soon enough with painful consequences for generations to come. For instance, in South Africa while Jan Smuts and the United Party appeared to be in firm control, D. F. Malan and the secretive ultra-nationalistic *Afrikaner Broederbond* were forging ahead in creating a hard-line purified National Party to oust the pro-English centre-right government, while promoting the interests of the Afrikaner nation – the *Herrenvolk*. In Europe meanwhile, Hitler was in his ascendancy, and Neville Chamberlain, Prime Minister of Great Britain, in a moment of fatal weakness, attempted to appease Hitler by turning a blind eye to his invasion of Czechoslovakia. The resulting World War blighted almost the whole of humanity. But the British Empire remained largely intact, and the British Royals went about their business.

Primary School Years
1947 - 1954

In 1947 my school was caught up in the excitement of preparing for a royal visit. I was nine years old then. Posters of the Royal Family - King George VI, Queen Elizabeth and their daughters Elizabeth and Margaret - suddenly appeared in the classrooms. We were told that our Prime Minister Field Marshall General J.C. Smuts had invited them. We had already heard from our teachers that General Smuts had done brave things in World War II, and that he was a good friend of Britain and its Prime Minister, Winston Churchill. This was confusing because we learnt, at the same time, that he had fought like an enraged lion against the British in the Anglo-Boer War. I was quite puzzled. How could enemies remain good friends after serious fighting?

In later years, I learnt that the General had even participated in founding the United Nations and, in fact, was the architect of the Human Rights clause in the preamble of the Charter of the United Nations. How ironical then that Smuts, back in his home country, was a staunch supporter of *white supremacy*, the policy and practice of the British in all its overseas colonies. Ironic, too, that soon after the royal visit and at the height of his career, Smuts and his United

Party were soundly defeated in the national elections of 1948 by DF Malan and his Afrikaner Nationalist Party. But then this was not unusual since Churchill and his Conservative Party, too, had been voted out in a similar manner in 1945, at a time when he was internationally acclaimed for his dogged resistance to Hitler and the Nazi scourge – for saving Britain from invasion and ignominious occupation.

We were taught to sing *God Save the King* at morning school assembly. Our voices were raised in pride and discordant gusto. The teacher-conductor stood on the stairs at the rear of the school, waving his arms as if he were an accomplished maestro. We children clustered under shafts of morning sunlight, in a parched and sandy playground of the AYS State-Aided Primary School.

Even with limited means, the Indian community was resourceful enough in attempting to provide for itself, in addressing social, educational, cultural and health needs. The AYS primary school was built in Mayville (an extension of Cato Manor) essentially to serve Indian children from an orphanage, the Aryan Benevolent Home, located adjacent to the school, both the initiative of a public-spirited charity, the Arya Yuvak Sabha (AYS).

The school building was, in fact, a large hall built of timber and corrugated tin, subdivided into classrooms by moveable partitions that fell short of the ceiling. Moreover, there were no doors serving the classrooms, only doorways each the dimensions of a standard door. One may easily imagine the cacophony of voices that criss-crossed the hall creating a kind of managed pandemonium – a unique environment for learning. The cane was liberally used in those days, its swishing sound and the accompanying sniffles and cries for mercy were immediate, scary, and distracting. Even now I picture myself flinching as the cane descended on my bottom or heard it go 'splosh' on someone else's. Girls got the ruler on their knuckles which was equally painful and humiliating.

Government or government-funded community schools were few. So initially, Indian parents sent their children to so-called *private schools* (usually reading and writing classes held in a garage or on a veranda of a private house with a casual untrained person in charge who charged a nominal fee). To accommodate the large number of children who turned up at a formal Indian school each year seeking admission, classes were often split into morning and afternoon sessions – *platoon classes*. I only gained admission to Class One (first grade) in a formal school at about the age of nine, hence completing high school at twenty or twenty-one years of age. Indian children mostly spoke English, and English was the medium of instruction from the inception of schooling.

I retain a vivid image of the principal, Mr K.M. Gounden. He was a much-feared spartan who would walk to school from home and back a distance of about seven kilometres each way. My family lived on his property in Cato Manor in rental rooms. My school principal and my landlord was an uncle on my mother's side. No wonder I felt confused and tongue-tied in his presence.

KM Gounden

~

On the appointed day of the royal event, hundreds of Indian children were taken by bus to Curries Fountain, a popular soccer stadium for Indians in town. Once settled in our bus, a female teacher standing next to the driver faced us. 'Now be quiet and listen,' she said in a soft voice, at the same time attempting to command authority over the excited din of chit-chat, laughter, and taunts. She held up a poster of people and waited until the children went quiet with anticipation. 'See, this is King George VI, and this his wife the queen.' She pointed to the poster as she explained. 'They have two daughters. You can see them here – Margaret and Elizabeth. Say after me Margaret and Elizabeth.' We screamed in unison the unfamiliar names: 'Maaget and Elaazabet. Maaget, Elaazabet.' The pained expression on the teacher's face puzzled me. She did not get us to practice any further.

'Ma'am Thulsi,' said a shrill voce. 'Are the people in the

picture white people?' A chorus of whispers erupted: 'white people, white people,' they giggled.

'That's enough now. Settle down. Take your seats.' And as an afterthought, she added: 'Behave yourselves when you get to Curries Fountain. Hear me. What did I say, Budram?'

'Eh?' said Budram with mischief in his eyes as he deftly pulled up a snot about to drip onto a girl with pigtails seated in front of him.

On arrival at the venue, we disembarked and were cajoled into lines. Each of us was then handed a small flag attached to what my carpenter father would call a dowel stick. With flags waving vigorously, we marched onto the field and into an area cordoned off and allocated to our school. Kids from other schools had already arrived and were seated in adjacent zones.

I only learned much later that the flag given us was that of Great Britain, the Union Jack. But South Africa at the time had its own flag, which was a compromise between the Union Jack and that of the two Boer Republics. This flag had come into being in 1928 some years after the British colonies of the Cape and Natal formed a union with the Afrikaner Republics of Transvaal and Orange Free State.

After Nelson Mandela assumed political power in 1994, this Union flag was given short shrift together with remaining vestiges of British and Afrikaner political hegemony. The current flag is striking and readily identified as a reclining letter Y in several colours symbolising South Africa's diverse population – the Rainbow Nation.

It never occurred to me (nor was it explained) why it was that only Indian children attended the event on that day. We children simply embraced it as a rare privilege – nothing unusual. Only later it may have dawned on us, if it ever did, that this was our first encounter as children of state-sanctioned segregation at work! White children would certainly have had their opportunity also with royalty. But would black pupils have been rescued, even for a day, from the tedium of classwork to be indulged with a free outing and bus ride just to see important white people, though from a distance? The occasion made little impression on me. I recall feeling bored and a little weary from the glare of the African sun. We sat crossed legged on grass, huddled like chicken, and peered up at the specially constructed ornate pavilion and podium where the royal family was ensconced together with a few other senior white dignitaries in military-like uniforms. The podium was far too removed and distant from us to hold our attention and curiosity. It was an effort, too, to keep waving the Union Jack. When they spoke over a speaker-system, the crackling and whistling voices of the Prime Minister and the King echoed all over Curries Fountain football field, as if mocking and mimicking their utterances. I certainly could not make much sense of what was being said and was relieved when it was all over.

'Did you all enjoy that?' Ma'am Thulsi enquired with little conviction in her voice as we climbed onto the bus, pushing and shoving. She looked as if she had just woken up and had not slept well. We said nothing. I pictured hundreds of Union Jacks being thrown onto a scrap heap by weary black municipal workers.

~

As children, we grew up knowing no life other than the one in which white people were superior and wielded power over us. They led privileged and materially superior lives, in secure leafy suburbs. Their sprawling houses were hugged by manicured gardens. Fierce dogs would sniff and growl at passers-by, their snouts pushing through the grills of ornate metal gates.

Like my grandparents, some Indians who had arrived as indentured labourers chose not to return to India after they had completed their indenture. Over time some Indian families started small market gardens several miles from the town centre. Soon, they became the thriving vibrant community of Cato Manor with strong bonds of religion and cultural practices. People lived cheek by jowl mostly in dwellings of timber and corrugated iron, interspersed by brick houses of the new rich such as the Seebran family who owned a modest fleet of buses. The area was characterised by rain-washed dirt roads and improvised pathways, commonly referred to as *shortcuts*. Grass and bush would have taken over the verges along these roads in wild abandonment, while the municipality looked the other way. I recall on school days bracing myself as I scrambled barefooted along a bushy, damp and potholed shortcut with other school kids, past open drains, and exposed bucket toilets. The steamy pungent smells would be overpowering and would stay with me for the rest of the school day.

On occasions, Whites attended Indian weddings at traditional venues such as a temple. The obsequious parents of the bride or groom would rush up to meet them, looking all flustered. 'Come Sir and Madam, this way please,' they would say with nervous laughter. 'So nice to see you, Sir and Madam. Make way, make way,' they'd fuss as these most favoured guests were ushered to the very front row close to where the wedding ceremony was taking place.

There they would sit aloof and god-like, wearing garlands of flowers placed there by their beaming hosts. Other guests would admire and even envy the host-parents for having white friends. Children seated with parents at the rear of the hall would stand tiptoe, to catch a glimpse of this rarity. For us, these were benign encounters from a safe distance, since even the thought of brushing against Whites gave us the jitters.

I recall, however, on occasions when my father was unemployed, that he was given casual carpentry jobs by Whites to erect shelves, cupboards, and partitions in offices in high-rise office blocks in the city centre. Over weekends he would take me along to keep him company. Being after office hours, the place would be deathly silent. Odd smells would be floating about, and I would be startled to hear an occasional slamming of a door somewhere in the building. My father was given piece-meal work by city counsellor JC Bolton and two dentists, Dr Barrow Bass and Dr Coward. My father's contact with JC Bolton grew into an enduring friendship that embraced his wife, Harriet Bolton, who was heavily involved in the trade union movement. When cautioned that he ought not to assume these people were his friends, my father would respond with hurt pride: 'How can you say that. They're not Whites, are they? They're Jews. And Jews don't treat us like dirt!' At the same time, when his good friend, Ganas, who lived in Delhi Avenue, dropped in to say hello, I'd overhear them talking above each other in troubled voices. My father had the evening Daily News in his hand.

'Look here Ganas, they're saying the Dutch people are going to take over the country.'

'You mean the Nats? The Afrikaaners?'

'Ya, ya, that's them, Nationalists. They're more worse you know than that United Party fella, Smuts.'

I would learn in my later years that an extreme right-wing conservative movement, largely representing the Afrikaner rural poor, had gained ground in South Africa during the period of World War 2. This movement admired Hitler's belief in the purity of the Aryan race. The Afrikaners were essentially of Dutch descent and staunch Calvinists of the ultra-orthodox kind.

The conservative National Party, once in government, entrenched itself by passing legislation to reshape South Africa into an apartheid state. According to the vision of Apartheid, Whites or Europeans would always occupy the upper rung of the ladder of privilege, followed by half-caste Whites (Coloureds). Indian descendants would be below Coloureds. The indigenous Blacks or African people of the country, who were by far in the majority, would have to be satisfied with some allocated space at the foot of the ladder of graded privilege. After all, asserted D. F. Malan, the first Nationalist prime minister: 'You see the Old Testament says clearly that natives are the children of Ham. That is why they need to know that their duty is to serve the civilised white man.'

It could be that the Afrikaner genuinely had an existential anxiety that as a small isolated god-fearing people he and his Christian way of life in Africa would, in time, be overwhelmed and obliterated by the burgeoning *black* masses of a *primitive* continent. The British in South Africa, on the other hand, were masters of an Empire. They had no fear of being driven out as white overlords over all coloured races. They were pragmatic, opportunistic and expedient in enforcing their policy of segregation. The master-servant arrangement was ultimately a commercial imperative to ensure a smooth flow of wealth from the colonies to the Crown. The black and brown races had to bow before their white colonial masters, addressing them as baas, sir, madam and so on.

Even though I was just ten years old when the Afrikaners came into power in 1948, I still have a sense of the alarm and foreboding this caused. It was a talking point for weeks on end. I would hear people voicing their fears as they went about shopping or sat on a bus with worried faces. 'They're going to put us all on ships and send us back to India, ya? What'll happen then?'

There it was in my father's newspaper. In large black letters. One word only. APARTHEID. Gradually, it became clear what the new word meant – white people on top of the wood pile forever. It soon touched our lives in painful varied ways. We learnt that it meant exclusive white privilege, entrenched in law, and enforced by a repressive, violent security apparatus. Black people called out the policy for what it was in reality: *apart-hate*.

They say that what may look solid may not be so. Often deep within sits the seed of its own undoing. In the face of mounting and sustained resistance from the oppressed people within the country, supported by international sanctions and outrage, the country's economy (the heart of Apartheid's very existence) began to convulse. The purveyors of Apartheid found themselves treated as outcasts by world opinion. Ultimately, Nelson Mandela, the undisputed leader of the oppressed majority, was released from incarceration in full gaze of the world. So it was that apartheid crumbled in dramatic fashion in 1994 much like the infamous Berlin Wall. This momentous event heralded a new beginning for South Africa.

But sadly, before Apartheid finally collapsed, family and community life suffered dearly, and many, many people were banished, driven from the country, or simply killed in gruesome ways by the security forces. It cannot all just be forgotten, I think. Our lives could have been so wholesomely different if it were not for segregation and Apartheid. Each of us, including my family, experienced day-to-day humiliations.

~

Even as a school kid, I recall being on the receiving end of white abrasive authority. The impressionable minds of children often perceive and register such events as frightening, if not traumatic. This would explain why some distressing memories remain vivid in me even to this day. Two experiences readily illustrate this.

In the first incident my family was chased by an angry white man. Here we were, my father and mother, brother, 5, me, 7 and sister, 9 enjoying a rare picnic outing in the Botanic Gardens in Durban. Around the corner comes this doddering, old white man in a white uniform, wielding a baton. 'Hey, you coolies, what you think you doing here! Get out. You're not allowed!' It was the park attendant, referred to as *parkie* in local slang. He was like a ghost taking form before my very eyes. I dropped my ball and stumbled over to my mother's side. My father spluttered instructions. We shoved plates of half-eaten chilli-bites and sandwiches into a basket and scuttled off in disarray. The look of distress and alarm on the faces of my parents was enough to send my heart racing. My mother had a tight hold of my whimpering brother's hand, my father had mine, while clutching the basket in the other. 'My ball, my ball,' I cried. 'Shut up,' my father hissed. 'Forget it.' My sister, carrying a rolled-up reed mat kept pace, glancing behind her repeatedly for fear the parkie would get her. But my mother, unaccustomed to running at her age, and constrained by her ankle-length sari and slippers, breathed heavily. I was truly scared for her. We relaxed only when we had safely boarded our bus and it was belting homewards. 'Why we made the white man mad, Amma?' asked my sister, having glanced at my mother a few times. I was all ears. But my mother sat grim-faced looking into the distance. 'Keep quiet and sit properly,' said my father.

At another time, my father and I boarded a double-decker or trolley bus (powered by two overhead lines) on a Saturday morning at the bottom of Mayville Hill opposite CN Rana grocery shop. We were on our way into town. As I had taken the trolley bus many times before, I was aware that we were permitted to sit on the upper deck only – but not in the very front row which was also reserved for Whites. On this occasion, we took the only seats available a couple of rows from the front. When two white passengers boarded the bus and came upstairs looking for seats, the burly and surly red-faced white conductor followed. The power he wielded was evident in his severe military-like uniform – black tunic with brass buttons down the front and a broad belt to which was attached his coin dispenser and wad of bus tickets. A black braided cap, not dissimilar to that worn by a pilot, completed his outfit. Upon discovering no seats for his privileged kind, he belted out a few expletives at us: 'Are you people blind! Can't you see these seats are wanted? Eh?' My father apologised in a feeble and contrite voice. But the conductor did not relent. 'Get off at the next stop and take the next bus!' I could not tell by their expressions what passed through the minds of the other non-white passengers, many of whom seemed to be staring at their feet.

In recalling these racially motivated events, for me both distressing and scary, I begin to wonder now why most Indians seemingly averted their eyes when something similar or even worse happened to black people out in the open.

One such example was the regular police harassment of Blacks in the city centre.

It was my father's responsibility on Saturdays to visit the markets for vegetables, meat, and fish. I really felt proud and grown up when he allowed me to accompany him, and to carry one of the laden shopping bags, sewn by my mother from off-cut vinyl.

'Is that heavy for you, son?'

'No, daddy,' I would say even though it felt like my arm would give way with the strain.

Having done with the vegetables at the Warwick Avenue Morning Market, we would proceed to the meat and fish market (Top Market). This meant we had to cross the Victoria Street railway bridge, always choked with sweaty and worried looking people, their clothes defining their impoverished status. I tensed whenever we approached this bridge. Would the police be there, lying in wait again? My first encounter of the police in action was enough to instil in me a lasting wariness of them. Certainly, this did not do me any good when, in later years as an adult, I had to contend with the dreaded security branch (SB) - probably little different to the Stasi of the communist-era East Germany.

One Saturday, two police pickup vans blocked our way, leaving just a small opening for the pedestrians. Here we were, my father and I, trapped in a melee of pushing and shoving natives, as black people were called then. It reminded me of cows being herded for slaughter. The smell of fear and resentment was welling up like toxic fumes from a drain. I thought they were simply angry because they may miss their buses or trains and be late for work. I began panicking when I could not see my father in the crowd. What if I am separated from him? I held onto my shopping bag and strained my eyes to spot my father's hat above the throng.

Black police constables in stiff khaki uniforms and helmets thrust their menacing batons at fellow black men, stopping them with looks of disdain. They herded and moved them toward waiting white officers nearby in dark navy uniforms, and guns at their hips.

'*Dompas* (dumb pass) *kaffir*,' a white officer barked at a cornered black man, holding out an impatient hand.

'*Nkosi*,' pleaded the elderly black man removing his battered hat and addressing the Officer as God. With a quick kneeling gesture, he handed over, with both hands, a small, much fingered passbook. The young white officer made a brisk check and threw the document back at the owner, who had looked all bewildered. Was he free to go or not?

No mercy was shown to another man who had not carried his passbook. A burly black constable dragged him away, kicking and resisting, and bundled him into the back of a pickup van. For a moment I saw his distressed face pressed against the metal-grilled opening at the back, as the van eased its way through the resentful crowd. A woman in the crowd rushed forward, wailing, and wringing her hands. She was comforted by other black people for losing her father, husband, or son, who she may not see again for a very long time. Yet another young black man in the clutches of the police, unexpectedly wrenched free and ran for his life, weaving through the crowd. The police gave chase, pushing aside anyone in the way with little consideration, returning a while later empty-handed and with sour faces. People in the crowd threw up their hands in relief.

My father, in the meantime, had moved through the cordon. I spotted him searching the crowd, calling out my name, his brow creased with concern. 'Here, daddy,' I answered, resting my bag for the first time.

'What's the matter with you?' said my father. 'Wooden legs? You want trouble or something, eh? Police business with natives not our business. Understand?'

No more was said.

In time, I worked out for myself the meaning of what I had witnessed so often on Victoria Street Bridge. Black men had to carry a pass day and night without fail. Urban centres, designated white areas, were out of bounds to them, except with special work permits. Those found without one were arrested for *loitering*, fined, and shunted off to remote rural villages – even though they may have never known rural life.

The passbook was one of the most hated instruments of Apartheid ever imposed on black men. The Blacks gave it their own name - *dompas* It was characteristic of politically oppressed black people to circumvent pain and humiliation with humour and ridicule.

On a recent trip to South Africa, I visited the Apartheid Museum in Johannesburg. I was profoundly moved. I entered via a turnstile marked *Whites Only* (rather than one marked *Non-Whites*) and proceeded along a narrow passageway leading to the reception hall. Pasted on the walls on either side of the passage was a display of authentic permits and passes imposed on black people by successive white governments to confine and regulate their lives. Each document featured a washed-out mugshot of the person who was once compelled to carry it. Lost-looking faces bereft of hope and dignity.

There is also a black and white photo of Mandela in that Museum, a handsome young lawyer then, flinging his dompas into an open fire. A group of Blacks gathered around him and follow his example. What a powerful and dramatic statement of defiance! Gandhi would have lauded this non-violent act of resistance, I thought.

~

Over my primary school years, I became increasingly aware of black people living in large numbers not too far away. They were much more in numbers than Indians. I grew accustomed to black people moving about in my immediate world. The Indian community, however, simply took them for granted, and had little to do with them socially or in any other meaningful ways. Apart from occasionally picking up casual work in return for food, black people, for their part, seemed to keep a wary distance.

Sudden frantic barking of dogs would alert us to their presence near our homes. A dog or two would race into the street almost colliding with the outsider. None of our houses had secure fencing. With ferocity and bared teeth, the dogs would go for the ankles. The hapless victim would kick and whirl and engage in a crazed dance, attempting to ward off the incensed dogs with his traditional carrying stick. I'd hear cries of 'nKosiami! nKosiami! Suuka!' (Oh my god. Oh my god. Get away).

As a child under ten, I cannot recall ever meeting a black man or woman as a person, as a human being. It was a decade or so before the material circumstances of Indian families improved sufficiently for them to employ Blacks for casual garden or domestic work, or as labourers.

As far as I could tell, urban blacks lived mostly in slum conditions, in informal congested shack settlements like the one at the intersection of Booth and Candela Roads on the fringes of Cato Manor. The area was known as Umkumbaan.

I have a vivid recollection of this chaotic slum on a hillside peppered with bush simply because I was once caught up in a fearful event there.

During World War 2, people had to contend with a strict weekly ration of basic foods such as rice, sugar, tinned fish, and condensed milk. Coupons were issued, one per household, and a member of each family would collect the allocated ration from a mobile food-van, operated by the army. The van would park at a suitable open ground near where mostly Indians lived. On one occasion, the van was stationed at Umkumbaan, largely to supply the concentration of black people here. My mother, together with other Indians, saw the opportunity to augment her meagre provision. They hastened on foot all the way to this site. I was dragged along.

The queue was long, and black people seemed to become restive, naturally fearing the supply would run out before their turn. 'Here, hold this coupon and bag. Stand in front of me,' said my mother holding me by the shoulder. When we got to the van, my mother spoke up. 'I bring this boy to collect for my next-door neighbour because the mother there is sick or something.' I had not a clue what she was on about, except that stuff was put into the bag I carried, before my mother got her ration. Some other Indians in the line did likewise – got themselves additional rations or did so quite genuinely to help an infirm neighbour.

Blacks milling on the hillside in front of their shacks caught onto what was happening. I began hearing angry and agitated calls '*amakhula,* amakhula' (Coolies, coolies – as indentured Indians were referred to by the British). There was agitated movement in front of the shacks, including a cluster of women brandishing sticks. I looked up at my mother who was whispering to the other Indian ladies near her. Suddenly an incensed throng descended from the hillside at a pace, screaming and ululating. My mother and all the other Indians scattered in terror. '*Ayoh Saami*', screamed my mother (dear god), grabbing hold of my hand and running through rain drenched grass and mud. I really thought I was done for. My chest hurt and my mother's spasm of coughing slowed us down. But we got away without injury. The bag of rations was no longer in my hand.

~

Despite the widespread scarcity and related hardships of the war years, my parents built themselves a modest house in the mid nineteen forties. How they saved enough money to buy a plot of land, I have no idea. Perhaps my maternal grandparents helped. The plot of land in Mayville, a relatively newer part of Cato Manor, was a challenge to build on as it was on a hillside, mostly clay and rock, and with an ungraded track for a road. But it was affordable. They first constructed a two-room *outbuilding (*traditional servant-quarters*)* on the site with a ceiling-less corrugated iron roof and moved into it. A bucket toilet was located outside, a few metres away. There was no bathroom, so we had to make-do with bucket-baths in the toilet space.

Once the main dwelling was completed, we moved there. The outbuilding was then rented to a Mr M.M Katti, a mild mannered middle-aged black man who had a shoe repair business at a shopping strip not too far away. A sign above his shop read '*MM Katti. Shoe Repairs.*' As far as I know, no Indian considered it unique or unusual for Mr Katti, a Black, to own this business. In fact, his customers were almost all Indians. Perhaps the local Indian community got to see him as a person, not as a native.

Mr M.M.Katti, spoke good English and dressed in Western clothes. His shoes always shone like glass. I recall taking him my shoes for repairs and that of others in my family. 'Hello son,' he would beam over his spectacles. 'Ah, your shoes. Yes, yes, I fix it.' He was the first black man I got to know well. My family also treated him with respect since he caused no problems and paid his rent on time. Mr Katti had girlfriends, although he had a wife and two little boys in a distant rural village. They would visit him once a year and stay for a few weeks. Humble, traditional in every way and god-fearing Christians.

Not only did my parents have a black man as a rent-paying tenant, but they also had a mixed-race couple (Coloureds) renting the basement of our house which had been converted into three habitable rooms. This would suggest that there was a level of co-existence and racial harmony among the non-white groups, dictated by economic necessity. Perhaps also the racial laws may not have been as restrictive during the war years, prior to the apartheid era commencing in 1948. It seems, however, the relationship between Blacks and Indians was tenuous all along. Even during the time of Gandhi (1893-1914), Indians seem to have kept the Blacks at a distance. In January 1949 Blacks in Durban rioted against Indians.

Black people who had been quietly resentful of Indians, went rampaging through Indian residential areas and business districts over a few days. The Natal Daily News and Mercury reported widespread looting, arson, killing, maiming, and raping. Fearful rumours spread like wildfire and engulfed Indians in mass panic. What was to be done? Where could we run and hide? The faithful Mr MM Katti came to our rescue. My father opened the back door with trepidation when he heard the tenant's urgent voice.

'Don't worry, Mr Mudaly. I guard your place. Your family stay inside. Must please lock all windows and doors. Close the curtains, okay? No noise, no lights.'

My family had no choice but to trust Mr Katti. The late afternoon drifted into evening and then into a long night of waiting and watchfulness. I was about eleven years old then, with a sister two years older and a younger brother. My sister and I tried to sit up with my parents, only dozing fitfully. My mother sat on the edge of her bed rocking and praying while my father all anxious roamed the house in the dark, peering through slits in the curtains. He pushed me away when I attempted to do likewise. But once or twice I did get a glimpse of spot fires in the valley below and along the Candela ridge beyond. The darkness was split by an occasional vehicle racing along Bellair Road, with blaring horn.

We survived the night and the next couple of days holed up in the house. So did our immediate neighbours. We learnt later that the rampage was eventually put down by a mobilisation of police with support from the armed forces. There were many stories of black people risking their lives to protect Indian families.

~

A government commission investigated and reported on the incident, as well as a joint committee of the Natal Indian Congress (NIC) and the African National Congress (ANC). Books have been written analysing the riots and speculating on possible triggers. But opinions tended to differ. Some blamed Indians for exploiting Blacks in their commercial dealings and for treating them as an inferior and outcast race. Others pointed to the social, economic, and political constraints colonial rule imposed on impoverished Non-Whites generally, which then generated internal tensions and divisions, increasing competition for scarce resources.

~

Interestingly, the latter explanation is now offered to explain the sporadic and ongoing eruptions of xenophobic violence in present day South Africa where black South Africans turn upon black migrants and refugees from elsewhere in Africa. In the most recent incident in March 2019, Malawians living in Durban were violently set upon by local Blacks spreading terror and destruction, leaving them homeless and with loss of livelihood. However, the ANC government, at a meeting of African Ambassadors of neighbouring countries, was insistent that the violence was a pure act of criminality, not prompted by xenophobia or economic factors.

I spoke to a ninety-year-old Indian friend in Durban recently on the phone. He had strong memories of the riots and was of the firm view that it was impossible for pockets of Blacks in various parts of Durban to have rioted almost simultaneously when there was no mobile phones or social media. 'You know what,' he added, 'if you asked me, the whole thing was orchestrated by someone. Nothing spontaneous here.' He did not elaborate.

The Indian community was traumatised and confounded by this episode. It certainly was a wakeup call. A level of distrust persists even to this day between the two communities. This was evident to me when I last visited

South Africa in August 2018. Black leaders at the extreme ends of the political spectrum expressed open hostility, accusing Indians of racism and of being supporters of 'white monopoly capital' – whatever that meant. However, black hostility is also directed at Whites who retain the larger share of wealth and economic power in South Africa, even after a black majority government has been in existence since 1994.

It makes me wonder if the entire nation suffers from generational trauma of racism, having endured a century of British colonial policy of divide-and-rule, and thereafter subjected to the pernicious structural divide of Apartheid where privilege was ranked and dispensed according to race and colour. I think perceptions are a fact of life. How we see the world around us, shapes our reality. We need to be vigilant and aware of our own perceptions and thoughts on race, ethnicity, and colour if we are to promote tolerance in a world fraught with complexity and diversity.

~

I am amazed how politically aware my father was – even though he had no more than primary school education and worked as a carpenter in factories. His employment tended to be precarious at best and he earned little to support my mother and us four children. However, he never failed to bring home a copy of the Daily News, a robust and liberal leaning daily. Although I do not have a mental picture of him sitting and reading it, he must have done so to have been so informed of current affairs and national events. I also became somewhat addicted to the Daily News in my high school years. I would wait for my father to arrive in the evening with the paper, snatch it before my mother sought it out to scan the funeral notices. In time, she, too, with no more than four years of schooling, became interested in reading all the social and political news, especially as this affected the Indian community.

Once I had left home to attend university, and later for a teaching post in Zambia, my mother would send me the Daily News, a fortnight's issue at a time, bundled, carefully secured with cellotape, and posted at affordable printed-matter rate. This was at a time of rampant state censorship. It was, therefore, not unusual to find the first few pages of each issue, which mostly covered political news, methodically blackened out with thick ink, one horizontal line after another. The funeral notices and obituaries, however, remained intact.

I now wish my father had shared his political interests and thinking with me, but he never did. And yet I recall him taking me to politically charged rallies in town in later years of primary school. A bold move indeed, especially since I do not think many other children were exposed to this kind of education. So it was that I became increasingly aware of the many good things in the world around us that were reserved for white people only, and the police kept a watchful eye that Non-Whites did not encroach on this privilege.

The rallies were held on a vacant lot in Durban, at the intersection of Grey and Pine Streets (renamed Dr Yusuf Dadoo and Dr Monty Naicker Streets). This meeting place came to be known as Red Square – the political flavour all too obvious. It exists now only in memory, as this open space later became a multi-level car park, Nichol Square Garage.

I picture myself at Red Square on a Sunday afternoon, standing with my father at the edge of a large and restive crowd of men, mostly Indians. Like my father, many wore similar English-style hats - worn tilted ever so slightly to the right. Speakers such as Dr Dadoo, Dr Monty Naicker, Dr Goonum and Advocate JN Singh would make strident, rousing utterances from a make-shift podium using a hand-held megaphone. Their utterances would reach my ear in waves.

'We can't ......allow.... the Nationalist Government ....to get away with these laws. They are unjust....... against the spirit of UNO.' The crowd would respond in thunderous, defiant chants: 'Hear! Hear! Power to the people. Hear! Hear!'

Then, perhaps, I would hear Dr Goonam, her husky voice almost muffled by the coughs and chatter of the audience.

The truth is, for much of the time I was unable to grasp fully what was being said or what the fighting talk was all about. I could barely see the speakers over the expanse of hats. However, the waves of energised cheering and applause would wash over me. I would feel strangely stirred and elated. Later, on the bus home, my father would tell me in a voice full of informed authority and pride; 'See son, they all Congress people (Natal Indian Congress). And communists too, you know, like this Dr Dadoo.' These were clearly heady days in politics for the Indian community. Not too long after, under the draconian Suppression of Communism Act 1950, Dadoo and activists of all shades, together with organisations which expressed views even mildly contrary to the policy of Apartheid, were banned, silenced, and subjected to police surveillance and harassment.

A squad of white and Indian security police would invariably be present at meetings and gatherings involving Non-Whites. They would make themselves very visible to intimidate people gathered there. At one Red Square rally, I recall looking about me in a moment of distraction and spotting a couple of white men on the far side, leaning casually against a large black car, taking photos – at least that is what it seemed to me. But I could not be sure. They were a curious sight among a sea of dark faces.

The last time Indians had been mobilised to resist unjust laws was in 1913 during the years that Mahatma Gandhi visited South Africa as a young barrister fresh from graduating from University College, London. He had been brought to Durban by Indian traders and merchants to represent them in their opposition to restrictive government laws which they saw as discrimination.

My father recounted to me the momentous event when Gandhi had, in defiance of laws restricting the movement of Indians, marched across the border from Natal into the Transvaal with hundreds of Indian men and women.

Gandhi in SA **Gandhi-led march in northern Natal**

Rally addressed by Monty Naicker wearing a Gandhi cap.

High School Years
1955-58

At the end of the last year of primary school (standard 6), we had to sit a province wide public exam. I did well and my name was first on a selection list of Indian boys admitted to Sastri College, the very first secondary school for Indian boys. My family and friends feted me for being 'such a smart lad'. So, at the age of seventeen, boosted by pride, I turned into a tall poppy.

The college carried the name of its founder, Sir Srinivasa Sastri, the Agent General of India, serving in South Africa at the time. It was officially opened in October 1929 by the governor general of South Africa, his Excellency the Earl of Athlone. A white principal headed an all-white staff. Situated in the city just below the Botanic Gardens and Curries Fountain Sports Stadium, the college was an impressive two-storey rectangular building of classical design with a line of supporting columns along a veranda, an entrance stairway, and a roof of terracotta tiles. An expansive lawn, a tennis court and a long driveway completed the picture of what elite Victorian private schools may have looked like in England.

I savoured the wholly new experience of travelling to school and back home by bus. My friends and I looked dashing in uniform – grey longs, blue blazer and a blue and gold stripped tie. Almost seventy years on, the traditional Sastri uniform is still in vogue, but the all-Indian boys' school has become an almost all-Black boys' school in a post-apartheid era.

Sastri College in 1955

The students have changed but not Sastri uniform.

Of course, my parents struggled to meet the cost of keeping me in college for four long years. I made a little pocket money from working weekends at Timol's Grocers at the bottom end of Grey St.

High school life generally and the demands of the curricula absorbed much of my attention and time. Vivid impressions remain of conjugating Latin verbs and deciphering Latin texts such as *Julius Caesar's Gaelic Wars*. I felt moved by the emotional sentiments ringing eternally true in the poems of Virgil and Ovid. And there was King Hammurabi the Great. Only his otherworldly sounding name remains to awe me, but his momentous exploits of antiquity have well and truly vanished from memory. I began to pay more attention to girls from Dartnall Crescent Girls College that I met regularly on the bus. This distraction was altogether an unfamiliar and unsettling sensual experience. But always lurking at the edge of my consciousness was a sense of tension in the air. A foreboding of threat.

~

The racial and political tensions were ever present like winter smog that sits over the Umgeni Valley. My father continued to bring home the evening paper, the Natal Daily News, with banner headlines of the latest racial legislation, and speculation on how soon it would be implemented. I remember the Native Resettlement Act 1954, the Group Areas Development Act 1955, the Riotous Assemblies Act 1956, the Reservation of Separate Amenities Act 1956, and the Separate Representation of Voters Act of 1956. There was public outcry and widespread opposition. The government was fully prepared and let loose the security forces, giving them a free hand.

One day late in 1958, I went home from school and my mother handed me a sealed brown envelope addressed to my father. It was not the usual kind of letter. No postage stamps, yet it looked official and seriously important. My mother clasped her hands and sat as I opened it. In a short terse sentence or two, we were told that Cato Manor had been proclaimed for future white occupation under the Group Areas Act. Soon neighbours came knocking on our door with copies of similar letters in their hand.

This event impacted profoundly on all our lives and livelihood. It inevitably thrust ordinary people into the cauldron of apartheid politics. Well-attended protest meetings were held. I recall attending one such meeting at the popular Mayville Theatre (local movie hall). Community leaders stood on stage and called for vehement opposition to 'these cruel and unjust laws.' Some from the audience, who had never in their lives made public utterances, stood tall, vented their anger, piercing the air with warning fingers. One or two speakers from the floor became emotional and had to be helped from the congested hall to collect themselves.

Grannies attended with grandchildren. Wives and daughters joined the men. In my experience, the community had never ever rallied together in this way. On reflection, what I had witnessed on that occasion was the emergence of a cohesive political consciousness in this community. Sadly though, mobilisation of this sort, although sustained for a little while, did not win the people reprieve. The government was determined. Thousands of families jostled (so as not to be stranded without shelter) for sub-standard cluster units in the sprawling new Indian Group Areas of Phoenix and Chatsworth. We lost out in a big way. There is little doubt the Group Areas Act fractured family and community life with long-term consequences.

Non-White communities in the rest of the country were also simultaneously dispossessed and relocated to remote (at times hostile and uninhabitable) places *en masse*. A few of these segregated new settlements became, over time, well known. Indian areas included Lenasia (outside Johannesburg) and Laudium adjacent to Pretoria. Soweto was the largest settlement created for Blacks on the fringes of Johannesburg, and Khayelitsha (and others) on the outskirts of Cape Town. The coloured people in Cape Town were uprooted from District Six, a historic, colourful, and vibrant settlement, and dumped in dusty windswept Mitchell's Plain and in a few other areas. Sophiatown, a predominantly black pre-apartheid township in Johannesburg was as rich as was District Six. It suffered the same fate. Having obliterated it, to further rub salt into the wound, the white group area created in its place was named *Triomf* (triumph in Afrikaans).

Fifty years on, Phoenix and Chatsworth, the two major group areas created in Durban for Indians, have turned into vast and densely populated suburbs of a greater Durban metro. Large sections of these townships looked rather scruffy to me on my last visit, reportedly marred by unemployment, drugs and crime. For some reason, Cato Manor did not end up as a white suburb even though the settled Indian community was uprooted and disposed of with such ruthless purpose. Nor was the prime urban land once called District Six near Cape Town resettled with

Whites. To this day it remains largely vacant, except for a small museum honouring a thriving community of a bygone era. But there is move afoot to return the land to the descendants who once live there.

On my recent visit to South Africa in August 2018, I had my nephew drive me through Cato Manor. The landscape had utterly changed. All the familiar landmarks had vanished – gone was Mayville Theatre where I had seen many a Western (in black & white) with such daring characters as Hopalong Cassidy, Durango Kid and the Lone Ranger; and where many a rousing meeting was held against the Group Areas Act; gone also was AYS primary school with the giant umdhoni tree in front where I had stood most Friday mornings memorising my ten spelling words (by heart) for the weekly test. So too all the familiar wood and iron houses, Munchie's one-chair barber shop, and the Moonshine milk bar where my brother was almost electrocuted while helping himself to half-a-pint of milk (in a familiar dumpy glass bottle) from an upright fridge during a freak lightning storm.

I felt appalled. Along one side of what was once Bellair Road, there sprawled an endless stretch of ramshackle shacks, all jostling for space. A picture of despair: Illegally strung power lines sagging like cobwebs over rusted iron and tarpaulin roofs, plastic strewn overgrowth, derelict cars, stray dogs, ragged children with assorted containers at communal taps, teenagers on rickety bikes criss-crossing the main road with brazen disregard, vacant-eyed men staring at passing traffic, women with shopping bags exiting buses, the dizzying sweet-sour smell of cheap cuts of meat sizzling on improvised open coal fires somewhere unseen.

Open festering drains gave off their peculiar pungent odours. The smells mingled with township sounds – blurred rap music, screams of kids at play, the sultry bark of a mangy dog, people carrying on loud conversations across open ground and from the open windows of a stationery kombi taxi (a feature of black urban transport). In fact, it was a chaotic mass of humanity living the reality of their everyday lives – an impoverished existence in a liberated and democratic South Africa. Where, I asked myself, was the evidence that the wealth of the nation was trickling down to the least among us – even after twenty years of independence?

Now as a relatively privileged Australian, I felt strangely uneasy driving through this chaotic informal settlement. Was I not intruding into someone else's space? This was no longer the familiar Cato Manor I had once known, my home territory. Amid my unease, another kombi-taxi abruptly pulled up in front of us to drop off and collect passengers. There was little we could do but wait as it appeared risky for us to overtake on this narrow stretch of road milling with ill-mannered dogs, bikes, and people. I hoped no locals would get a whiff of us stranded here, and alert others. In which case, I feared we would likely be promptly encircled by locals suspicious of our presence as outsiders. On reflection, I wonder if this sense of threat was irrational and unfounded. Or was it racially tinged residues of traumatic events experienced by my family and me in my early years?

~

The Group Areas Act was, as I have already mentioned, only one of several unsettling events of my high school years. It was, however, the Treason Trial of 1956 that really ratcheted up the tension in the country and drew the attention of the world to the brutal reality that South Africa was effectively a police state. The Treason Trial mobilised concerted international condemnation of the policy and practices of the South African Government. Nelson Mandela, leader of the ANC, and 156 other activists of all colours were arrested and tried for high treason, allegedly for plotting an insurrection. After a prolonged trial, they were found not guilty and released in sensational circumstances. The whole episode gave unprecedented exposure to the freedom struggle, raised the profile of Mandela and his co-accused, and boosted the resolve of the oppressed peoples to persevere. Active resistance against Apartheid had become very much a struggle involving all races. For instance, liberal white women formed an organisation called the Black Sash to engage in non-violent resistance. The silent vigils of the Black Sash became iconic and highly visible - and loved by newspaper editors for the graphic photo opportunities the vigils provided. I once came upon such a dignified vigil outside the Durban City Hall. The image of this line of women with black sashes is etched in my memory.

Black Sash in silent protest

In the same year, 1956, as the freedom struggle was intensifying, a broad-based political conference of a multiracial nature was convened in Kliptown outside Johannesburg, by members of the congress alliance. The culmination of the meeting was a statement pledging a vision for a free South Africa and a program of action to achieve this vision. This document came to be known as the *Freedom Charter*. It was widely considered as having almost similar historical significance as the Magna Carta for Britain.

Increasingly women, especially black women, came to the forefront to protest and agitate against the intolerable impositions of apartheid on daily life and family wellbeing. They fought for themselves and fought for their husbands, brothers, and fathers who they had witnessed suffering harassment, humiliation and even imprisonment. On 9 August 1956, in an act of supreme courage, twenty thousand black women (supported by women of all other races) marched to the Union Buildings in Pretoria to petition the government against the Country's pass laws which were to be extended, compelling black women to carry the *dompas* as well. This event is now observed annually in South Africa as National Women's Day.

In the midst of all this turmoil and tension, I had to prepare for my final and most critical high school exams. The atmosphere was not the most conducive for study. Hence, the grades with which I passed matric (year 12) were, at the time, too distressing to be spoken of. I left high school no longer a tall poppy. I felt humiliated, and my family bewildered. They had long fancied their eldest son becoming a doctor – with the help of a super scholarship.

Not now. Not with my scores. My fallback option was to enrol for a science degree at the University of Fort Hare, in the Eastern Cape Province, a long way from home.

University Life and Challenges
1959 -1963

Fort Hare had been established in 1916 by Christian missionaries under the name South African Native College to provide higher education for indigenous Blacks. Following a name change years later, a sprinkling of Indian students was admitted annually.

I was overly excited to leave home and engage in a rare adventure with other ex-Sastri College friends. Securing an overnight sleeper-berth on the train from Durban to Alice (where Fort Hare was located) was the easy part of my travel arrangement. To be on the safe side, I made my booking three weeks in advance of my departure. Then came a shocker.

'You know, you'll not get a ticket,' said the railway booking clerk, an Indian himself, 'without a permit to enter the Eastern Cape?'

'But why? I gasped.

'Indians not allowed. That's it,' he said as if it was a natural immutable law.

It was only then I remembered my father telling me ages ago that Indians in South Africa suffered influx control restrictions. Even as late as 1970 Indians could not move across provincial borders without a permit.

My head spun. And there was more panic when I learnt that the permit would only be issued after police vetting. Not just any police, but the dreaded Special Branch itself. The job of the SB, as it came to be known, was to flush out people suspected of anti-state activities, as defined by the government.

I felt feverish the whole time I waited. As the days dragged on without an outcome, my anxiety mounted. What if I was refused a permit, or it did not arrive on time? I turned up at the offices of the Department of Indian Affairs almost every day for news. Finally, the fateful day of my departure arrived. I was all packed to board the train that evening, but there was still no permit by midday. In despair, I made a last forlorn trip into town, convinced by now that all was lost.

But as luck would have it, my name was on a short list of other applicants cleared by the police for travel into the Transkei. It was 3 pm already. My train was scheduled to depart at 8 pm.

I made a hectic dash home with the good news. The dash, in fact, was a twenty-minute jog from the offices of Indian Affairs to the bus rank, followed by a forty-minute tardy bus trip. Come on, get-a-move on, I fretted. The tell-tale signs of stress were unnerving me.

That evening my family stood on the platform at the Durban Central Station to see me off. My mother was in tears. Her eldest son was leaving home for the very first time. My father gave me a rare hug. He had a strained look. My brother seemed indifferent. 'Can I have your room?' he said.

Fort Hare here we come! (Author on right)

Fort Hare University

In many ways Fort Hare opened my naïve eyes for the first time to the political reality of South Africa. Until then I had lived in a cocoon, in the segregated world of working-class people of Indian descent. It was almost as if Indians were a distinct species of animal in a confined game park, yet always aware and wary of the presence of other species using the very same water hole. Encounters among the different species were rare and largely predatory. In short, there existed an explicit distance between the races physically, socially, culturally, and politically – with a few rare exceptions.

However, at Fort Hare I found myself sharing a dormitory with black and coloured students. I experienced some as quiet and friendly. Others were loud, inconsiderate, and vaguely threatening.

There was brotherly Gumede, spectacled and serious who was studying to be a priest; Hendrikse, his face inflamed with angry pimples, always keen to share something amusing; Beezley, the hunky and wild rugby player from Eastern Cape always ruffling the atmosphere in the dormitory with his unwashed physical presence; the lanky coloured, Peter Marsh, who wore an aura of silent menace much like Jack Palance in the classic movie *Shane*; the obese and chronically anxious Indian student Manilall; the small and humble village African, Molefe, who occupied the bed next to me. I found him sitting on his bed most evenings studying, with a blanket over his shoulder. He would give me a timid smile but say little. I soon realised that he was gifted in maths and physics. He later qualified as a medical doctor and served his rural community with compassion and distinction. I got on well with all of them. I was perhaps popular because I readily shared the spicy contents of my food hampers from home – which arrived fortnightly without fail by parcel post. It was hilarious when I was feted to an improvised 21st birthday party in the dormitory. Someone even found empty alcohol bottles to adorn the table.

How truly fortunate I was that Fort Hare provided me with a rare opportunity to cross racial and ethnic lines, to have had close encounters with Blacks and Coloureds. To appreciate them as people, as individuals and colleagues each with a distinct personality tinged with unique cultural

Dormitory mates at Fort Hare (Author: centre row left)

Author (bottom right) celebrating his 21st birthday

and ethnic influences. This experience certainly opened my eyes to a life out there beyond the narrow, curry-flavoured confines of Cato Manor. I began to feel the essence of a *South African-ness*.

For the first time, too, I found myself taught by Indians, Whites and Blacks. The lecturers and professors were, without exception, competent and gifted teachers, and incredibly supportive of students. They earned my undeserved respect. This was a period of close cross-racial encounters which helped shape, expand, and deepen my consciousness, both politically and socially. I felt proudly aware that I was following in the footsteps of past students at Fort Hare who later became involved in the African liberation struggles of the nineteen sixties and seventies, and whose names are now internationally recognised. These include Nelson Mandela, Seretse Khama, Oliver Tambo and Chris Hani. The latter, a contemporary of mine, became a formidable leader in the ANC military wing. Yet I remember him as a lean and gentle youth, standing casually at the entrance of his student room, welcoming me with a sunny smile.

The country had great hopes for Chris Hani to take over the mantle from Nelson Mandela in government. Sadly, however, he was assassinated in 1993, on the eve of South Africa's new dawn. Clive Derby-Lewis, a Conservative member of parliament, was sentenced to life imprisonment for arranging the killing. His statement to the Truth and Reconciliation Commission read: 'As a Christian, my first duty is to Almighty God, before everything else. We were fighting communism, and communism is the vehicle of the anti-Christ.'

Communism for the Afrikaner Government was anything that stood in the way of Apartheid, the pillar of white privilege. In this sense, it was no different to the McCarthyism of the nineteen fifties in the USA where all-and-sundry were persecuted for so-called subversion and terrorism - for being anti-American. But that awful time in history is now almost forgotten. In fact, a Communist Party exists in post-apartheid South Africa and serves in government, in partnership with the African National Congress.

As things turned out, my sojourn at Fort Hare was short-lived. The university was declared a *Bantu College* under the Nationalist Government's Separate Universities Act, which meant that, in future, students would be compelled to attend racially segregated universities. The many indigenous black tribal communities were collectively and conveniently designated as Bantu by the Government. We expressed our outrage by boycotting lectures and milling around the campus with placards and engaging in sit-down protests. I was in the thick of the concerted student and staff opposition to the government move. This was quite a new experience for me: I was fearful of the consequences on the one hand yet exhilarated by the mesmerising pull of mass protest.

We shouted slogans until we were hoarse. We marched around the Student Union building and down a mile into the town centre of Alice, drawing out into the street curious onlookers - shoppers, shop-assistants, and office workers. A few Whites from upper-level open windows leaned out with scowling faces. A strong police presence attempted to contain the resistance.

The Student Representative Council convened several meetings of the student body to decide on more drastic actions. But these joint sessions were eventually abandoned without a clear outcome. I was among those who felt quite frustrated at how rowdy and chaotic they became. Anxious and cautious students, not wanting to risk their university careers, clashed with more radical students who were proposing fire and brimstone. Adding to the confusion, was a small disengaged and disruptive rabble who saw the situation as one hilarious joke – an occasion to engage in relentless banter. They competed with one another to mock and mimic speakers, drowning out debate in bursts of laughter, whistling and catcalls. Poor Mr m'Gutumela, a short, dark, and thickset senior student with a serious pitted face, had it the worst. His pronounced nasal twang reminded me of the whining of a cat in distress. His 'Why, Mr Chairman,' immediately elicited a spate of 'Woo-whyeee, Meester Chaarman.' Even I, at times, could not keep a straight face.

When the government appointed a new pro-apartheid rector, he and his entourage of security officers received a most unceremonious welcome. A surge of students pushed, shoved, and taunted them. They did not react but seemed stoic. Clearly, they had come prepared for such strong opposition. They were there for the long haul.

Students Boycott Lectures

New Rector with Security

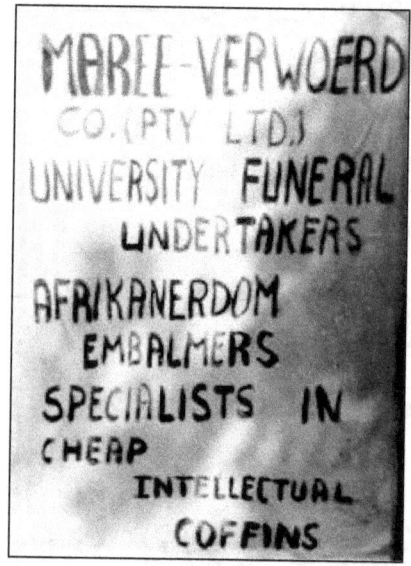
Slogans displayed by students.

Despite our concerted agitation, an exodus of students from Fort Hare proved inevitable. Many of us decided to jump before being pushed.

~

Having quit Fort Hare, for the next four years (1960-63) I studied at the University of Natal in Durban for an Arts

Degree. The irony was that this university also practised strict segregation in accordance with the government's Separate Universities Act. (A university in Durban exclusively for Indians was in the process of being established.) White students attended the Howard College campus, an iconic Victorian-style building located on the Berea ridge with a panoramic view of the city and harbour, far below. Students other than Whites (designated Non-Whites), however, attended classes in what was called the *Non-European Section.* Marion Buildings, adjacent to the City Campus of the University of Natal, was a shoddy multi-storey warehouse in Lancers Avenue, off Warwick Avenue, and across from markets and bus ranks – a busy and congested working-class fringe of the city. The lecture rooms were on the rented second and third floors. There was no lift.

The building was also a block away from the notorious Lancers Bar. I had no choice but to walk past this pub on days I attended lectures. I would feel painfully disgusted to see an occasional Indian woman in a sari staggering outside the bar, eyes glazed and intoxicated, ranting, and swearing at ghosts in her mind. Wary pedestrians would quicken their pace, giving her a wide berth. Her bare dirt-encrusted feet, her lips burnt pale from excessive drinking, and her hair unwashed and wild as feral bush. I was clearly in denial. Alcohol-addicted Indian women simply did not exist in my blinkered reality.

Although I was a full-time student, my lectures were invariably in the afternoon and evenings. This was to accommodate the white lecturers who taught at the main campus in the mornings and commuted to the non-white section in the afternoons. The all-white lecturing staff were, by and large, English-speaking academics with integrity who excelled in their subjects. However, they rarely commented on the segregated nature of the university or fraternised with us.

I soon joined the Student Representative Council (Non-European Section) and engaged in student issues and activities. We liaised with the white SRC on a few matters – the annual charity floats parade being one. This parade through the city was organised to assist the Durban Community Chest to raise funds for not-for-profit welfare organisations. Although our floats paraded together, the non-white students built their floats quite separately at an independent venue.

I am uncertain now if the non-white SRC was ever relevant to the students it supposedly served, or successfully advocated on any issues of grave importance on their behalf. What remains embarrassingly vivid in my mind, even to this day, was the time and money (allocated by the university from student fees) squandered by us at every meeting on take-away meals. We would start the meeting about 6 pm, attend to a few items on the agenda, then routinely engage in a ritual of scanning a take-away menu from a café downstairs, and then call out our preference to whoever volunteered to go and get the orders. While waiting for the person to return, we would distract ourselves in chitchat where political gossip would prevail. Then we would haggle over who ordered what, as the brown-paper packs were passed around. Time would pass. The chair would attempt to bring the meeting to order and pick up on the agenda again. 'Let's go, guys. Come on, settle down.' But even weighty issues would end up being masticated with our bites of bacon and egg sandwiches, then drowned with coffee.

Now, I gaze with wonder at the photo of the non-white SRC. We certainly were an all-male bunch of Indian and Blacks - everyone handsome, healthy and in the prime of his life. As far as I know, at least six of these are now deceased and the whereabouts of the others unknown to me. Such is life.

Segregated SRC (Author in front, second from left)

NUSAS (Author: back row second from left)

During my tenure on the SRC, I became an active member of the National Union of South African Students (NUSAS), which at the time was dominated by white students from the relatively liberal English-speaking universities. There were no more than a handful of black members. Afrikaner students from the Afrikaans speaking universities had a parallel national students' union. I recall sitting at an old Olivetti typewriter in the dining room of my home in Mayville, late into the night, composing laboured letters critical of some policies of NUSAS, or its stance on a burning issue of a political nature. The apartheid government frowned on NUSAS and kept it under police surveillance. Adrian Leftwich, the very vocal president of NUSAS at the time, challenged government policies with courage and fervour, and championed the cause of us non-white students.

Years later, however, I read a report in the mainstream media that, before his death, Adrian had confessed to providing the Security Police with incriminating information on some of his closest NUSAS colleagues, as a trade-off for favourable treatment. The shock of this disclosure made me wonder if Adrian had, in fact, been a police informant all the years he was a student activist. NUSAS, founded in 1924, eventually disbanded in July 1991 as its relevance became questionable in a rapidly evolving political climate.

~

On one occasion, while the SRC was meeting, we were interrupted by excited loud voices in the corridor. Thami Mhlambiso, in the chair, interrupted proceedings and stepped into the corridor to check what the commotion was all about. He rushed back to announce that a large column of protestors from Umkumbaan, was approaching the city centre.

'Let's go, guys,' he urged, gesturing with urgency. 'Let's show solidarity.'

Without thought or hesitation, we scampered down the two flights of stairs of Marion Buildings and out into the street, almost colliding into pedestrians hurrying in the opposite direction and looking visibly scared.

'What's going on, mama?' A man outside the downstairs café shouted.

'A stampeding mob,' blurted a large, coloured woman, catching her breath, as she lumbered past.

The traffic had come to a chaotic halt. We heard a chorus of male chanting. The rousing black protest song grew louder and louder as we hastened towards Gale Street. I felt quite nervous and uncomfortable. Although I had participated in relatively disciplined student protests and demonstrations at Fort Hare, I had not done so in a highly charged and volatile situation where the participants were disaffected and impoverished black men. I felt rather uncertain and anxious about joining them. Perhaps the only reason I did not pull back was that Thami kept us all in sight. It would have been shameful for me to hesitate at this crucial moment. Then, too, I felt reassured sticking close to my black SRC colleagues, Earnest Gallo and Boy Matseke.

Then the moving crowd of protestors was upon us, a throbbing and bobbing mass of sweat-drenched black men, jogging in unison, wielding fighting sticks above their heads in shared defiance of authority. Many men were without shoes. They were poorly dressed. Some had strips of rags tied to their foreheads like bandanas.

The column had force-marched like Roman soldiers over twenty kilometres from Umkumbaan. This was a remarkable feat of endurance. How was it possible? Almost five abreast, the protesters took up the width of Gale Street

I remembered that it was late afternoon. A sultry working Friday. The air was heavy and humid as we attempted to join the moving mass on the run, falling into its rhythm of stomping and chanting. I almost lost my footing in a desperate attempt to thrust myself into the flow. Luckily, someone caught and pulled me in. Merging with the protesters was strangely mesmerising. I was no longer me, a separate person. I melded into some larger collective, emotionally charged and almost single-minded. I felt no fear. It intrigues me how a rowdy protesting crowd metamorphoses into a mob.

In reliving the experience now in my imagination, I'm reminded of Tennyson's poem The Charge of the Light Brigade:

> *Theirs not to reason why*
> *Theirs but to do and die*
> *Into the Valley of Death*
> *Rode the six hundred*

The sweltering air was shattered by the menacing sounds of rapid gunfire. In a second, the seemingly amorphous group splintered into units of countless human beings. We scattered in all directions like a disturbed army of fire-ants. The much loathed and invincible security forces had ambushed us at the intersection of Gale Street and Berea Road. Carefully concealed Saracen tanks (armoured personnel carriers) emerged from several directions all at once. We ran for cover, for dear life, gripped by a primeval fear – each person for himself and God for all. I do not recall how I survived. Fortunately, my SRC mates and I eventually found our way back to Marion Buildings in Lancers Road, disconcerted yet foolishly intoxicated by the danger we had exposed ourselves to.

On the following day, newspapers gave full accounts of the event, illustrated with graphic photos. For me it was a near-death experience. Sadly, I now have no recollection of what triggered the march, if it was led by any brave and inspirational leaders, what number of protesters were involved, how many of them were killed and injured, nor how many were arrested, found guilty and sentenced. An archival search of the *Daily News* and *Natal Mercury* yielded nothing. Perhaps these questions are now purely academic.

~

Apart from this one gripping incident, university life was much of a settled routine. Nevertheless, I found it full and engaging, and much preferred to home life. The appeal was certainly about meeting and socialising with university friends – girls included.

At the time, I lived with my family. Travelling by public transport was no issue. On most days I would return home well after 9 pm. But the Indian bus I would usually take did not operate a late-night service. The alternative was a trolley bus (electricity powered double-decker bus) which I alighted at Model Garage on the main road. I had little fear walking the two kilometres home in the dark in all weather. Even the tall swaying shadows cast by a full moon was a familiar sight. At this time of night, the streets were eerily deserted, with only an occasional vehicle speeding past.

There was one spot on my route, however, which I would find somewhat unsettling. At the intersection of Trimbourne Road and Jansens Avenue, there stood a large old Dutch-style mansion with a veranda on two sides. It sat far back from the road, squat and gloomy, protected by four or five giant fig trees along the fence-line, their awesome canopies reaching out over the roads on either side. I never set eyes on the occupants of this palatial house. It was likely built and occupied by Whites who, long before Indians moved into the area, owned large estates. But now only the ghosts of dead occupants flitted about in the dark corridors. I would hold my breath and quicken my pace as I passed, consoling myself all the while I was simply being silly.

My family were invariably asleep when I climbed the back stairs and quietly let myself in. Clearly my mother and father had no concerns for my safety. Yet, almost sixty years on, when I visited South Africa, I found there was widespread fear of all sorts of crime – home invasion, mugging, car-jacking, and wanton killings. I was constantly warned not to venture out on my own, and to be mindful of crime-ridden, no-go zones. Most people claimed to have been attacked or robbed at one time or the other. The new normal is for homes to be secured by elaborate alarms, electrified fences, or to be part of a gated complex with security checks at single entry gates.

Not that crime was unknown in the nineteen forties and fifties. Petty and opportunistic thieving was common. My family, and the Indian community generally, was wary of vagrants, disaffected and unemployed black men, who occasionally stole clothes from clothes-lines or walked away with garden implements left lying about – especially when the family dog was asleep on his job or, together with other roused dogs, was out pursuing a female in heat.

I recall a burglary that left us quite distraught and unsettled for a long time. It happened at the time when we were living temporarily in a two-room outbuilding in Mayville while the main dwelling was being completed. My parents and four of us kids slept in the one room, while the adjacent room, with a separate entrance, served as kitchen, dining area and storage space for our meagre possessions – mostly collected by my parents when they married in 1936. This room was broken into at night and a lot of stuff taken. When my mother woke at dawn to go to the toilet located outside, she found the door wide open and a few of our clothes and kitchen items strewn about. Her scream was enough to wake the dead. My sister and I sobbed to find that the few chickens we had in a pen next to the kitchen were also taken – including a pet chicken with a broken beak which we had nursed and raised from the time it was a fluffy yellow chick.

A widely held perception now among Whites, Indians and Coloureds is that they alone are the victims of crime, and the perpetrators are mostly Blacks. Not so. From recent media reports, I get the impression that Indians and Whites are equally involved in high-level white-collar crimes. I have also heard a cynical view that behind every corrupt black man there lurked a corrupt Indian.

In the 1940s and '50s, it was not uncommon for Indian women shopping in the city to have their gold *thali* necklaces ripped of them by brazen black pickpockets. The rumour was rife that some of the many competing Indian jewellers in the Grey Street area were, in fact, behind this lucrative racket. Even my mother believed this story.

In a post-apartheid South Africa most black people, still marooned in apartheid-era segregated townships, suffer even more from endemic crime. Unrelenting poverty and the ever-growing disparity between the super-rich and the impoverished majority are glaring factors explaining the current sad situation. The expression *conspicuous consumption* aptly describes how wealth is flaunted in South Africa. Even I, as a visitor from affluent Australia, was staggered by the many glitzy shopping malls and casinos, the countless recent-model BMWs and Mercedes to be seen, and the extravagant mansions in exclusive suburbs. A fast-growing black elite has embraced this lifestyle with fervour. The upwardly mobile, post-Mandela young Blacks are referred to as the *born-frees* or entitlement generation. Freedom riders of another kind.

However, this is not true for most of the black youth. Youth unemployment is rife. The much-touted post-Mandela miracle has yet to touch their lives. They are, understandably restive and cynical.

~

On reflection, it is clear to me that growing up as an Indian (and a Non-White) in South Africa in the 1950s and '60s, had largely shaped my perception of my immediate world. My reality seemed infused with notions of colour, race, and ethnicity. Interestingly, Hazel Carey, a former South African of coloured background, captures almost similar sentiments in her 2016 memoir (*Ubuntu – My life in Other People*). According to Hazel, one of her friends observed that seeing colour was ingrained and automatic in the South

African psyche. *'We don't just see black and white but all the colours in between. The exact shade determined where you lived, whether you could vote which beach you went to, which part of the bus you sat on and who you could sleep with.'*

From childhood, I was immersed in the beliefs and unchallenged prejudices of my parents and of my immediate community. The people in my everyday world were slotted into boxes - Whites, Indians, Coloureds or Blacks. Whites were, naturally, above us and Blacks were beneath us. That is how it was. Should I feel appalled? Should I pass judgement on my parents and my community? Should I blame them for *my* prejudices? Chabani Manganyi *(Being Black in the World,* 2019*)* is deeply pessimistic about the corrosive impact of our exposure to institutional racism. *'We will need a miracle to undo the damage of psyche indoctrination wrought by Apartheid.'*

I must confess it took an awfully long time for me to realise I harboured inherited prejudices. Travel and cross-cultural interactions cast a light on these, making them visible to me. The challenge then was to dispel them, with persistence and perseverance, like getting rid of resistant curry stains on a business shirt. Not at all an easy task.

As I progressed through high school and into university, I began meeting and interacting with Whites, Coloureds and Blacks at a more equal level – although I was always wary not to breach the country's apartheid laws. Initially this was largely with coloured and black male colleagues. I recall once inviting home a few of my close friends from the University of Natal. Although this was rare and unusual, I do not remember what the occasion was that prompted such an event. The foursome included two girls (an Indian and a Coloured), and two men (an Indian and a Black). I felt at once proud and rather self-conscious when they all arrived. My parents appeared visibly ill-at-ease, not knowing if we were breaking the law or that they would be in trouble with the police if neighbours reported us.

When my friends left, my mother quizzed me about the girls. 'Not Tamil girls, eh? Clara – what kind of name is that? And this Poonwanthi – what's her father's name? He said okay to bring her here?'

I was not sure what she was on about – perhaps that her precious son would be spirited away by two girls not of our ilk. My father was more taciturn and circumspect. His only comments were: 'Don't spoil your studies, son. Girls come later.' My black friend got no mention. It was as if my parents did not wish to acknowledge his presence.

But here is the thing, the great good man Gandhi himself seemed to have harboured racial prejudices when he was active in South Africa. In fact, the Washington Post of 15 Dec 2018 reported that a statue of the Gandhi was removed from the University of Ghana after a petition was circulated by university staff accusing him of espousing racism. They alleged that Gandhi, in his capacity as a barrister representing the interests of local Indian merchants in colonial Natal, had made a case to the British Government that Indians ought not to be subjected to the same restrictions as lowly 'kaffirs', since Indians, of Aryan stock, were *infinitely superior* to Blacks. As a barrister trained in England, it seemed to me, Gandhi acquired the mentality of Victorian England – the white man's view of Africa as *primitive*. Not only that, but Gandhi gave himself a complete makeover, dressing and looking like an English gentleman – a dark skinned enthusiast of the British Empire. Only bitter experience in subsequent years compelled him to change his outlook.

~

All too soon my university life days were over. I experienced a wistful letting go of all that intense fellowship, strident student politics, stress of study, assignments, and exams - and the carefree social life. There were brave smiles all around, hugs and parting drinks and best wishes about finding a job. Finding employment as a teacher in an Indian school was a fearful new spectre. For several long weeks, it loomed large and refused to budge. It stood stubborn at the foot of my bed as I opened my eyes each morning – until the unimaginable happened.

The news spread like a wildfire among my university friends. The newly independent nation of Zambia (previously Northern Rhodesia) was recruiting foreign teachers at virtually three times the salary I would earn teaching at home in a segregated government school. Indian teachers with equivalent qualifications were paid much less than Whites under Apartheid for similar roles. Of course, Blacks received much less than Indians. My parents received the news from me with scepticism.

'Really? Are you sure? Zambia? Where *is* Zambia? So farrrr away, other side of Rhodesia? The government won't let you go, you know.'

The more I explained, the more apprehensive and confused they became.

'Going to a country run by native people, to teach native children, that's very risky isn't it?' said my father.

'You don't know what you're talking about,' added my mother. 'Suddenly you're too big for your shoes, eh?'

'But please Ma, think of the money I'd earn and send home,' I pleaded. I saw it as a once-in-a-lifetime opportunity. I was both fearful and dizzy with anticipation as I digested the real possibility of venturing out to teach in a distant country – way beyond the suffocating stranglehold of an apartheid state.

Applying for a passport to leave South Africa was a daunting process. My previous experience of applying for a permit to study at Fort Hare had prepared me not to be overly optimistic. At the same time, I had gained some skill in dealing with the apartheid bureaucracy. In due course, an officially embossed letter arrived in the post instructing me to call at the offices of Indian Affairs (Passport Section) with a photo identification. I was over the moon. My pulse was racing when I arrived at the appropriate counter. And then there it was, in my hand – a green document. My passport with my very own photo. So it was that the unthinkable happened.

It was with no little trepidation I crossed the northern border of South Africa at Beitbridge into Rhodesia. But the security check was brisk and cursory. So unpredictable. I was in a car with three others, all starry-eyed and heading north to secure our fortune, much like prospectors during the gold rush days. We were fearful and feverish with anticipation as we drove through the night from Beitbridge to Kazungula, the border crossing into Zambia. We covered the distance of 850 kilometres with only brief pit and smoke stops. In entering Zambia, we had breached finally the *apartheid barrier*. What a spectacular moment!

Part 2
Breaking Through the Apartheid Barrier

Zambia
January 1964 – December 1967

It would take a couple of days and nights by car and a local bus for me to arrive at my first teaching post in a remote rural part of Zambia. Of the many South African Indian teachers given postings by the Zambian Education Ministry, I alone was shunted to Serenje, a one-horse town on a major gravel highway to the newly formed United Republic of Tanzania.

My first bus trip from Broken Hill (now Kabwe) to Serenje, some 186 kms away, was both traumatic and memorable. Immediately on boarding the bus, I realised that I was a rare spectacle for the local Zambian passengers. Perhaps I was the very first foreigner to travel on a local bus. Hence, the many puzzled looks and nervous smiles and mutterings! The bus route was known famously as the Great North Road. It was a pulverised unsealed road from Kapri Mposhi, to Mbeya on the border of Tanzania.

I had barely room to breathe since the bus was packed. I had to contend with a very congested bus hurtling at breakneck speed and churning up a great cloud of sand in the process. Passengers and their possessions were knocked about by the whipping, swaying motions of the speeding bus. The nightmarish journey seemed to go on forever. I wished it to end soon as I barely coped with the choking dust combined with the acrid smell of countless sweaty bodies, the smells of anxious trussed-up poultry, and sacks of local produce and fertilizer. This was all complemented by the strange smells emanating from the local foods being consumed on board! I had to also bear as well as possible an intense cacophony of competing sounds produced by animated passengers, unhappy fowls, and a straining engine. There was simply no place to hide! What a relief it was when the bus briefly stopped a few times to drop off people.

Serenje proved to be a rare, challenging, and unique experience. The school complex was still to be built when I arrived there – six months before completion. It was to be a boarding school for boys from a vast rural catchment. Self-contained cottages were being constructed for staff. While the building work was proceeding, I was put up in a mini caravan called a *terrapin*. This I shared with a new teacher recruit like myself, Mr Peterson, a young Coloured teacher from Cape Town. Our time was largely spent taking delivery of books, stationery and other equipment for the new school and compiling an inventory.

We were a complement of seven teachers - three Zambians, a Dutch priest, a female teacher of Scottish background, and, of course, Petersen and me, both unmarried South Africans. The principal, Mr Bouchard, was a lanky French Canadian in his forties. He and two of the Zambians had their families with them. Each of the staff was allocated his own 3-bedroom cottage, still smelling of fresh paint. The priest, however, lived at a mission station.

What a cosmopolitan lot. One of the Zambians was into drinking and rubbishing his pupils for being rural and uncouth. His jolly first cousin resented the white man who headed the school because he believed a black man (which was him) ought to have been appointed principal. After all

Clockwise from top left: Teaching staff (Author standing on the right). Author's first car and his 3-bedroom cottage.

Zambia had won its independence from British colonialists. He expressed his views openly to me, which made me feel compromised.

'See now, this white guy only knows how to give instructions. Do this, do that. I swear that whenever he sees me, he's thinking, "Don't you forget I'm the *bwana* here."'

What could I do but appear attentive to his spluttering? I would pull out my handkerchief immediately he turned to leave.

'Aagh man,' he'd continue, 'the days for the white man are over. I'm telling you it's finished.' He would shuffle a bit and break into a sweat.

The principal, Mr Bouchard, mostly went about his responsibilities with unruffled diligence. I was certain he sensed the passive hostility in the corridors of the boarding school. Perhaps he simply shrugged it off and chose to keep his head down, knowing his lucrative expatriate contract would soon be over. I attempted to be in his good books and with the rest of the staff. The Dutch priest, the Scottish woman and my colleague from Cape Town, all active Christians, remained cheerful - steering clear of local politics.

The third Zambian was a young and fun-loving new graduate fresh from college. He did not seem too interested in his older countrymen or about their gripes. Whenever free, he would disappear into the night in search of opportunities universally favoured by virile, young men. I was sceptical that he would have much luck in this bush outpost. But then he may have been capable of special hunting prowess.

~

Serenge boasted a Christian teacher training college, a small cluster of modest houses for locals, a post office, a Boma (a guest house-cum-office for visiting government officers - a vestige of colonial times), and a well-stocked grocery store catering essentially for a poor rural community, all black Zambians.

The shop, however, was an Indian-owned family business – the large Badat clan lived at the rear of the shop, having migrated from India in the nineteen fifties. Brave and resourceful pioneers, like the European explorers of earlier times. They had relocated with their wives and children to the *back of the beyond* with the single-minded purpose of amassing wealth.

The Badat General Supply Store was a large, cavernous structure of wood and iron with a timber veranda. It was poorly lit. You name it and they most likely had it. Most of the basic needs of rural people with little cash was sold in small affordable amounts. The shop oozed a distinct smell – a blend of paraffin, firewood, sisal hemp, cloth, sorghum, tobacco, and maize meal. The smell reminded me of our dog, Rover, back in Durban, rain-soaked, dripping, and miserable.

The Badat brothers spoke the local language, Bemba, fluently and tended to keep up a light- hearted conversation with the male customers. The women continued to chat among themselves with expressive sounds and gestures while their eyes roamed over the open sacks of maze meal, grain and beans. It was all so foreign and intriguing to me. I wished I could have understood the banter and joined in their laughter. The customers would leave seemingly well satisfied with their purchases. Clearly the Badats, with their shrewd business skills, were the winners – and the customers none the wiser.

For Peterson and me, the Badats were a lifesaver. They were a cheerful and friendly lot. Many a time when I was bored and craving for curry, I would take myself to the Badats, a twenty-minute walk from the school campus along a dusty yellow dirt road. Even though I would invariably arrive there uninvited, warm hospitality always awaited me. And I would leave late, satiated with curry and rice.

Soon I was into my second year at Serenje. My life as a resident teacher settled into a routine. I was getting accustomed to my pupils – their strange names and personalities and I was connecting with the staff and with other expatriate people in the village. I even bought my very first car for a modest sum from the Dutch priest – a sturdy, 1959 second-hand VW beetle which had already done some two hundred thousand miles but was still going strong. It became my prized possession. I learnt to drive on a largely unused airstrip a little outside the town. All in all, then, it was a relatively enjoyable and eventful year for me. As promised, I sent a good part of my salary home to help my family.

My mother was the only one who kept in touch with me – by snail mail. A hand-written note every few weeks would arrive by post - a few troubled lines carefully written on ruled paper. My mother had been unwell for years. Corrosive worries eroded her health and emotional wellbeing – worries over an absent son, worries over my father's precarious income from week to week, and above all, fear of an uncertain future now that every household in the long-settled community of Cato Manor had finally received an eviction notice in accordance with the Group Areas Act.

'We need you to be here to help us decide if we should accept the little money the government is offering for our house. Your father is not good in these things. He depends on me. But I know you can't be here.'

My mother had stinted and saved the money for a deposit on a building plot in Reservoir Hills. I think she had a vision of the family progressing, aspiring for a better quality of life. I thought it ironical that she had turned dispossession into a potential advantage. An indoor flushing toilet was her dream. And a proper sealed road. My mother's protracted illness had handicapped her in many ways. It was humiliating for her to use a potty as she was unable to take the back stairs and then walk down a sloping backyard to access a bucket toilet. And the steep gravel path to our house deterred a taxi from collecting her at the door whenever she needed to go to the doctor or to the hospital.

The letters from my mother always left me with a sense of guilt. Why wasn't I around to help at a critical time for the family? I decided I would make every effort to return home on a visit in the next summer school holidays. But it was not to be. The gods, it seemed, had ideas of their own.

My short stay in Serenje came to an unexpected and abrupt end on a Saturday in summer. I crashed my precious VW on the treacherous Great North Road.

~

The accident was perhaps predictable and did not surprise my colleagues at school. After all, I had barely taught myself to drive and did not even have a driver's licence. I was also unfamiliar with the hazards of pulverized dirt roads, and ignorant of the notorious instability of a VW beetle (with a rear engine) on such roads. I was no less than a brazen young fool. Moreover, this attitude was quite inconsistent with my being a teacher who was expected to be a role model for impressionable Zambian pupils – especially boys.

The accident happened on my way back after having serviced the car at the nearest service station which was in Kitwe about 180 kilometres away. Boy, was I lucky!

As I hit the unsealed road, I became aware of a slight heaviness in my chest. Concentrate, I told myself taking a firmer grip of the steering. My old car did its best riding out unrelenting stretches of corrugation. It felt as if I was working a pneumatic drill on a slab of concrete. Repeatedly checking the rear-view mirror, I prayed no speeding vehicle would descend upon me through the sandstorm raised by the VW. If this happened, I would have to give way – moving into treacherous loose sand.

Insistent hooting followed almost immediately by a short, sharp metallic thud at my right rear. My world went into a tailspin. Calamity experienced in slow motion. This is it, I thought. I am done for.

A voice calling, remotely as if through fog. 'You okay there? Hey, you hearing me?'

I squinted but could not see anyone above me, as it was shimmeringly bright. Why couldn't I move? How did so much sand get into my mouth? Sand all over.

Someone tugged at my arm. There was excruciating pain.

Next, I recall being driven in a car, wedged in the passenger seat. The driver, from what I could tell through bleary eyes, had a large, sweaty black face.

'Hey bwana. Hold on, okay. I get you to doctor fast, fast.' He sounded anxious. 'You sleep now.'

I grunted with some relief. My world was a muddled mess. I felt awful. Bloody bumpy car. God, I thought, I'm going to throw up any minute.

After a long while, I found myself lying on a cold hard slab, mounted waist high. My body was numb with pain. A thin sheet, smelling vaguely of hospitals, covered me. The room was cramped and cold and dingy. Silent. Oh no, not a mortuary!

I turned my head ever so slightly and was startled to see a man kneeling on the ground next to me - a bearded slightly bald white man in a white lab coat. He was bent over, clasping his hands. Was he saying a prayer? I blinked but the image did not disappear but straightened up.

'Ah, you're awake.' He adjusted his glasses and peered at me.

I tried to sit up, but the man placed a firm hand on my shoulder.

'What's this place? Where am I?'

'It's Chitambo Mission Hospital. You know it? On the highway to the Tanzanian border.'

'And you?' I said with a nervous sniffle.

'Oh, I'm Father O'Connell, the Mission doctor. You were brought here by a Good Samaritan. Found you on the roadside, he said, near a mangled VW. Shocking.'

'I'm not dead then?' I blurted, still feeling out of control.
'No, no. Oh no, not all,' he smiled, revealing an uneven set of discoloured teeth 'I sedated you. You were delirious. You probably don't remember.' He pulled up a high stool and sat. 'You're lucky. Broken bones and bruises, mostly. No internal damage as far as I can tell. Can't be sure, you know. I don't have proper stuff for a thorough examination. We're

just a small rural hospital.'

I felt a little alarmed. It must have shown in my face.

'Don't worry, an ambulance is on the way. Broken Hill (Kabwe) Hospital is better for you. That hip will take some fixing. But these jutting collar bones,' he said going over them with his fingers, 'I'm afraid you'll have to live with them. They don't mend easily.'

I lay in Broken Hill hospital for some three months with a leg suspended in traction. I was never to return to Serenje, to bring closure to my life there. I never got to say goodbye to staff, pupils or to friends in that close-knit community – and I never got to say sorry to my VW beetle for wrecking it good and proper!

My family in South Africa was in the dark about the accident and my hospitalisation. I had told my mother in a letter that I intended to spend the summer holidays exploring Zambia. She died soon after, pining for her son. I was compelled to travel home for the funeral. On crutches.

On my return from Zambia after the funeral, I was transferred to Lusaka Hospital as an out-patient. My rehabilitation (mostly exercise physiotherapy) lasted three months. The upside of my accident turned out to be the city lights of Lusaka, the urban capital of Zambia. How amazing is that! For a young person like me (a city bloke), Serenje had been smothering. No frills, no thrills.

~

Accommodation in the capital for civil servants was scarce and in great demand. Hence, my relocation to Lusaka, it seemed, was only made possible by the generosity of a fellow South African teacher, Raj Dayal, who, when approached by the education department, readily agreed to share his government allocated flat in Connaught Road.

It was one of five flats in an elongated two-storey block, a featureless building much like an army barracks. But the flat itself was spacious and comfortable, with a large living area on the ground floor, a bedroom, and a kitchen with an attached pantry. Upstairs were two further smallish bedrooms plus a toilet and a separate bathroom. Most times, a single row of cars was to be seen parked side-by-side in the front yard, which was unfenced and gravelled.

We called it Libala Flats, but I am unsure if this was its official name. All five flats were occupied by expatriate teachers who taught at Libala Secondary School, about seven miles away in Libala Township. Perhaps this was why I was also posted there. It proved very convenient as I then travelled to school and back with my flat-mate benefactor, Raj.

Shared flat (2nd from left)

Libala was not too different from my previous school but had a larger enrolment, and the boys lived with their families in the community. The principal was a Mr Molotsi, a cultured and urbane black South African. Imagine that I would come all the way to Zambia to meet and serve under a black South African. It was certainly a steep learning curve for me.

The staff comprised South African Indians, Blacks and a Coloured, a Russian and a Polish woman, a large man from India (Pathan), and several white expatriates from Britain. I cannot recall any Zambians on the teaching staff.

I had arrived in Zambia in January 1964, the very year the country attained independence under Kenneth Kaunda, the man in a safari suit waiving a white handkerchief. All about I saw euphoric, cheering black people dancing as if a long drought had broken, for the moment forgetting their impoverished circumstances. The men wore tunic-like t-shirts of inexpensive cotton with motifs marking Zambian Independence. The women wore ankle-length wraps made of almost similar printed cloth. Many people had bare feet. The white expatriate community looked troubled and uncertain of their futures. They huddled together in the expatriates-only clubs. In Lusaka, they were concentrated mostly in the town centre close to the seat of parliament and the hub of government departments, private and public schools, colleges, and hospitals. Black Zambians, on the other hand, lived on the fringes, in relatively poor and congested townships, an enduring vestige of colonial rule. For now, the old order prevailed, although subtle indications of change were evident.

I realised very soon that we non-white South Africans were the *new expats* since we were employed on the same terms and conditions as the overseas colonial expatriates, with identical entitlement to a privileged life. The local

Blacks remained outsiders, second-class citizens. I cannot recall giving much thought to this glaring disparity. A shameful pointer to my blind spot!

The white expats set the pace in Lusaka, a frenetic and restless pace. To a degree I allowed myself to be sucked into this lifestyle. So did the rest of us South Africans. The social life was generally lived at a superficial level, characterised by partying, drinking, and womanizing. Unlike the sedate, boring tenor of Serenje, life for me became exceedingly stimulating - and exhausting.

The trauma of my car crash and the death of my mother was no longer hurting. I was also beginning to forget the soul-nourishing meals with the Badats. In place, I embraced the open hospitality of Joe and Kamoo Kajee, exiles from South Africa. Kamoo would laugh and shake her head as she opened the door to her flat. 'I told Joe the hungry bachelors would soon come knocking.' She always cooked a little extra curry for me, Raj, and a couple of regular ANC cadres like the sociable Julius.

The African National Congress (ANC) had a vital presence in Zambia at the time. Since creating a military wing, Umkhonto we Sizwe, and mounting guerrilla incursions into South Africa, Lusaka had become one of its operational centres. And Libala Flats somehow turned into an informal hangout for ANC cadres passing through or temporarily based in Lusaka. There was much coming and going. So, apart from our full-on involvement in expatriate social circles, fraternising with ANC people, both politically and socially, grew into an important focus of my life. I got to know a few cadres quite well – mostly Black and Coloured South Africans. They were all warm and friendly young men in their early thirties. Some were disciplined and serious-minded, awaiting their imminent deployment to the front line. Others appeared restless, troubled, and readily given to alcohol and womanising.

Not long after meeting two of the cadres and taking to their friendly disposition, we were shocked to learn that they had been shot and killed near Plumtree, Southern Rhodesia, in a skirmish with South African security forces while attempting to infiltrate into the country. The news saddened and jolted us. For me politics was all talk, but for these cadres the reality was otherwise. To commit to armed political resistance meant putting one's life on the line.

My ego went up a couple of notches when I met the likes of Oliver Tambo, the ANC President, and Tennyson Makiwane, head of the ANC mission in Zambia. Later in casual conversations with someone, I would deliberately create the impression that I too was actively involved in the freedom struggle. In hindsight, it seemed the ANC was a little lax with security in Lusaka. No one ever warned me to be careful. The cadres spoke to us freely and earnestly about what they were up to, even sharing their anxiety.

On one occasion during school holidays, I was requested by the ANC to drive into Southern Rhodesia on a scouting mission, to check how active the security forces were along the northern border with Zambia. I was assured that I would not be in any risk as I was legally outside the country on a valid passport. Hence, the security forces would not pay me any attention.

'Hey man, just keep saying to yourself you're a tourist, and no one will suspect.'

I could not quite follow the logic of this assurance. Did

it put me at ease? I cannot recall, but I think I felt honoured to be assigned this important task by none other than Oliver Tambo himself.

Oliver Tambo

It was my very first (and only) brief and close encounter with this man of world stature. He certainly made an impression on me. A short and stocky man, broad shouldered, with a cheerful face and a receding hairline – which gave him a shiny prominent forehead. His peppercorn hair and full-facial beard were speckled-white. All-in-all I thought he appeared very distinguished.

He fussed and beamed as he spoke. Mr Tambo was in his late 50s at the time, and with his heavy, black-rimmed spectacles and wise-looking eyes, could easily pass as a dedicated and humble African pastor - in the mould of the late Chief Albert Luthuli, the president of the ANC before him.

'You'll put these on, okay,' he said, holding up a pair of sea-blue underpants, and pointing to two concealed pockets. 'See, it's even the right size.'

Not surprisingly, this rare image has survived most

vividly in my mind. What secret items went into the concealed pockets, has remained a mystery. The round trip took me a few days of driving, but the precise details of the mission have eluded recollection. If I had any reservation about this mission, it was to do with driving hundreds of kilometres into Southern Rhodesia on my own at a time when Ian Smith, the wily Prime Minister, had snatched independence from Britain. This illegal act greatly heightened tensions in the region. But I was also, after my last accident, still a little nervous about driving. This was despite acquiring a valid driver's licence within six months of arriving in Lusaka and buying myself a second-hand Fiat.

In hindsight, I believe I was quite naïve at the time and somewhat blinded by the thrill of engaging in a cloak and dagger mission. Perhaps it was pure luck I was not stopped and questioned by the security forces at one of several checkpoints I was waved through. The obvious learning from this experience was that I should in future be more circumspect about my political involvement.

~

Thereafter, I looked more to what opportunities Lusaka had to offer to advance my skills and augment my personal and professional experience – mindful that my time in Zambia would sooner or later be over.

Firstly, as an English teacher at Libala, I produced a play with the year nine pupils. I did this almost single-handed. Aiming high, I leaned on the prestigious Lusaka Theatre Company to allow me the use of their posh theatre. Up to then it had been an exclusive whites-only facility. I chose *Everyman* a medieval morality play, by an unknown author, with the universal theme of man's greedy pursuit of personal material wealth, not heeding the inevitability of his death and having then to give account of his good deeds while alive. The moral of the play made a strong impression on the students. The Nigerian playwright Ulli Beier had originally adapted the theme to fit local Yoruba culture. I was captivated by an English translation of this Yoruba version by Obotunde Ijimere. When we read the play together in class, my Zambian students found it hilarious, yet they were able to relate to its authentic African context and cultural texture. They were more than eager to participate in bringing it alive on stage, but without having any idea of how demanding this may prove to be. 'Sir, sir,' they clamoured shooting up their hands. 'I want to be in it. Please sir, take me.' Mr Molotsi, the principal, was dubious about the idea. He stood up behind his desk with hands in his pocket and laughed with incredulity. Come on man, you sure you want to do this thing? Talk it over with your head of department.'

~

The project succeeded beyond expectations. The students delivered a performance of calibre and acclaim. The theatre had limited seating capacity but was packed with parents, teachers, Libala students and a few members of the Lusaka Theatre Company. At the end of the show, they crowded the foyer hugging, handshaking and showering the actors with compliments. We have not seen anything like this before, was the recurring refrain. It seemed as if this was a watershed moment, a new beginning for an independent Zambia. I felt a deep sense of satisfaction that I had bonded with black Zambian parents and pupils at a personal and professional level, a bonding that overrode my worry I may have had that they would be wary of me as a person of another race and culture. On reflection, I think the play was somewhat prophetic for its time in that it anticipated the recurring story of corrupt and plundering despots subverting the emerging independence of impoverished nations in Africa, Asia and Latin America.

Hand-drawn program, and a scene from Everyman

My second achievement in Lusaka was undertaking and completing a research project for a Masters' degree in psychology. While in Serenje, I had registered with the University of South Africa (UNISA) to study for a post-graduate degree by correspondence (distance education). Lusaka provided me with a much greater opportunity to find a suitable research topic. With a little effort, I managed to persuade Zambia's one and only psychiatric hospital (Chianama) to allow me to access a sample of adult Zambians on its register of outpatients. Adult and older black Zambians, many village, and rural folks, were mostly the ones who flooded the waiting room from early hours of the morning. In my screening research, I asked patients to copy what was put before them, which was a set of nine geometric drawings called the Bender Gestalt Test. The idea was that a clinician could quickly tell the degree of mental disturbance present by simply inspecting the copy drawings of each outpatient. This would then enable the more disturbed patients to be given priority.

In this way, I was able to meet the necessary requirements for my Masters - to demonstrate a capacity to define a research topic relevant to clinical psychology, design the research, undertake it and, finally, analyse the data and produce a report. Despite all my diligent effort, I secretly doubted its usefulness for Chianama. I honestly think I was being rather naive in believing that a psychological tool, based on a very western notion, would make much difference in this complex third-world situation. Before leaving the hospital, I handed a copy of my report to Dr Manangwa, the head of the Outpatients Department. The nurse-assistant had just given him the file of the next patient in an awfully long queue. He gave me a harassed look then glanced at the file, the nurse, me and my report in his left hand. All he said was 'Hmm,' as he placed it on a heap of files in the out-tray.

My third and last achievement while in Lusaka was teaching English to adults, in the evenings, at the Evelyn Hone College. It was a stimulating and valuable learning experience which complemented my other interests and commitments. It also enabled me to meet new people outside the usual ANC and expatriate circles. Because I taught a small group, I got to know a few of the adults quite well. This unfortunately resulted in an incident which caused me much angst.

~

In the time I taught in Zambia, I travelled back to South Africa a few times over the school holidays to catch up with family. I would travel by car with friends. Once though I used the train. From Lusaka it took me almost two days to reach Durban. It was a picturesque and varied route, crossing the Zambian border at Livingstone and the Victoria Falls, then passing over the length of Southern Rhodesia (now known as Zimbabwe) and into Botswana, before finally reaching the South African border-crossing and passport control at Mafeking. However, what I did not expect was that the South African security police would board the train in Bulawayo, a town deep in Southern Rhodesia. This was at a time when Ian Smith, the racist Prime Minister, had declared his unilateral independence from Britain.

Soon after we left Bulawayo, I happened to lean out the window from my non-white coach as the train came around a bend, bringing into view several of the first-class coaches. Many other passengers were doing likewise, that is leaning out of their compartment, delighting in the exhilaration of the moment created by the rush of wind, clatter of the train and the drifting past of undulating landscape of rock and trees and remote little villages.

It was then that I spotted Angela, her auburn hair fluttering in sunlight. She caught my eye, smiled, and waved and called out 'Come over.' Angela was a vivacious young white woman, of Portuguese background, who had been attending my advanced English language evening class at Evelyn Hone Adult College. So, we stood and chatted amiably in the passageway of her first-class coach for a while. She was also on her way to Durban to visit her sister.

It was quite a harmless encounter from our point of view. In any event, when the train pulled up at the border crossing at Mafeking, passengers had to get-off to have their passports checked and stamped. This was done at an improvised and open counter on the platform. I joined a queue. When it came to my turn, I held out my open passport to the seated white officer with the deference expected of non-white folks. The sullen-faced officer glared at the passport, then at me.

'Hier is die coolie wat'n wit vrou gesels het,' he scowled (Here's the coolie who was chatting up that white woman), handing the passport to a burly puffed-face Afrikaner standing next to him.

I felt my ears burn as I was dragged away with little ceremony.

'Ek maak jou op, jy bugger,' ('I'll fix you up, you bugger.') barked the security officer in full view of the other passengers. The Blacks on the platform shook their heads in silence, apprehension on their faces. Angela was nowhere to be seen.

I found myself in a window-less little enclosure next to the ticket office. Two other officers joined the red-faced brute. All three shouted and sneered and threatened me with blue murder. I would be detained indefinitely they said unless I confessed, came clean.

'What were you doing with that white woman?'
'What's she to you?'
'Will you be staying with her in Durban?'
'Do you know any kaffir terrorists in Lusaka?'

So went the rapid-fire questioning. I sweated and felt parched at the same time. Fear. Shit, I thought, this is too terrible. What is to happen to me? Will the train leave me behind?

'Come on, the truth, man. You're wasting time,' scolded the tall one with a twitching left eye. The heat in the enclosed room was clearly becoming unbearable. The interrogators grew redder by the minute and, together, they gave off a smell like boerewors drenched in rancid beer. I was past worrying about the temperature.

I pleaded innocence. Told them the truth. Wrung my hands. I begged, pleaded but they simply were not impressed with my entreaties.

The train tooted ready to depart. I almost peed. They consulted among themselves.

'Okay you can bugger off. But don't worry man, we'll have you tailed the whole fuckin time you're in Durban. Verstaan? (Understand?) You're not smart as you think. We'll get you.'

The train slid away from the platform as I re-entered my compartment and slumped into my seat. The three others in there averted their eyes. I was left shaken and humiliated – and fearful of what may happen once I got to Durban. What if I am prevented from returning to Zambia! Did the SB also interrogate Angela? Did she witness what happened to me?

Despite their dire threats, the SB failed to front up in the three weeks I was home. However, chronic worry and anticipation of what might happen, effectively deprived me of the joy of being with my family. I felt mildly feverish the whole time like I had a low-grade viral infection. I kept the whole traumatic episode away from my parents.

With the holidays almost over, I was more than eager to return to Zambia, again by train. I felt comforted by the thought that I would slip out without further harassment, and soon reach the relative safety of Lusaka. How mistaken I was! Once again passengers disembarked at Mafeking for passport clearance. Ye again I found myself hauled before the same three SB thugs in plain clothes. This time I was instructed to remove my luggage off the train. I was not going anywhere soon, they said. Once more I was pushed, shoved, and barked at. They were using terror-tactics to rattle me, to get me shitting in my pants. Their English, in slurred Afrikaans, was full of menace and vindictiveness.

'Is your woman on this train, eh? We'll find her, you bloody coolie. Then we'll put you in the tronk (jail) for good or packed off to India.'

The train was held up for almost fifty minutes while the first-class coaches were thoroughly searched. I had no idea if Angela was on board or not, as I had not had contact with her in Durban.

In the meantime, the protracted delay was making the passengers rather restive. Most would have had no idea why the train was being held up. For a moment, the SB officers were distracted from me when the train conductor turned up, cap in hand and wiping his sweaty face with his forearm. He appeared displeased his train was held up and berated them.

'Hey julle here. Neem 'n besluit. Laat die passasier gaan of jy hou hom. Jy besluit oor vyf minute.'

I had a smattering understanding of Afrikaans. It was obvious I was being discussed. The conductor was complaining about the hold up. Just then the security officer who had searched for Angela got off a first-class coach at the far end of the platform and made towards us, indicating at the same time with an empty hand gesture that he had not found her.

It was a mad scramble to get myself and my luggage

back on board. I screamed at someone at the open compartment window to grab my bag as I thrust it up to him, and almost instantly rushed to take hold of the handrail at the stairs and jumped aboard as the train gave a long toot and re-commenced its journey. I was breathless, my heart pounding.

The very last picture I had of the feared SB, was of three hefty thugs standing near the ticket office, chatting, and letting off puffs of cigarette smoke. Silhouetted against the afternoon sun, together they projected a single merged shadow which reached across the platform like a slithering sea monster. Nearby stood a black woman with a mop and bucket watching the train pick up speed and disappear, oblivious of my dramatic escape from the clutches of terror only moments earlier.

Within minutes, we had crossed the border into the relative safety of Botswana, and I sighed with relief.

Angela did not return to the evening English class at the College in the new term nor did I ever see her again. She was on my mind for a long time as I puzzled and speculated over what may have happened to her. The security police showed no further interest in me over this event. But then I never travelled home again from Zambia by train. In fact, when I finally grew disenchanted with Zambia, I headed for Britain not South Africa.

~

In time, the novelty and excitement of an urban lifestyle in Lusaka began to dissipate. As the saying goes: too much of a good thing wears out the soul. I felt jaded and unhappy in myself. But why? The fact was that deep down I was lonely. I was a young man in search of love, for an enduring and meaningful relationship. Somehow this was not happening for me. At least not in Zambia. The last girl I had dated at Natal University for a few years quit on me when (according to her), her orthodox father insisted she marry a very suitable partner he had found for her of their caste and ethnic group – Gujarati.

What also caused me unease was my growing awareness of how unsettled the white expatriate community in Zambia was, more especially the couples and families I had come to know well. They seemed to be drifting – and I was drifting along with them. I observed an unravelling of social and moral cohesion at close quarters. In my view there was much too much drinking and partying. It concerned me that their kids were being dragged along (and short-changed of parental attention and a settled home life) while their mums and dads were in pursuit of elusive pleasure. It seemed relatively easy for unattached men like me to engage in opportunistic casual liaisons with married women. Was this yet another symptom of the pervasive malaise I sensed? Or was this just a case of men and women having a fling on the side? Would there be anything more ravishing for a young man in his prime than to be sitting in a car driven by a young woman in a mini-skirt – the fashion craze initiated by Mary Quant in 1964? Was it just coincidental that the men in question would be classified non-white under apartheid laws of South Africa, and the women White? And if this flirting and these liaisons had occurred back home, the people concerned would have fallen foul of the Immorality Act, another one of the pillars of Apartheid. It was the *colour thing* that was bugging me. I had carried this preoccupation with me from apartheid stratified South Africa. Wherever you go, there you are is a Zen saying. But my personal unease was further compounded by a practical factor – an uncertainty about the terms of my ongoing teaching contract.

The political situation in Zambia after independence was changing rapidly. The expatriate community, including South Africans, began to feel insecure in their well-paying jobs. The first black government under Kenneth Kaunda let it be known that the privileged conditions under which foreigners were employed could no longer be financially sustained – nor politically or morally. Not long after came an ultimatum that we would have to transfer to local conditions of employment (meaning accepting huge cuts in salary and related benefits) or accept termination of existing contracts. Our relatively settled world started unravelling. There was much feverish discussion on what was to be done. How could we secure our future careers? I worried about how I could continue to sustain the financial lifeline to my family in Durban. The thought crossed my mind that perhaps I could switch to a career in psychology. But how and where?

'Yeah, you should chance it. The possibility is certainly there,' encouraged Peter and May Brook, a friendly middle-aged couple from England whose second teaching contract was nearly over, and who were headed back home. 'Look, we'll ask around when we get back.'

'Love, didn't our neighbour Mark mention that he worked at the British Psychological Society?' said May.

'That's exactly right,' said her husband, his eyes lighting up.

I felt a surge of hope, of expectation almost verging on

fantasy. I mulled over the possibility of going to Britain. I sounded out Raj's girlfriend who was Scottish. Thereafter, I wrote to the British Psychological Society (BPS) and sought their advice. In about ten days, a letter awaited me when I got back to Libala Flats. I tore opened the envelope with stamps carrying the face of the Queen. The information in just two paragraphs was precise and unambiguous. *'Even with the qualifications you have listed, you will not be allowed to practice as a psychologist in Britain. You will have firstly to be registered with the BPS as a probationary psychologist. Thereafter, undertake a period of internship as a psychologist.'* I felt deflated and alarmed.

A couple of months after I had received the letter, I packed up and flew to London. It was my very first experience of plane travel – a long and claustrophobic flight. I left behind a complex and, in many ways, unique phase in my life, my close friends, my Zambian world, the nurturing bond with my school and pupils, my memories, and so much more. My family in Durban required much convincing that my decision was the right one. 'No, it's not risky at all. Believe me, I'll be okay. Definitely. Didn't I say so? Yes, I'll get a job and continue sending money home.'

My Zambian interlude, free from the stranglehold of Apartheid, had proved vital in expanding my worldview and my sense of self. While Fort Hare made me realise I was not just an Indian but a born South African, a chip of a larger fraternity, Zambia helped me to become aware of Africa, a mighty continent that stretched way beyond the southern tip. And that I was a child of Africa whose blood 'flowed in my veins' (David Diop. *Africa My Africa*). As a teacher in all-Zambian schools, my closeness to indigenous peoples was enhanced. It had also deepened my insights into another culture. My first up close and personal encounters with white people also occurred in Zambia which prepared me for my spell in Britain. But the most significant influence on me was, no doubt, my contact with the external wing of the ANC. I was drawn into the aspirations of the struggle, formed personal relationship with a few cadres and office bearers and gained some understanding of ANC strategies, tactics, and the inevitable human cost of fighting for freedom. My political consciousness was expanded immeasurably.

Britain
February 1968 – 1 June 1969

I landed in Britain in February 1968 without having secured an internship in psychology. I had taken a calculated risk, which pretty much meant *no internship, no income.* My anxious mind saw no promise or awe in London the city of my inspirational primary school teacher, Mr RN Singh. Instead, I had stepped into a London shrouded in winter - bleak, wet and bitterly cold. I imagined Jack the Ripper skulking in the darkened streets waiting for his next kill, or Sherlock Holmes in cap and cape, following a trail of muddy footprints in determined pursuit, undeterred by the swirling fog.

As I recall, R N Singh was tall, well-built, and handsome with a cheerful face. He used to wax lyrical about Britain and London, the country of Shakespeare and of other great English writers and poets. We pupils were quite unfamiliar with the people he named or the landmarks he spoke of. But we were captivated by his narration. Especially when he concluded each account with a starry-eyed: *No person should ever be happy to die before walking the streets of*

London, the centre of the world. Although I carried that refrain within me for years, I do not think any kid in class entertained the notion of ever getting to this place called London. Our lives were too constrained by poverty at the time, and our aspirations circumscribed by an awareness that we lived in a white-affluent world in which we were outcasts.

On recollection, I would say it was silly of our teacher to drum London into us since we would not even have travelled to the next suburb or to towns nearest Durban such as Pinetown, no more than 20 kilometres away. As for RN Singh, he never ceased urging: 'You kids must believe in yourselves. Trust me, you can do it if only you keep trying.' We would sit with our mouths open, elbows on desks, chins resting in our palms. He would scan the classroom, as if he was looking right into us, knowing exactly what we were thinking. 'Get out there tonight, into your backyards, and try touching the stars. Don't give up, you hear.'

RN Singh (1953)

The incorrigible Mr RN Singh did eventually get himself to Britain (so I heard years later). The story goes that his family life fractured soon after he arrived there; that he simply lost the plot, succumbing to the 'temptations' of London. His life ended at a relatively early age in some unfortunate circumstances in the city of his dreams! I could only speculate what may have been his undoing. Did his soaring dream lose momentum and crash into a London drain?

A generous couple I had known in South Africa ages earlier agreed to let me live with them temporarily while I found my feet. Theirs was one of the typical cloned working-class tenements, attached in a row and spilling onto the pavement. It was on Edgware Road at the very end of a metro underground line.

London turned out to be a profoundly depressing experience. For days on end, I'd peer through lace curtains at the sullen mist and rain. Day after day the view from my window was a wash of wetness, chill, and gloom – drenched bare skeletons of trees, dank earth, steel grates, wet asphalt and gutters running with incessant rain. People in dark winter coats, hoods, hats, and black umbrellas went about with dogged resignation.

With little guidance, it took a while for me to work out what kind of employment there was for psychologists with no work experience. Fortunately, the British Psychological Society pointed me in the right direction. I sent off my first batch of applications for internship positions in psychiatric hospitals (asylums).

Each day I would wait at the window about noon,

checking the footpath every now and then in case the postman in his distinctive yellow mackintosh, was making his way towards me lugging his bulging postbag over one shoulder. The first few responses I received were one-line regrets. Most days the items dropped through the slot in the front door were household accounts.

Here I was, very much on my own, in a cold dank house for much of the day as the couple would leave for work by seven in the morning, only to return after dark. At times, the toxic combination of boredom, loneliness and my uncertain future was quite difficult to manage. My perpetual worry was that my meagre reserve money would soon be depleted before I found employment. Most days I would venture out for an hour or two to get a newspaper. But there was only so much one could do to fill up the long despairing days. At times I regretted abandoning my settled sunny life in Lusaka.

After a wait which seemed forever, the postman finally delivered me good news. A psychiatric hospital in Scotland was prepared to take me on as a psychologist intern. It felt as if I could breathe with ease again. All this while I had hidden my desperate plight from family and friends – largely to save face. Living a lie can be quite demoralising. Pretty soon, however, my relief gave way to anxiety fed by a nagging doubt. Misgivings multiplied. What was I letting myself in for to take up employment in a largely closed psychiatric institution perhaps still run in the Victorian tradition of mental asylums? How would I survive in Cupar in County Fife, a remote little town far removed from urban life? Would it be Serenje all over again?

~

Stratheden Hospital

Having little choice, I thanked my hosts and boarded a train for Scotland. The journey was a protracted one but interesting as I had the opportunity to see much of the countryside across England and into glorious Edinburgh. Thereafter, I crossed the famous bridge that straddled the Firth of Forth into Macbeth's country, rugged, expansive, and eerily wind-swept as always – but now peppered white with the previous night's snowfall. If one listened attentively to the gusting wind one might still pick up the shrill voices of Macbeth's witches uttering prophecies. What would they prophesise for my future?

Before long I found myself becoming accustomed to moving about in adult lock-up psychiatric wards, drenched in sickly-stale odours - a combination of tasteless hospital cooking and harsh detergents and disinfectants with which the glossy green walls and floors were routinely cleaned. Not to mention the smell of decay from chronically disturbed, over- medicated patients. These pungent odours seemed more intense in the elevated temperature in these wards, thanks to hot water radiators located all along the walls.

Stratheden Hospital: remote and bleak

The wards were crowded with patients lolling asleep in well-worn chairs or just shuffling about as if they were lost souls in Dante's purgatory – women with hairy chins and men with drooping shoulders and baggy pants. Many of the patients had been committed by psychiatrists ages ago and almost forgotten by their families. However, a new bold movement was emerging in psychiatry at the time – turning psychiatric asylums into so-called therapeutic communities. The case was being made at the time that adults committed to long-term psychiatric care often became chronically incapacitated on account of their prolonged institutionalisation, lack of social stimulation, and excessive and harsh medication regimes – drugs and electric convulsive treatment (ECT).

I was profoundly impressed by this emergent perspective in mental health. More so when I learnt that one of the pioneers of this movement, at the time, was Dr Maxwell Jones who had been born in South Africa. New thinking generated enlightened improvements in the treatment and care of the mentally ill in large parts of Britain. Overseas countries also became interested and initiated mental health reforms. However, as with most movements, the momentum for reform dissipated over time. The argument was that the therapeutic community model was over-glamourized by some proponents. It was not a panacea for the ills of the long-entrenched psychiatric asylums.

I was permitted to live on the premises of the hospital at nominal rent, which suited me just fine. However, the accommodation turned out to be a cramped windowless single room located on the second level of one of the dingy hospital blocks. The nursing and medical staff had comfortable and dedicated living quarters close to the administration complex. I wondered if this in any way reflected a poor regard for psychology and psychologists. On weekdays, I had lunch in the staff dining room. Rhubarb tart, a Scottish favourite, was invariably set before me without fail on Fridays, after the main course. I recall cooking a curry for myself whenever the blandness of western meals got too much. I did this on a small hotplate, kneeling on the floor. As I possessed a single little metal pot, I could not be overly particular about the order in which the ingredients went into the pot. It was a case of all together now and hope for the best! Even an occasional curry dish helped me to retain my Indianness.

The Psychology Department was a relatively recent innovation, no more than a year old. The team comprised a clinical coordinator and three interns, including myself.

~

For a while I was taken up with my new life in this relatively strange and foreign setting. Soon I had two good friends – one of the psychologists, John Glover, a lanky, shy Scotsman with large hands, a baby-face and an odd rolling laugh. He drove a Mini. John introduced me to pipe smoking and Scottish draft beer served in large tankards. In winter, the draft beer went well with a palm full of beer nuts. The other friend was Dr Jivanathan, a psychiatric registrar from India. He loved to make sweetmeat from milk – boiling the milk until it separated into curd and whey, and then happily straining out the whey with his handkerchief. What remained was a sticky-sweet lump to savour. Neither he nor I bothered about the questionable use of his handkerchief.

I bought myself a car, a second-hand Hillman Minx, pale green in colour.

At Stratheden the relatively small band of psychologists found it a struggle to be acknowledged. The doctors and psychiatrists did not give us the impression that our presence and contribution had any relevance in the assessment and treatment of patients. We were envious of the nurses and social workers who seemed to fraternise relatively easily with the medical staff.

Day after day we would lug our psychology assessment kits to the wards and try our level best to elicit the attention and cooperation of patients who were, to varying degrees, disorientated, and diminished in normal functioning. Our reports to the psychiatrists would follow conventional manualised guidelines, all looking and sounding much the same. We would receive little feedback, if any.

Of course, it could be that the advent of psychologists in psychiatric hospitals in Britain was still an untested novelty in the nineteen sixties and seventies. There was a determined movement to do away with Victorian era asylums and to change and modernise mental health care in hospitals. And the employment of psychologists in hospitals was assumed would contribute to this change.

My first winter in Scotland tested my grit to the very limits. Coping with bone-penetrating cold while trying to stay on my feet on icy snow was the least of my worries. But my work also required me to drive to outlying clinics. That was a big ask. Every other day I would have to find my car under a generous deposit of over-night snow and then unfreeze the lock before labouring to get the car started. Driving on icy roads brought back the unsettling feeling I had back in Zambia driving on loose sand and gravel. Once I even rolled my car after skidding on black ice. It felt as if I was falling off a moving plane in slow motion. There was a stark sense of inevitability and impotence. Fortunately, I escaped this accident injury-free. And my car was, thankfully, repairable.

Even as I adjusted to the lifestyle and working culture of the local people I got to know, I could not help but be acutely aware that this was very much a foreign world, more accurately, the territory of a distinct white group of people, the Scots, distinguished by their peculiar accent, and their partiality to such things as haggis, rhubarb pudding, tartan kilts and bagpipes. And, apart from the sweetmeat psychiatrist from India, I was the only other dark-skinned person at the hospital – staff and patients included. For that matter, I had not bumped into a single non-white person in the shops downtown. Yet again, this preoccupation with colour troubled me. I thought I ought to confront and interrogate it. After all, I was now a practising psychologist.

The uncomfortable truth was that I seemed to see people through the prism of colour. Perhaps growing up non-white in South Africa, I had become conditioned to feel relatively more secure when I was among people of colour. Yet it seemed more complex than that. Britain, Scotland, Cupar and, ultimately, Stratheden Hospital were, together, so far removed from the familiar world of my childhood that, deep down, I could not quite let my guard down and relax. I felt somewhat out of place. If not marginalised, I felt I was being patronised. Clearly my perception of reality was questionable. We simply assume we see with our eyes what is out there. Not so. What we perceive is a reality distorted by our fears, preconceived beliefs, and cultural biases. In hindsight, I would accept that I'd become overly sensitive relative to my lived experience of Apartheid. In other words, I had become predisposed to a kind of racial vulnerability.

At the time, unfortunately, I also had an issue with the local police. I had a temporary visa to live and work in Britain. An ID pass was issued to me called an Aliens Certificate, which I was to produce on demand to a policeman or an immigration officer. In addition, I was required each month to report to the police in person. On one occasion when I forgot to do so, a policeman came looking for me at the hospital, eliciting a few raised eyebrows. I felt quite angry as this seemed to me no different to police surveillance of non-whites in South Africa. Of course, there were other foreign staff at the hospital who were also temporary residents. They did not see anything sinister or untoward in the conditions of residence. They took it as a quite normal immigration requirement. Nothing to fuss over.

Years later, I wondered if seeing the world in black and white and shades of brown, necessarily meant I was a racist. Perhaps not. I do not think I was bigoted or wilfully negative in my appraisal of people according to the colour of their skin. I saw people and groups as being different to me, but not beneath (or above) me according to class or caste or race. It became a problem only when people usurped power and dominance by virtue of their colour, class, caste, or race. I was of the view that the populations of the world were all of one race, the human race. In the wise words of Ajahn Chah, a renowned Thai Buddhist Monk, *'There are always differences. Get to know those differences. But learn to see the underlying sameness of all things, how they are all truly equal, truly empty. Then you can know how to deal with the apparent differences wisely.'* (A Still Forest Pool, 1985).

I had intended that after fulfilling the BPS requirement for internship, I would stay on at Stratheden for a while longer gaining more professional experience and expertise. But after a year, I changed my mind. The Buddha believed that *dis-ease* was at the core of human existence. I found myself once again increasingly unsettled with what I had, and, naturally, I wished to shake off this unpleasant feeling. Perhaps if I upped and moved, I would find the grass elsewhere more appealing. I latched onto this thought with remarkable zeal. The attractiveness of quitting Stratheden took hold. The genii had been let out! I found compelling justifications. For one thing, Cupar was far too parochial and unexciting for young single blokes. Then too, the job was not as fulfilling as I'd expected. I had changed from being a teacher to this profession called 'psychology', believing it offered greater status, the next best thing to a medical doctor.

~

On reflection, I would say there existed a much deeper, personal theme that would better explain why I felt the way I did at the time. It was a kind of *unease* I had been aware of years earlier – during high school days, and all through university. It accompanied me to Zambia and sat beside me on my flight to Great Britain, staying close. Loneliness – or was it the dread of abandonment, falling into a void. Hence, I had always hankered after companionship, the reassuring presence of close male friends and, increasingly, an enduring female presence.

I did not look forward to or enjoy being on my own. I felt somewhat lost during school holidays. At Fort Hare I felt separated from my close buddies as they were in another hostel. I'd go looking for them at every opportunity. At times I made my way across the soccer field to the annexe where they lived, only to find they had gone off on some little adventure – without me!

At Serenje in Zambia, I would escape to the Badats on afternoons and weekends when I felt particularly low, and there was not anyone about to chat with. It was at a time when I had fallen out with young Petersen the only other South African teacher at the school.

At Stratheden, come the end of a working day, my colleagues would take off home to their cosy families. John Glover would knock on the door to my office, open it gently and poke his head in. He would nod with a broad smile, indicating it was time to pack up for the day. 'Have a good evening' or 'Have fun.' I would, of course, have no home awaiting me but the gloom of a one-room cell in a dingy corner of a psychiatric hospital. I am reminded of the words of Pankaj Mishra *'I felt a shiver of loneliness, and in that feeling was blended the strangeness of the evening in the large gloomy house in the middle of nowhere.'* (An End to Suffering, 2004):

Naturally, I would feel vaguely unhappy and envious. With no TV, no mobile phone, wifi or computer to distract me, I would generally turn in early after chewing absentmindedly on a piece of desiccated rye bread. On odd occasions, Dr Jivanathan would invite me over, which was always a most welcome relief to the monotony of my own company. But I would baulk at the thought of sampling more of his handkerchief-strained sweetmeat.

I soon concluded that my precious life was being wasted in Cupar. This was not a life for me, not for a young man in his prime. I craved, instead, the type of company I had taken for granted in Lusaka, forgetting that I had quit that world when I could not take any more of it.

Solitude was foreign to me. Yet, interestingly, Haruki Murakami the acclaimed Japanese writer has explained that he, on the other hand, was the kind of person who never found it painful to be alone. This was why he loved running. *'The desire in me to be alone hasn't changed (in years). Which is why the hour or so I spend running, maintaining my own silent, private time is important to help me keep my mental well-being. I just run. I run in a void. Or maybe I should put it the other way: I run in order to acquire a void.'* (What I Talk About When I Talk About Running, 2008).

Thoreau famously promoted the virtues of solitude in his book *Walden* after an experiment of living alone. It is true there are those who live alone by choice and relish it. Not so others for whom life circumstances have relegated them to suffer a lonely existence. Many men and women live alone following the loss of a partner or perhaps after the traumatic end of a relationship. And what of the countless people imprisoned by despotic regimes for political reasons, and held in indefinite solitary confinement?

I began to grow increasingly homesick. I continued to ruminate and firm up reasons why I ought to return home. I needed to convince myself beyond doubt that quitting Stratheden and Britain was not to be construed as failure or lack of endurance. To this end I wrote a lengthy letter to

Lionel in London, who had been a good friend since my high school days in Durban.

The letter is dated 24 February 1969. Here is the unedited version.

I have decided that my decision to return to South Africa must now be irrevocable. I have spent the last few months persuading and conditioning myself to all the possible consequences of this decision. Of course, I'm still far from happy. But then I have been long enough alone to think things out.

It is becoming ever more difficult to reconcile my continued presence here even though I feel I had about enough of it. It is constantly asked of me why we feed on the hospitality of Britain when we claim not to like the people and their ways. Why do we? Is it such a haven from South Africa? I for one did not honestly come here expecting non-racial utopia. But I had hoped to feel a sense of intellectual exhilaration and release, and relatively more secure socially and emotionally than I had felt in Africa. Certainly, I did not expect to feel so rotten so soon. The face of Enoch Powell, recent immigration laws, a rebel Rhodesian flag over London, and such like things are like bees in my bonnet. It is not easy to move among British people the whole day long and not feel incensed. Those who call me 'friend' and look suitably apologetic only exasperate me the more.

If it were only for the 'political' issues, I might perhaps intellectualize them and give them a certain remoteness and, in this way go on with my more immediate tasks with a measure of emotional detachment. However, this is not to be, since I have to contend with prejudice and duplicity in my everyday dealings with the people here. Contact with coloureds (the likes of me) is minimal and largely in necessary work situations only. You meet with guarded superficial postures – smiles that mock your foreignness. Could I help my sense of alienation? After all, sustained human relationships are so essential for personal growth.

I feel particularly vulnerable when I have to contend with barely concealed prejudice and deception in my association with women. For here my manly vanity and intelligence are called into question. Yet I sometimes wonder if we, growing up in South Africa, have not grown hypersensitive skins – seeing racial prejudice in every setback, hurt or rebuff. On the matter of sex itself, I do not mind admitting that with age I am beginning to long for fulfilment in the context of a secure interpersonal involvement. The hit-and-run or shot-in-the-dark strategy has lost its dare and relish. At the same time, I am uneasy about laying myself open to any such involvement for fear that I may be easily persuaded by a possible marriage to relinquish South Africa for ever. How easy it would be to grow forgetful. So here am I following my sexual urges through mindless shadows, seemingly indifferent to the leprous withering of my soul.

While we are out-of-reach of the Juggernaut, our fear of direct involvement (in the struggle) is allayed. Who would not cringe instinctively from thoughts of physical and mental harassment, restrictions of personal comforts and means of livelihood? But with us there is a further extension to our anxiety. Perhaps I do not know my level of endurance (in the hands of the Security Police). How much would it take to crack this carefully cultivated belief in my intellectual identity, my good worth? At what point would my 'shadow line' be crossed? From a distance of safety this may be a fascinating preoccupation – if not alarmingly perverse (and that may have been Oedipus's undoing). I am not blatantly brave. I too am anxious for myself - the law of self-preservation! But this anxiety is countered by an inner impatience when I realise that the worst that could befall me in South Africa would be laughably insignificant when compared with the price that others have had to pay.

(And they have been changed in their turn
Transformed utterly A terrible beauty is born.) – WB Yeats

After all, I have done little and know even less. But I do want to descend from this ivory tower of mere intellectual involvement and return to live under apartheid, amid the betrayals, anguish, humiliation and debasement. I need to stand in the very midst of that amorphous conformity. Only then I may have a fuller estimation of myself. For me this is crucial.

You would not deny that Britain is full of our chaps. At least, enough to go hysterical over ideologies, man the protest movements, and to chide all the naughty liberals. There are times when I feel suffocated by the liberals oozing sympathy and support for me simply because I belong to one of the oppressed black races. And too often have I caught myself in a posture of dramatized bitterness before a white audience merely for the effect – to elicit that look of pained embarrassment. I am sick of all this intellectual verbosity and pretence. (Benedict Nightingale in New Statesman; Eldridge Cleaver next to the little Red Book on the coffee-table; Che Guevara plastered round the bathroom; gay chatter about 'direct action' across the imitation soul-food. Very good, but at what point do you cut the crap, get out there and make revolution?)

I was forgetting – there is another reason that profits us to remain abroad. Easy financial grants from various well-meaning agencies (?). It may be fashionable, and even cosy, to be a professional political refugee these days. You can see places free and be a 'student' for an indefinite period.

Frankly, I do not regret coming to Britain. It has been an instructive experience. I must not minimize the fact that Britain is unique vantage-point from which to view the world. Since coming here, I seem to have developed a deeper understanding of the South African situation in the context of historical, social, political and economic events the world over. Perhaps the mass media have been largely responsible for this understanding, in the sense that they have been a remorseless pointer to the oppressions that exist in places other than South Africa, and, indeed, a pointer to the relentless pattern of human endurance, struggle and sacrifice in the face of despairing odds. I am put to shame. How can I wait for others to put things right in South Africa, to make the place bearable so that I could return in safety? And should I wait, how long would I have to wait? 'One can argue that in the long run apartheid must fall and fail explosively; but can one also argue that in the long run we – that is, we of the present generation – will all be dead' (source of quote unknown).

In any case we cannot all get out with our discontent on our backs – especially when the government gleefully helps some out with one-way tickets. I believe that if we are not directly involved in the liberation movement abroad, our best use would be within the country. You mentioned that the Indians in Durban, for example, are growing ever complacent and conditioned to their material servitude. Don't you agree that there is the possibility that if all visible signs of discontent were to disappear (both as a result of government 'persuasion' and voluntary secondment), there would be a grave situation where the present generation and the next would have little or no inkling of the past struggle or the hope of a different future? Then, surely, all those who have gone before would have gone in vain. Therefore, the need for people like us to parade our discontent in South Africa – and talk of hope as if we believed in it – as long as this is possible.

There are lesser reasons for my wanting to return home. One of these is professional. I have been unable to find a suitable area for research (doctoral). But the field of mental illness in South Africa among the non-Europeans is largely unexplored and holds great possibilities. I think I would get a greater sense of satisfaction and involvement working among our people. Another reason, of course, is my family. There are internal dissensions and signs of disintegration. Salvage work may be necessary. For these many years I have been fortunate to have escaped the petty and wearisome stresses and responsibilities of family life. All I seem to have been doing is dispensing 'sensible' advice by post. About time I took on some of the menial responsibilities in person.

In the time I have been away from home I am aware that I have grown accustomed to living alone, of having developed personal whims and private attitudes. Now, this aspect of me and this way of life seem threatened. There will have to be necessary adjustments. We shall wait and see...I used to think that the life of a vagabond held infinite charm, untold possibilities. Now I know that one CAN grow weary of the very opportunity to travel. A few more faces or new places. Can't tell the difference. Might even have seen them before. Do you recognise this feeling – of creeping age? Moving about has its points, glamour for one thing, but it has its toll also – in terms of wasted human relationships. Don't you known that it is difficult for me at times to believe that I lived in Zambia for four years. What have I left to show that it did happen? No news, no letters; faces and voices having receded to matted insubstantiality.

It's after midnight, and about time I ended this marathon. Woolly thoughts and typing errors are becoming obvious. I hope I have not embarrassed you unduly or outraged your critical eye by wading into such personal details. The detail has been intentional. Firstly, you gave me an opportunity to work out my thoughts on paper. Secondly, I am hoping that you will retain some of the reasons given in this letter and offer an independent commentary in the years to come in the light of changes within me as a person, and events without me fortuitous or planned.

You take care,
Best Wishes
Bala

My reaction in re-reading this letter now in my eighties is one of incredulity. Was this really me? No, it could not be. At best perhaps a remote version – very remote.

In fact, I found some of the views, emotions, and expressions somewhat embarrassing and excessive. In the words of Hamlet: *Me thinks he doth protest too much.* Posturing on a grand scale. I even felt a little uncomfortable transcribing the contents word for word for this memoir. Should the letter be part of this memoir? Was it wise to do so? What impact might it have on friends, colleagues, and family, I wondered. Strong views expressed with equally strong emotions. It may perhaps strike readers as odd and puzzling, especially those older folks with tenuous memories or those who were born post-apartheid era.

But then I sat up, jolted by my seemingly unsympathetic reactions. What is this all about? Disowning and distancing myself from the person I once was? Surely as an old man with eighty years of life experience, I ought to have a depth of understanding of the psyche of young people and how they coped with adversities and challenges in the world in which they find themselves?

Now on reflection, I marvel that the letter was written at all. I recall using a cranky old Olivetti typewriter. And I was not skilled at typing. This I can tell by the numerous errors on the carbon copy I have retained. I am impressed that Bala, as a young man, had the courage and honesty to commit his innermost thoughts and feelings to paper, for selecting a friend as an independent witness to his inner musings, and for having had the foresight to preserve a copy for posterity. Being privy to the contents now has helped me to assess how my life unfolded over the last half a century relative to expressed fears, thoughts, and imaginings.

As for Lionel, I lost contact with him after visiting him once briefly in London about 25 years ago. We did not remember then to touch on the contents of the letter – which is a pity. Come to think of it, I have no idea if Lionel replied to it.

In March 2019, a mutual friend re-connected me to

Lionel still living in London and quite unwell. We spoke only very briefly.

In early 2016 for reasons which I do not recall, I shared the contents of this letter with Yacoob, another of my enduring friends from high school days. His prompt reply is shared below.

My thoughts on your letter to Lionel. You obviously suffered from the same sense of dislocation as that of the refugees and migrants who come to you for treatment. I must admit I went through a similar soul-searching exercise even when I was in Zimbabwe. Although I made a few friends in Salisbury (Harare), they did not share my views or interests in what I thought was important. I went through a period of heavy drinking and was glad to be transferred to Bulawayo. There I was a housemaster looking after kids who were boarders. For two years I chilled out. Fortunately, I met Baboo, Marcus and Shef who provided a friendship and understanding that I needed badly. I realised then I needed a partner who would share my joys and lows in the secure knowledge that she would be there when I need comforting and a keen sense of balance in the view of the world. You don't need me to analyse your sense of alienation even though you were apparently in the company of 'sympathetic liberals'. I had similar arguments with some acquaintances who when I pointed out the effects of being colonised and being subjected to the cult of white supremacy including the horrors inflicted by the British on the indigenous populations they retorted with 'why did you come to England then?' Your questioning of whether having left South Africa and probably making a permanent break might have been justified then but in the light of our present circumstances seems invidious. At that time there were too many working for example in the ANC proselytising. Your contribution might have been of negligible consequence. In fact, there were far too many hangers-on lurking in the corridors apparently contributing to the cause but in actual fact, living off the liberal sentiment. As for distancing from family responsibilities and loosening of ties, this is a sentiment I can well understand as I questioned the wisdom of staying away. Hence my decision to spend some of the time in South Africa so that I could get to know the family a little better after the long separation. We took this decision not without a lot of soul searching. If it works out, we would be more than satisfied, in fact delighted. If not, well we will put it down to experience. We are going to South Africa in March in order to furnish the flat we bought in December.

I did not anticipate that he'd be so thoughtful and frank. More than that, I found Yacoob's response most empathic and eloquent. He suggested that our early experience away from South Africa indicated remarkable similarities – an anguished sense of alienation; non-white young men seemingly trapped (and grappling) in a colonial world in transition. It was reassuring to realise that I was not the only one conflicted in the way I was as a young adult attempting to forge an identity. I'm reminded of the late VS Naipaul, a prolific writer awarded the Nobel Prize for Literature in 2001. He was born in Trinidad of Indian parents whose ancestors were also indentured labourers taken from India by the British. Naipaul it seems chose to live in Britain for long spells contemplating the harsh historical realities of European colonialism, experienced by generations of third world nations as so much inflicted suffering and exploitation.

Having shared our sense of alienation and longing for home, it's ironical that in reality Yacoob and I later chose to exile ourselves from South Africa. Permanently. While Yacoob has lived in Britain continuously for over forty years, with a periodic urge to return to South Africa, I have now myself been an Australian citizen for just over thirty years, with little urge to move back. At the same time, I find myself (unlike most ex-South Africans abroad or at home) caught up almost obsessively in the media portrayal of daily events and happenings across the country – mostly distressing news about corruption, crime, poverty, natural disasters, and political machinations.

Looking back now on the tail end of my time at Stratheden, I find it intriguing that even when the urge in me to quit and return to South Africa, my natural home, was strongest, I seem to have readily postponed it when Dr Jivanathan suggested I use the opportunity, while still outside the prison of Apartheid, to visit India.

Overland to Ancestral India

It was early 1969. I had turned thirty. Since leaving my family in Durban in 1964, I had spent four years teaching in Zambia and over a year at Stratheden, Scotland, preparing for a career in psychology. 'Enough is enough, son,' said my father in his five-line aerogram air letter. 'You come home straight away, now.' It was scrawled with a heavy hand, a carpenter's hand.

On the way to my dingy room in the west wing of the hospital, after an unproductive day with patients, I stopped for a chat with Dr Jivanathan in his comfortable doctors' quarters. We had become good friends. 'My Indian brother,' he would call me. He was easy, light-hearted and had a dimpled smile. I felt relaxed in his presence. A pot of chai was brewing on a hotplate, the aromatic smell of mixed spices wafting my way uplifted my mood. Of course, Dr Jivanathan was eager to know more of my plans to return home. 'Not made booking yet? Arreh man, but why?' He had a cheerful sing-song way of speaking. Today was no exception. In return, I would mock him about his funereal attire - black suit worn seven days a week without fail, tightly buttoned at that. I did not let on that his black outfit not only made him look very professional and distinguished, but also added much to his handsome youthful appearance.

'You know,' he said 'I'll certainly miss your company when you're gone. But I tell myself,' he added in a brighter note, 'surely Bala you got to visit me one day. Yah no? My wife will welcome you with open arms, open arms. She's so happy I found a nice friend here. And my daughters too.' With that he pulled out a family photo from his wallet, gazed lovingly at it before handing it to me. It was a black and white photo, a little fuzzy. Wow, I thought, two glamourous teenage daughters in saris. Simply ravishing. I must get to India!

'Let me know when you're coming yah? I've got contacts all over - Delhi, Bombay, Calcutta.'

I savoured my cup of chai. Dr Jivanathan slurped from his saucer, blowing at the rising steam before each slurp.

'This time is your chance to make homage. India first home, South Africa second, nor? Maybe you'll still find like cousins and aunties in Madras.'

Until that moment, I had no feelings of affinity to India. I had not given a second thought to the notion that India was my ancestral home. Not like Australian-born whites on pilgrimage to Britain or Ireland in earnest quest of their lineage, their ancestry – even attempting to read barely discernible names on crumbling gravestones in ancient churchyards.

Later, lying in bed after a spartan meal of crusted rye bread and tea, I got to speculating. I imagined arriving in India and going in search of my ancestral village in Madras. Then a much-anticipated visit to Dr Jivanathan's daughters. I had a vison of the girls at the door with bright and eager faces. I sat up startled by a daring thought. But why not take in India on your way home? said a voice. That is preposterous, I argued. Do not even entertain it. But the voice persisted. The thought was still there in the morning, exciting and alarming me in equal measure. The more I spoke about the ridiculous idea with colleagues at the hospital, the more it took form. 'You'd probably do it if you hitched yourself along the way to one of those backpacking American hippies,' said John my beer drinking friend with a sparkle in his eyes. 'But that's almost not likely to happen.' His comment simply spurred me on. Backpacking, hmm? I thought.

~

Before long I had read up all that there was available on backpacking overland to India, especially of challenges and risks. I joined the worldwide Youth Hostels Association. I researched the popular backpacker routes across Europe and Asia. All this I did in a state of heightened fever. Dr Jivanathan and I visited the local library in Cupar and poured over maps of Europe and Asia. I would be travelling from England through France, Italy, Greece, Turkey, Iran, and Pakistan. That is it. I began phoning and sending letters to these embassies querying about visas, receiving, and completing application forms, and finally sending off my passport for visa endorsements. This was at a time when google search and emails did not exist. I had to trust the reliability of Her Majesty's Royal Mail. Days and weeks went by before the visas were finalised. Patience and forbearance were sorely needed.

The Pakistan embassy was annoyingly slow. In the end, I went to London myself. Even then I was pushed around.

My application sat in a tray unattended. And when I fronted up, the application and my South African passport were scrutinised by three separate Embassy staff, the one handing it to the other, speaking all the time in a language I could not quite grasp. They were clearly suspicious and hence hesitant to issue me with a visa. With desperation on my face and voice, I pointed them to the already approved visa endorsements from the other countries. They stared at my face and the photo in the passport. 'You Africa, eh?' one queried. 'Yes, I'm South African' I responded. Then quite unexpectedly one of them, a large man with dishevelled greasy hair said 'Okay, okay, we accept your visa application. You pay now and give me passport.' At that he shook his head from side to side to make his point. In my presence, three stamps were pasted on a page, stamped and three words added: Visa applied for. 'We send application to chief passport office in Iran. You go there, please, to Teheran. Okay?' What rigmarole, I thought.

Before returning to Cupar by train, I visited the tourism office in India House and bought myself an open train ticket to enable me, as a tourist, to travel first-class all over India. It was unbelievably cheap. But the envelope-size ticket was as flimsy as airletter paper. Over the many weeks of train travel in India, I worried constantly of mislaying it, accidently wetting, or soiling it. And what would I do if it tore at the folds?

Once back at the hospital, I began preparing in earnest for my departure. Giving notice to the hospital superintendent, writing to my father and getting rid of my meagre belongings as I needed to travel light. I bought myself a pair of sturdy boots, a set of light weight wash-and-wear travelling clothes and a large almost sack-like backpack. Being ignorant of how to prepare for backpacking, I trusted the judgement of an enthusiastic young sales staff at a camping store in Edinburgh. Since my motor vehicle accident in Zambia, I have had to contend with a shortening in my left leg by about three centimetres. The consequence – the length of every pair of long pants had to be shortened on the left side, and the left sole and heel of every pair of shoes raised. The cost of shoe repair was sometimes more than the cost of the shoes.

Money worries proved to be a bugbear. It is called *obsessive budgeting* – how much could I really afford to spend? How to carry the money safely when cash and traveller's cheques were the only options (No bank cards then). In the end, I carried mostly cash in British sterling, concealing small amounts in my backpack and on myself – in a pouch tied around my waist and concealed by my shirt, and some notes in my socks.

It did not seem my psychology colleagues planned to give me a send-off of any kind. I found myself so caught up in anxiety and excitement about the trip, that I did not give much thought to how I felt about quitting my job at the hospital. It had lasted a little over a year.

~

I boarded an early morning train in Cupar for Edinburgh where I took an express to London. My intention was to get to Paris by the evening to avoid paying for an overnight stay in London. There were only three white teenagers in this carriage. No sooner had the ticket conductor passed through, than the teenagers began fooling around, shouting and jostling. Soon tiring, all three moved to a seat closer to me and began shouting out 'Hey Pakkie, go back home.' Or variations of something similar. Obviously, the taunting was aimed at me in the hope of eliciting a reaction. I felt quite unnerved. It reminded me of times in Durban when Whites in authority abused us. But I held onto my backpack which stood between my knees, and pretended not to hear them, keeping my eyes fixed on the rapidly passing scenery. Fortunately, when two more adult passengers got on a few stations down, the teenagers promptly found some other focus for amusement.

I was in London by early afternoon and took the first available connection to Dover. My unwieldy backpack was slowing me down. Much stronger shoulders than mine were needed. Oh well, I will just have to deal with it, I thought. Once in Dover, I found my way to the ferry terminal which was relatively easy. Crossing the English Channel (my first) by ferry was a pleasant change from being confined to a seat on a train for long hours. I did not mind that the sea was a little choppy. A few passengers smiled at me with curiosity. I may have been one of a very few dark-complexioned people crossing into Europe rather than gate-crashing into Britain.

It was late afternoon on a Wednesday when the ferry docked in Calais in France. Luckily for me it was midsummer, and the sun was still high in the sky. My anxiety gave way to a measure of elation. Setting foot on French soil meant my overland trek had truly begun. No turning back now.

I had not realised that it would be another three hours at least before I reached Paris. And once I arrived at the Paris central station, Gare du Nord, things began to unravel. It was peak time, the end of a working day. The noise and the people with morose weary faces all in a mad scramble to get home or determined not to miss their next connections. Alarmed and disoriented, I looked about. A crowd at the far end appeared in a celebratory mood. They were milling outside a packed pub. Could they be a university or football crowd I wondered? A newspaper placard featured a face familiar to me – Charles De Gaulle. Superimposed on it was a fist with a thumbs down gesture. Only much later I learnt that the French had had their first stage presidential election that day. De Gaulle had apparently resigned months earlier after losing a referendum. I'd seen him in the past on television news. A stern-looking man as tall as the Eiffel Tower with a prominent nose. Always in military uniform.

I had assumed it would be relatively easy to find a five-night accommodation in a youth hostel nearby. But I was proven wrong. Firstly, none was within walking distance from the station, and secondly, I needed clear directions to get to any of them. Hardly anyone would stop to help me. Did they brush me off simply because I addressed them in English? Or was it my colour? Why skirt past me without even slowing a little? A few gestured and muttered 'Nor, nor.' It was getting later and later every minute. In desperation, I stood in the way of an elderly woman shuffling along with her shopping cart, trying to negotiate her way carefully through the crowd. She wore glasses and had a friendly face. She could see I was frantic. She shook her head saying she did not speak English. I clasped my hands and rested my head against it like on a pillow. I made a snoring sound. It worked. 'Ah, ah,' she said and gestured me to follow her. We ended up at the metro ticket counter.

There she spoke to the ticket clerk and handed me over to him and went her way. The counterhand explained in accented English that the youth hostels were in nearby suburbs, assuring me I could get to any in short time by metro. 'Here go to this one,' he said writing down a name on a slip of paper. He sold me a ticket and explained how to get to the appropriate platform and which train to look for – and the name of the station where I would get off. 'From there you walk not too far,' he added. Before I could ask him another question, he turned briskly to assist others banked up behind me. I hurried on, still anxious about finding the way on my own.

The metro system appeared quite different to what I had grown used to in Britain. Here the trains appeared quaint and Lilliputian as if they were designed by Charlie Chaplin. Because all signs were in French, I was uncertain of my bearings and disorientated by the foreignness of this place. I showed people my ticket and asked repeatedly if I was headed for the right platform and the right train. Thankfully, I did get onto the correct train. As I emerged from the station into the open, I was startled to see that streetlights had come on. It was nearly 8.30 pm Paris time.

I walked some ten minutes before finding my youth hostel, a well-lit old European-style mansion. Immediately I entered the reception room a cluster of young people made way with uncertain smiles. I set down my backpack and felt the strain on my neck and shoulders ease. I wiped my sweaty face, adjusted my spectacles, and faced reception with visible relief and expectation. The woman attendant in her early forties gave me a bright hello which sounded more like *hullo*. She had a child of about two at her hip who stared at me without blinking. Yes, she had a vacancy in a shared room with bunkbeds, she said, but only for the next two nights. Would I take it? But there's ample vacancy in a sister hostel in the next suburb, she explained. She would phone and get me in there for five nights if I so wished. But I would have to get there in the next forty minutes – before closing time. Only twenty minutes by Metro. I felt myself stiffen. No, no, not back into the night, I thought. I cannot handle more of that, not when I'm starving.

I secured the two nights. One of the other guests, an older man who had just stepped in and got himself a drink, offered to show me the room with the vacant bunk. He grabbed my backpack with little effort. I gratefully followed. It was close to midnight when I eased myself onto the upper bunk and covered myself with a thin sheet which smelt of soapsuds. Only that very morning I had bade farewell to Scotland, Cupar and Stratheden Hospital. And now I was falling asleep on an upper bunk in an unfamiliar place outside Paris.

I was up early the next morning. I had not slept well worrying over what I should do – move to another hostel for three more nights or head on to Italy. I was undecided. At breakfast, I got to chatting with other backpackers at my table, most of whom had a smattering of English. Everyone readily exchanged travel information. The morning liveliness was infectious. This is the way to go, I told myself. Connect with others. I teamed up with two others to spend the day in Paris exploring the landmarks. Uncertain of how freely to dip into my limited cash, I decided against spending on tickets to go up the Eiffel Tower or a visit to the Louvre. Instead, I went on a city coach tour. I took lots of photos, at times troubling other tourists to get me in the pictures. (Poor quality black and white prints thrown out over time, but now regretted). The day was warm. The tour ended near the central train station. I went into a café inside and scanned the display of cakes and sandwiches, settling for a croissant with cheese and lettuce. As I strolled about in the concourse eating, it struck me I had not yet sorted out how to get to Rome, my next destination. How silly of me, I thought. I resolved to be diligent from now on and to plan ahead. On checking the international train schedule, I found several trains left for Italy daily. Thereafter, I walked along the Seine. I also strolled into a few older parts of Paris. Lots of foreign tourists were wandering about gazing and marvelling at the historical buildings and architecture. All the while I debated about when I should leave France. Now that I had seen Paris, was there anything else worthwhile spending a day or two on? Suddenly, I was certain I should make for Rome the very next day. (It became a standing joke later among friends that I had seen Paris in a day!). I went ahead and booked myself on a sleeper express departing Paris at noon and arriving in Rome early evening on the following day – a journey of about twelve hours. The downside of this was I would sleep though spectacular parts of the French and Italian Alps along the train route – an opportunity never to be repeated. Oh well, I cannot expect to have it all, I thought.

Before checking out from the hostel, I rearranged my backpack, shoving my spare pair of shoes to the very bottom. This made the backpack a little more stable when stood upright, and less likely to topple over. I also caught up on writing letters to my family, and to my friends in Cupar.

The train to Rome was several coaches long. I had to lug my backpack almost halfway down the platform to find my coach. The three-seater compartment smelt fresh and clean. The two other passengers, a balding man in his forties and a boy about eight, had already made themselves comfortable. The man acknowledged me with a polite smile and promptly helped lift my backpack onto a rack. The boy did not make eye contact but kept chatting in Italian with the adult, who I assumed was his father. He wore a striped blue and white cap which he fiddled with all the while, as if it helped him frame his sentences. The man responded with patient grunts and occasional questions. For the first few hours of daylight, I had glimpses of the urban sprawl of Paris and the less glamourous, rundown, and congested fringes. Soon I became preoccupied, wondering what challenges awaited me in Rome. I was relieved when a train attendant turned up to make our beds.

I could hear passengers moving about in the corridor. By my wristwatch, it was only six in the morning. We were not scheduled to arrive in Rome before eight thirty. But the anticipation in the air also got me wide awake. The boy and the man were yet to stir. As I was on the upper bunk, I had to descend without waking them. Thankfully, when I returned from the washroom, I found them up and rummaging in their bags while the bedding had been folded and pushed aside so we could all sit.

Rome's Termini Train Station, while confoundingly large and busy, had a most helpful tourist office which I made full use of over the time I spent in Italy. People were more helpful than in Paris – in fact excessively helpful. The office found me five night's accommodation in the

Alessandro Downtown Hostel, 200 metres from the station. As I had enough time for Rome, I had no intention of rushing about the Eternal City in just a day. I returned each morning to the tourist office to work out which historical sites I could manage that day and how best to do it in an affordable way. I felt I was gradually learning to be a sensible and discerning novice backpacker. Hence, I was more than satisfied with myself for visiting the main attractions in Rome – ruins of ancient Roman Forum, the Colosseum, Palatine Hill, Trevi Fountain, and the Arch of Constantine. I walked about surveying the excavated ruins of the Forum, all the while roused by my imaginings from Shakespeare's *Julius Caesar* - this is where Caesar was murdered, this perhaps where Mark Anthony stood and stirred up the rabble to vengeance, and the corner where Cassius and Brutus met and agonised for the last time before going into battle.

I still recall how I almost missed my paid-for tour of the Colosseum because I had foolishly persuaded myself that in the ninety minutes I had before the tour, I could find the one and only Indian café in Rome. A Japanese girl I met at the youth hostel, said she had eaten there and almost got into a fitting cough when she accidently bit on a chilli. Sadly, I did not find the place. I wandered far too far away in my eagerness for curry and thoroughly lost my bearings. Luckily for me, a young worker in overalls while giving me directions, noticed I was not following him. He motioned that I should jump on the back of his scooter. He drove me at a speed along a narrow curving road and down a hill – with me holding on tight and shielding my face from the strong breeze. And I made it to the Colosseum just as my group was being ushered into the monument. Here I puzzled over the extravagant size of this Roman stadium. Surely the population of ancient Rome could not have been so large as to fill the stadium. I also felt revolted by the guide's detailed account of the gory sports relished by the enthusiastic spectators – the killing and maiming of lions and other wild animals and, in full public view, butchering the gladiators who lost in combat.

While I gave the Vatican City a miss because of the exorbitant entry fee and the endless queue of patiently waiting pilgrims, I went on a great coach tour to Florence and Pisa some four hours north of Rome. I enjoyed the rugged scenery together with the small walled towns and hill-top guard towers along the way. I saw for myself the exquisite soft light which bathed Florence, and which landscape painters found irresistible. I recall standing in front of the Tower of Pisa and marvelling at why it had not yet fallen flat on its face. There were many people on the coach who spoke English and who I befriended – although there were not many dark faces to be seen, and initially people seemed uncertain and wary of talking to me. It was extremely hot and bright, and I had not remembered to carry a bottle of water. On one of the coach-stops, a man raised his eyebrows when he caught me drinking water at the sink in the toilet. It tasted perfectly okay to one who was not overly fastidious.

~

The nine days passed swiftly, and it was time for me to set off for the next stage of my overland journey to India. I boarded a local bus to Brindisi where I intended to take a ferry to Greece. It would take about seven hours for me to get across. I read that the modern highway from Rome to

Brindisi followed the ancient Appian Way, the sturdy road built by the Romans about 300BC.

I was happy to have company all the way to Athens with three backpackers whom I had befriended in my Rome hostel – two American youths travelling as a couple, and a German mature-aged woman student enjoying a summer break from university.

We stayed overnight in a cheap hostel in Brindisi and caught an early morning ferry which landed us in Patras mid-afternoon. I spent much time standing on deck with others delighting in the sunny calm weather and the azure blue of the Ionian Sea. The name itself conjured up in my mind the exploits of Odysseus, although I was not sure if he had sailed the Ionian Sea.

Local buses were readily available from the port at Patras to various destinations. While the German traveller and I boarded the first bus to Athens, the Americans opted to hitchhike their way there, even if this took them a few days. I recall the journey was not comfortable in the least. The bus was old and laboured along. It made several stops at villages along the way, dropping off and picking up passengers who appeared to be mostly poor and elderly. They carried bags of shopping, leaving little room for my backpack. They spoke loudly as if sharing their troubles and complaining about government services. At least this is how it sounded. Of course, I could not help smiling when I remembered the cliché *it's all Greek to me*.

At one stop, there was an unexpected security check. People became quiet and produced their documents as if they were accustomed to this intrusion. Thereafter, the bus drove through drab shopping strips and lacklustre houses that were occupied but clearly incomplete. Trees and bushes were sparse and seemed parched and sullen.

The bus eventually rumbled into Athens Central Bus Station, which was crummy, crowded and depressing. It was 12 June 1969. I felt uneasy to see gun-toting military personnel at every street corner. I am not going to like this place, I thought. My German friend and I changed small amounts of money into drachmas. Together we worked out how to ask for directions and hailed a taxi to the nearest youth hostel. From eavesdropping on conversations in the bathroom, I soon learnt that Greece was under the rule of a trigger-happy military junta. As long as foreign visitors kept their heads down and mouths shut, they were safe to move about - but only to designated tourist sites.

In three days, I was done with Greece. In Athens, I trudged up the Acropolis to have a close and personal look at the Parthenon, one of the most celebrated world heritage sites in the world. The skeletal remains in off-white marble were truly magnificent, enhanced, of course, by glorious summer sunshine. The distant view of Athens from the mount was equally stunning. But it was far too congested for me.

The only other historical place I remember visiting was the Temple at Delphi about two hours by bus from Athens. There was no longer a temple to be seen but a few columns standing gallantly on slabs of foundation stones. The rest was left to my imagination. I had heard much of the ancient oracle's cryptic answers which, I suppose, kept kings and other distinguished worshippers guessing. For less gullible visitors, however, there was a more sobering message on a marble face. Carved in Greek, it read in translation: KNOW

THYSELF. Two telling words! The temple was located high up on a hill embraced by a rugged landscape with rich green vegetation. The air was rarefied and cool with a solitary eagle floating remotely in a clear sky. I felt momentarily uplifted and transported to ancient times.

∼

Now, fifty years on, in recalling challenging moments of this overland madness, I marvel that I did it without a Lonely Planet Guide or the ubiquitous Google readily at hand. Getting to Istanbul from Athens was my next fraught destination. I kept my ears open and spoke to others at the youth hostel who had either just come from Turkey or intended to go there. But the information and advice I picked up was either inconsistent, varied, or confusing. 'You can do it by train,' said one. 'No, cheaper by bus,' said another. 'But which border crossing are you headed for? asked an older man feeling his unshaven face. 'You mean there's more than one?' I asked. 'How long will it take me to get to Istanbul?' A girl with a tanned Italian complexion said knowingly 'But no way to get straight there. First to Ioannina, yah?' Attempting to process all this information gave me a headache. What was most helpful was when one of the backpackers produced a travel map and traced for me optional routes from Greece to Turkey with related border crossings.

In the end I convinced myself to take an overnight train to Ioannina on the northwest of Greece, and then catch a regular bus from there to Kipoi (Kipi), a relatively short trip of less than two hours. Crossing the border here would bring me to Ipsala on the Turkish side.

Once I left urban Athens, I had the distinct impression I

was travelling back in time. The people and countryside appeared not just rural and relatively impoverished, but more of an earlier age. The men on the bus to Kipoi were mostly short and stocky with darkish complexions, and older women were invariably dressed in black – black stockings, black flat-soled shoes, black below-knee skirts with long sleeves and black headscarves. I was reminded of fairy godmother stories of my childhood, of witches similarly dressed in black, whizzing past on broomsticks. This sense of a time warp was reinforced when I spotted an occasional ragged-looking young man transporting loads of what seemed like firewood on rickety donkey-carts. And of course, a few large, bearded billy goats in the field stared at the bus as it lumbered past.

People appeared indifferent to my presence. Surely an Indian man with a backpack on a local bus ought to be a rare curiosity, even if unwanted? I did not know how to handle this lack of acknowledgement, apart from feeling a little uneasy. Fortunately, I was distracted by blaring Zorba music on the bus. I refer to it as Zorba music because it sounded much like the music of the movie *Zorba the Greek* which had delighted me years earlier with its rich masculine exuberance. Sadly, all traditional Greek music played on the lyre and bouzouki sound much the same to me.

For countries where there was a visa requirement, I had made sure to have one clearly endorsed in my passport before leaving Britain. But for some odd reason, I had not obtained one for Turkey. Hence, when I presented at the Turkish border post in Ipsala early on 17 June, I was issued with a transit permit with explicit instructions that on arrival in Istanbul I should go directly to the relevant office to regularise my stay in Turkey. This I did.

~

By now I was becoming quite adept at understanding and adjusting to the different currencies and finding my way around without being able to read street signs, bus and train destinations, and menus. With food, I felt safest when I trusted my eyes to recognise what seemed familiar. Ah yes, that's chicken on the spit with flatbread. However, from Turkey onwards I suffered intermittent stomach problems. The urgency in my voice to find a toilet was obvious to people in the street but making myself understood was always a challenge. I would try gestures with variations of toilet - even 'where's the shitting room?' It was a nightmare when I ended up in a squat-toilet which was wet, stinky and without toilet-paper! A few times I got to the convenience only to find a weary-looking toilet attendant at the entrance collecting a fee. She would point me to a notice on the wall – unintelligible to me. Bugger me if I did not have the correct coin just when I needed it!

The four full days I had visiting the sights in Istanbul were particularly pleasant when, by chance, I linked up with three other backpackers travelling as a group, two women and a guy all a little younger than me. I was 31 at the time. They were university students fresh and clean, gentle, and intelligent. I felt warmly drawn to them. Lynne and Eleanor were friends from the United States and Ron was a Canadian. One of the women (I cannot now recall which one) was blonde, lean and tall as Ron – and (I thought) they made a good pair. The other was relatively shorter and about my height. She had a single long plait. There was this photo of all four of us posing in front of the famous Suleymaniye

Mosque in Istanbul in bright sunshine, a cheerful photo now sadly gone missing.

We stayed in the same youth hostel, and at breakfast we would plan together each day's itinerary. I recall this time as being most exhilarating and great fun. We laughed a lot. It was, however, to be the first and last time I enjoyed such good company on my overland trip. In December 1969, many months after I returned to South Africa and was rather troubled and caught up in finding my feet, I received an unexpected letter from Lynne, typed on pink paper. It lifted my spirits and reminded me of the best days of my overland adventure. I was taken aback recently to find this letter among heaps of discoloured correspondences from family and friends dating back to 1959 when I had left home for Fort Hare University.

Washington DC
4 December 1969
Dear Bala,

It has been a long time since we met that I am not sure you will remember who I am. This picture was taken in June – perhaps it will remind you of the time the four of us spent together in Istanbul. My letter has been prompted by my reading the journal that I kept this summer. I remember that we had a very spirited discussion about euthanasia, that you were studying to become a psychologist, and that you left by train for Tehran the day that Ron, Eleanor and I took a boat up the Bosphorus.

I hope your trip to India was as successful as our trip around Europe. We got very tired of travelling in the end, but it was such an incredibly educational experience that it was worth the fatigue. We had agreed to meet Ron in Paris but found out on arrival that he too had wearied of travelling and had gone back to school in Canada.

Now Eleanor and I are both back at school, dreaming about returning to places like Istanbul and discovering new places like South Africa. I had hoped that three months of sightseeing would cure my wanderlust, but it does not seem to have done that.

If you ever can come to the U.S., please know that you are welcome at our home.

With best wishes

Lynne

Lynne remembered correctly that when we bid farewell, I had headed for the Istanbul Central Station to catch a train to Tabriz in Iran. What she could not have guessed, even remotely, is that I had almost not made it onto the train. I arrived in good time, booked my seat and, as the station was crowded and noisy, I decided to wait at the entrance, squatting in a corner with my backpack leaning against a pillar. There were a few scruffy Western backpackers to be seen, casual, chatting and puffing away. The smell of whatever they smoked was cheap and revolting like damp rotting hay. It reminded me of the pungent smell of *dagga* (marijuana) in Durban in the filthy back alleys near the market.

Suddenly four or five police (*Jandama*) rushed at us from within the station with military-style guns. Alarm, alarm. Local people scattered. I stood rigid against the pillar where I had been squatting a minute ago. I got shouted at in Turkish, before being thrust behind four other backpackers, girls included, and marched into the station. The young backpackers exchanged frantic and furtive looks whispering rapidly, one having a fit of coughing. It soon became clear to me that the police had a strong presence at the station. I suspected the complex they herded us into included interrogation rooms and perhaps even temporary detention cells. I was separated from the others and literally dragged with my backpack to a small room. Terrified and confused, I pleaded my innocence. One policeman yanked my backpack from my grip, opened it and emptied the tightly stuffed contents onto the floor. He scattered the stuff about using his boot and rifle butt. A police dog was brought in which sniffed at my belongings with ears pricked and tail in the air like a security antenna. Another policeman demanded my passport and train ticket, He examined the photo closely, and took it to a photocopier. They gestured I take off my clothes and bend over. I recalled someone telling me that his mother often reminded him to change his underwear whenever he went out. 'You never know', were apparently her words.

    I kept glancing at a wall clock above the photocopier. My train would depart in forty-five minutes. It's okay, it's okay. You will make it. Just be calm, I said to myself. I was gestured to dress and pack. Feverish and in haste I tried to stuff everything back into my backpack. Bugger me, it would not quite fit. I was perspiring no end. A policewoman stepped into the room, picked up my document and disappeared. This is it, I thought. My mouth was parched. I was haunted by rumours of backpackers arrested by Turkish police on mere suspicion, endlessly tortured and held in indefinite solitary detention.

After what seemed a lifetime in hell, the woman in uniform returned with my passport and ticket. 'Go,' she said. Other police joined in. 'Go, go! Now.' However, their sour expressions said they were displeased to be instructed to let me go. I stumbled out and dragged my partly open backpack to the platform where my train was ready with the heavy engine chugging away in readiness. I never gave a second thought to whatever may have happened to the others taken in by the police. The thing is, even if I had run into them again, somewhere sometime, I would not have recognised them.

~

I remained anxious and vigilant on the train, sleeping but fitfully. I did not mind the day and a half it took me to journey across Turkey – as long as I made safe distance between myself and the horrid Jandama. I was thankful when a young Iranian man with a pale and delicate skin, kept me engaged in chit-chat. He was eager, he said, to practise his English. 'Once I complete my degree at Tehran University, I will join my sister in Boston.' In return, he later helped me to catch the right bus to Tehran.

Mid-morning of the next day I crossed the Gurbulak-Bazargan custom checkpoint and arrived in the Iranian city of Tabriz. It was 22 June. I looked around noticing how different Iran was from Turkey, although both were Muslim countries, and both had many elegant mosques gracing the skyline. For one thing, all signs were scrawled back-to-front in wispy swirls. To me the Persian script looked a mirror image of itself. What a pain, I thought, how am I ever going to find my way around once I get to Tehran? At least in Turkey I was in the company of friends and we deciphered things together.

I chose to travel by local bus to Tehran because it was affordable. It was crowded with loud and talkative young people who may have been high school students. When the bus arrived at the western bus station in Tehran, a girl sitting next to me pointed the way to a hostel smiling bashfully as she did so, clearly understanding my query but not saying a word. The hostel was small, scruffy and in a back street, but good enough for me – an easy walk to the bus station and to a cluster of rain-washed buildings with shops of sorts.

In the three days I was in Iran, I remained pretty much in Teheran largely exploring the Grand Bazaar and nearby sights making sure not to get lost in the process of wandering around. One afternoon, I plucked up courage and boarded a city circle bus. The landmark for my return stop was a single bowser filling station and a burnt-out minibus in a ditch opposite. Whichever way I turned, I was confronted by an imposing portrait of the Shah of Iran and his wife. At the time it was Mohammad Reza Pahlavi who was in charge. I had a vague recollection that a few years earlier the Americans had kicked out a democratic government under a man called Mosaddegh, helping the Shah to retake power. From the bus I saw how big and relatively modern Teheran was. There were more young people out and about than older folks.

For dinner that night I had a bottle of coco cola and a packet of what seemed like local made potato chips with an odd tuna-like flavour.

~

I had not forgotten the parting instruction given to me by the Pakistan Embassy in London. 'Take passport to immigration people in Tehran office, okay?' Although I felt vaguely hesitant, I knew it had to be done. I sat at the edge of my seat, as a taxi drove me to the embassy. The meter just kept ticking over. I could not trust the fella, I worried. I felt foolish when he arrived at the embassy gate with time to spare.

I explained why I had come. 'Passport,' said the man, peering at me. He wore wire-rimmed glasses and smelt of snuff or tobacco. 'Okay, I see you Hindu, ya? Laats of Hindus make house in South Africa. Gandhi too. You see, I know everything. Everything.' He shook his head and glowed as if overly pleased with himself. I stood there not knowing how to respond. He pulled out a large, stained handkerchief, blew his nose, folded it thoughtfully and returned it to his pocket as if he were miming an act on stage. 'Visa for you Hindu not granted,' he said with a hint of disdain. Pakistan for Muslims only. Okay?' That was that. He instructed the guard on duty to show me the door. I had no time to ask for the refund of the visa fee I had paid in London. I felt furious but walked away timidly, not wishing to make a scene.

By the time I returned to the hostel, I had almost resigned myself to the thought that it was all for the best. After all, wasn't I beginning to tire of living out of a backpack, being on the move all the time, feeling starved of news from family and friends, and waking each morning to uncertainty? But how was I going to get into India if not overland? And what about exotic Kabul, the Khyber Pass and Peshawar – places on my wish list? I sat on my bed weighed down by this unexpected and troubling problem. And there was really nobody I could consult or receive support from. I rummaged in every place I had hidden money before leaving London. How much would I need for a one-way flight to India? I must not cash any of my traveller's cheques, I thought.

I was impatient for the hot and sweaty night to end. Up before the break of dawn, I got to packing up without the motivation to shave or shower and went to the petrol station at the end of the street. The attendant, a drowsy morose old man was not too pleased that instead of petrol, I only needed directions to the airport. All I got from him was a gabbled 'Mehrabad fruit agar,' which sounded like he was directing me to a fruit market in the next village. I paid him to phone for a taxi.

The taxi driver grunted with half a smile. I immediately recognised him to be the one who had taken me to the Pakistan Embassy the day before. 'Airport,' I said flapping my arms and pointing to the sky. 'Ah, Mehrabad fruit agar,' he said turning on the ignition. I heard the second call of the muezzin to prayer. It was still six in the morning.

Luckily for me, there was an Air India flight early that afternoon. The ticket cost me a little over the hidden sterling notes I had unearthed, so I was compelled to cash one of my traveller's cheques. No joy in that.

It was to be a long wait. The airport was beginning to liven up with earnest passengers hastening behind porters with their luggage or shuffling forward in queues. I found a quiet seat and stretched out, my mind unsettled and body feeling the wear and tear of protracted travel – adjusting to changing time zones, disrupted sleep routines, and eating poorly at odd hours. Now I had a runny nose and a soggy handkerchief. I cheered myself by the thought that in a few days I'd be calling on the beautiful daughters of my friend Dr Jivanathan, which reminded me of the list of contacts he'd given me. I had better pull out that sheet and have it in readiness. The first person I would hopefully meet was Mr Mohan Singh in New Delhi,

~

The flight touched down in New Delhi at about midnight – seven hours from take-off. I had no idea it would take so long, but as I had slept most of the way I felt a little refreshed. A dense, oppressive humid smell hit me full in the face the moment I emerged from the plane – a stale sweetish smell of curry, sweat and decay. It also seemed like the whole of India was awake and whispering incessantly from a remote place, all together. A combination of peculiar smells, chaotic sounds, dirt, and sweaty heat stalked me wherever I travelled in India.

It was almost three in the morning by the time I cleared passport control, customs, and collected my backpack. Everything was dizzyingly complicated and moved at a snail's pace. A young man with a famished face, in bare feet hassled me wanting to carry my backpack. He wore a cotton dhoti and turban, both in much need of a good wash. I had to restrain him with a firm 'no' and a fierce expression. I soon found that this kind of pressure from porters, taxi and tuk tuk drivers and other touts was a common feature of India, an impoverished country with millions of illiterate and unemployed. I just had to learn to be more patient, I reminded myself, without becoming overly stressed. It proved not an easy task.

I whiled away time at the airport until around eight in the morning. There was a café which sold spiced tea (chai) and fermented rice cakes (idli). The tea was hot, unhealthily sweet and refreshingly potent – a heady brew. I was already beginning to get the feel of India – a giddy mix of aversion and appeal.

When I phoned Mr Mohan Singh's office and asked to speak to him, a female answered in a sing-song accent. He took the call immediately. 'Oh yes, I was expecting you. And how's Dr Jivanathan? Okay, okay I come collect you at ten?' I thanked him and said I was quite happy to wait. He suggested I stand at the Delhi Tourism kiosk in the foyer. I told him how to identify me and that I had a large backpack.

Mr Singh turned out to be a Sikh in his early forties, bearded and in an ochre turban, a long-sleeved light business shirt and black pants. No tie. He was amiable and chatty with good English, all of which immediately set me at ease. We travelled into the city on separate *tuk tuks* (covered scooters). He and his mother, uncle, sister and two brothers all lived in a two-level flat in a convenient but congested part of Delhi. We deposited my backpack in the flat and then walked to a *gentlemen's only* club around the corner near the popular Nehru Park. It was approaching noon, and the summer sun was at its fiercest, the glare difficult to handle. 'You'll need dark glasses like these,' he said. 'I may have one to spare.'

Entering the club was like escaping equatorial heat for the pristine cool sanctuary of a cave. The effect was created by drawn blinds, soft lighting, and slow-moving fans. The quietness was unreal. The members seemed to speak in hushed voices. My host ordered me a chilled coconut and lime juice, while he chose iced coffee with pistachio ice-cream, both served in stainless steel glasses. I still recall the feel of condensation each time I lifted my glass for a sip.

Later we had a light lunch at Mr Singh's home prepared by his mother, a slight built elderly woman in a typical Punjabi outfit – a long loose cotton skirt and a matching baggy pants worn under the skirt. She smiled a lot as she served us to make up, I think, for her lack of English. I was shown where to shower and rest for the afternoon, while Mr Singh returned to his office. I felt extremely grateful that my very first day in India had turned out this way.

After dinner, to my great relief, Mr Singh offered to sit with me and plan my India itinerary. I also had the opportunity to chat to Mr Singh's family. Of course, they asked many questions about their friend Dr Jivanathan and what it was like working in a Scottish hospital. But they were equally curious about my family and life generally in South Africa under Apartheid. They knew all about Gandhi's work there as a lawyer. I felt sheepish when questioned about why I spoke no Indian languages. It was near eleven when the family was ready for bed. I had been yawning much before then and was quite blown away with the sleeping arrangements. One after the other, we climbed onto the balcony veranda through an upstairs sash window. Even Mr Singh's mother did so with her skirt tucked between her knees. Not everyone changed into nightwear. There was a line of metal-framed beds alongside each other. A thin mattress served each bed laid on cross-woven hessian strips firmly bound to the bed frame. A light sheet and a pillow completed the bedding. The evening had cooled a little. Within minutes, I fell into a deep sleep.

I was woken by the incessant call of birds – rooks and sparrows. It took me a few minutes to realise I was in India and had slept out in the open. It was 4 am by my wristwatch. The sky above me was already a shimmering orange. Not a speck of cloud. The only movement was of black kites drifting high up with wings fully extended. The call of magpies and crows came from somewhere closer. I was the only one still in bed. I got up wondering how I was going to manage the extreme Indian summer for weeks to come.

Over the next two days Mr Singh took me sight-seeing. I rode pinion on his motorbike. No helmet. I learnt that to survive as a driver in any Indian city, you need to be agile, sharp-eyed, and skilled in risk taking – and have no qualms about blasting your hooter every second. At one point, just as we were approaching Parliament House (*Sansad Bhavan*), Mr Singh stopped abruptly for a large brahmin cow the colour of sea sand. Traffic behind us banked up rapidly. The cow stood in the very middle of the road, turned its head our way with a look of dreamy disdain and dropped a bucket of dung right there before us. Eventually a taxi driver got out and persuaded the cow to move on. 'Chal, chal,' (go, go) he urged in frustration. The power of a holy cow!

On the third evening I was ready to move on to my next destination, Lucknow. I was sad to leave New Delhi, largely because of the warmth and hospitality lavished on me.

It was to be my very first experience of train travel in India. I soon found that the train stations were much the same all over the country – congested with famished and weary bodies sprawled all over the platform, day, or night. I had to be careful not to tread over any of these waiting passengers or accidently kick any of their precious little bundles wrapped in old clothes. Countless taxis and tuk tuks caught in traffic snarl-ups, blasted their horns in frantic disregard. Porters and touts competed to harass potential customers in the dust and heat. Every station encounter for me was a melee of madness.

Mr Singh showed me how to find my allocated first-class seat. 'Check the list displayed outside the ticket office,' he instructed. 'Each coach has a letter and a number. Your name and seat number will appear next to the coach detail. Simple, yah?' Thankfully, this lesson stood me in good stead without fail. I noticed that second-class and third-class coaches were always bursting with passengers. I found first-class train travel in India relatively comfortable, with each sleeper compartment for only three passengers.

Mr Singh saw me onto my coach before saying goodbye and good wishes.

~

I slid the door open to my compartment and found it already occupied. A man sat in the far end near the window. He looked up and glared at me momentarily and then closed his eyes, resting his chin on his chest. He is no good, was my immediate assessment. I had better be careful. I propped up my backpack on the seat at the opposite end, close to the door, and rested my head against it. The man, fully in my sight, was about forty, unkempt and unshaven – rough looking. What could I do but remain vigilant? As the train pulled out from the station for its long overnight journey to Lucknow, I heard a grunt. Only then did I realise that there was another man asleep on the upper bunk, not visible from where I sat.

As the night wore on, I found it increasingly difficult to keep my eyes open. Other times, I made as if I had fallen asleep, but kept one eye open ever so slightly. I became obsessively convinced the man in the far end was eyeing me and my backpack. How come this unsavoury person was travelling first-class? He must have a motive, I thought.

I awoke to metallic tapping on the compartment door. It was a waiter come to announce that the restaurant carriage was open for breakfast and orders. My unsavoury man was having an exchange with the invisible one on the upper bunk – in Hindi. A pair of bare legs dropped abruptly from the upper bunk. 'Hello.' He was addressing me, this youthful faced, light-looking man. I was startled that he spoke the Queens English. 'Where you're from?' I'm sending my man to buy breakfast. Can he get you something?' 'No, I don't have small rupees,' I said. 'Don't worry, I'll pay.'

Not too long after, the train arrived in Lucknow. Not only had I survived the night but learnt a valuable lesson. How readily I had allowed faulty assumptions to lead me astray and, in the process, misjudge good people. The young man turned out to be an army officer on leave from a stint on the Pakistan border. The other was his man servant.

As a first-class ticket holder, I was able to rent a guest room at the station at Lucknow at a very reasonable charge. I was relieved to find it amazingly clean with fresh sheets and a functioning ceiling fan. Three nights maximum, I was told. I was even more impressed to learn this facility existed, in limited ways, at most major rail stations, together with inexpensive curry cafes at either ends of the platform. Hence, my travel across much of India took on a routine. I would book myself a station guest room as soon as I arrived in a city and then take short trips to a few selected places of interest – affordable ones. If it got too hot for me while out and about, I would duck into an air-conditioned place, often an airline office. Several times, I recall, being asked to move on as soon as a diligent staff member became aware of my lingering presence. Many a time I aborted my tour and returned to the coolness of my room at the station.

For whatever reason, I found myself constantly hungry no matter how often or how much I ate. Food was always on my mind. Whenever I had a room at the station, I often had two dinners or two lunches, moving from the meat café at the one end of the station to the vegetarian café at the other end. Even so, I continued to lose weight, and the clothes I wore hung on me. I had not had a haircut since leaving Cupar. Washing clothes and showering became infrequent.

~

My next stopover was at Varanasi (Benares), a city saturated in history, religion, and tradition. I went to the steps of the Ghats on the Ganges River to see for myself the cremation of the dead, on improvised pyres all along the water's edge. The acrid smell of burning flesh, incense and flowers saturated the air making me want to vomit. I dared not venture too close, but even from where I stood at the head of the ghat (platform), it was obvious to me that the bodies only half charred were ending up in the river not too far from where countless people were dipping themselves in pious fervour. I certainly did not feel I would wish to witness this macabre ritual a second time. I headed back to the station not in the best frame of mind. Locals were making their way across a shunting yard to the station, stepping over rail lines between parked train coaches. I foolishly followed, only to trip and stumble, hurting an ankle. The throbbing discomfort lasted days, hindering and slowing me down. Hence, I had to give up on a few places I had planned to see.

After a few more stops on the way from Varansi, I arrived in Madras (Chennai). In a letter dated 6 August written from Madras to my brother, I say '*I arrived in Madras a couple of days ago. Rather disappointed with the place. Tamil is all over in spoken and written form. Very amusing at times.*' And I go on: '*The people look mean, dirty and famished. Temples, temples all over. I'm somewhat tired of the whole business.*' It does not seem as if I identified with the Tamilians as my ancestors. I don't say 'Wow, I'm finally among my people. I look so much like them.' Nothing of this sort. How intolerant and disparaging can one be. The nasty side of me is telling. I now feel so very ashamed.

I was pleasantly surprised to meet a Tamil-speaking Muslim in Madras, a Sultan Khan living in Angappa Naik Street. He was one of the many names on my list of contacts from Dr Jivanathan. I visited him in his crockery shop where he readily shook my hand, welcoming me to Madras. He took me to his house behind the shop and pointed to a hammock suspended in the open veranda near a tap. 'Please make yourself comfortable,' he said and returned to his shop. I was tongue-tied. What kind of hospitality is this? I thought. I stuck it out for two days, the hammock being my entire living space – apart from the adjacent tap. Sitting and lying on the hammock for hours on end, I felt the swaying as if I were on a small boat out on open water, fishing. Mr Khan did not come to check on me nor did I see any of his family. Only a curious cat came by once or twice to brush against my legs. I used an outside squat-toilet and ate at a nearby café. On the third morning, incensed by the way I had been treated, I packed up to leave Madras sooner than I intended. Seething, I went to see Mr Khan and give him a piece of my mind. He, in turn, was appalled. 'Look here, Mr Bala, you Hindu, yah? I tell my wife you not happy to sleep inside Muslim house. Not eat halal food. Religion, you know. I'm so sorry you leave now. But you not told me you very upset. But why?'

What a mess, what misunderstanding. Here was Mr Khan scrupulous in believing I would feel polluted by entering a Muslim home, and me assuming that he'd treated me, a guest, in a most shabby way. Much of the strife between Hindus and Muslims, between Pakistan and India may be ascribed to such misunderstandings stemming from a history of mistrust and animosity grounded in religion. I was reminded of how the Pakistan Embassy in Tehran had refused me a visa.

The possibility of visiting India had appealed to me simply because this was where my grandparents originated from. I had thought immersing myself fully for a time in the land of my ancestors would inspire me and bring out the Indianness. I would take to the country, its people and culture – like fish to water. In the process, I might just uncover distant family members still living somewhere in Tamil Nadu.

Dr Jivanathan had suggested it. 'You may find family there. Like cousins.' But now physically here in Madras, I did not feel all that motivated or inspired to go cousin hunting. But then, even if I had wanted to take a shot at it, I had no idea how to begin the search or where to start. The fact is, I had done no prior homework, no preliminary research. In truth, I abandoned the project even before making a start. When I reflect on that time in Madras, what is clear is that I could not identify with the true, authentic Tamilians there. We had grown a world apart. I had lost my mother tongue, Tamil, and with it had gone much of my South Indian culture. Culture, I learned is a dynamic thing, ever adapting to changing circumstances. In South Africa, I would still be taken by other Indians as a Tamilian, not Hindi, not Gujarati and certainly not a Tamil speaking Muslim. It is just that I'd turned into a very different kind of Tamilian, no longer the original Madras brand.

~

Admittedly, I was also tantalised with the prospect of meeting the two gorgeous-looking young daughters of Dr Jivanathan. For an unattached young man, attractive girls were simply irresistible. After my disappointment in Madras, I felt I could do with some excitement to cheer me. So it was, I decided that this would be my last stop before heading for Bombay (Mumbai) from where I intended to board a ship home. Because I was low on funds, my father had agreed to pay for my ticket.

After all that anticipation and build up, I could only manage an overnight visit to the family. But it was well worth it. The sisters, Rani and Seehta, received me with glee. They spoke English after their own fashion, swaying their heads from side to side, expressing pleasure – a characteristic gesture I had noticed across India. Soon I had a distinct sense they were competing for my attention. They were modestly dressed in saris, moved gracefully, and were softly spoken. Yet they seemed bold and unusually forward with me, I thought. 'Shall I take your photos?' 'Yes, oh yes,' both chimed happily, and disappeared for a few minutes to make themselves look even prettier.

I felt secretly drawn to Seehta who was relatively taller, lighter in complexion with wavy hair - very much taking after her father. A potential Bollyhood star. The other, Rani, wore glasses and appeared a little shorter, darker, and more the homely sort.

Sisters Seehta and Rani

That night I slept in a room with little more than a large bed encased in a mosquito net suspended from the ceiling. I had visions of the sisters frolicking in my dream. Soon after I had turned in and was dozing off, when I had the strong impression in my half-sleep state that the girls were at my bedside gazing at me intently through the netting. I sat up with a start but saw no one. Imagined or not, this was very odd and puzzling.

I had played with them for the thrill of it, but they may have had a more serious purpose in engaging me, I thought: to find an eligible husband. I had strayed into their home, a handsome young man I thought, single, a professional with a potentially secure future and, what is more, someone well-liked by their father. In another life, perhaps if I had had my way, I would have considered marrying them both. That is the chauvinist in me!

In capturing my thoughts about and conduct with Seehta and Rani in this way, I provide some insight into the kind of person I may have once been, and how I may have related to women. Now I am left somewhat ruffled and contrite. If still alive, they would be in their '60s. I hope life has dealt them good health, much joy and wholesome families.

I bade them goodbye early the next day. Were the girls sad to see me go? Did I leave them in hope, with promises? I cannot now recall. But I puzzle, even now, that I have no recollection of their mother or any other adult chaperone in the house. It is a complete mystery.

~

When I arrived in Bombay, I left my backpack at the luggage section at Bombay Central station, found a tuk tuk to take me to the home of Mrs Meena Kothane, a distant relative of Dr Jivanathan. I had requested my father and my younger brother to send her the money to buy a ticket for my return to Durban by ship. I had explained who she was and had given them her postal address. 'So finally, I lay my eyes on you, Bala. See you in flesh and blood. Come, come in. Meet my family,' she fussed with much warmth. She was a buxom woman with dancing earrings. The end of her sari kept slipping off her shoulder.

I had to remove my shoes at the door. Although the house was small and cluttered, I was invited to stay with them, sleeping on a couch in a back room. 'Yes, I got the money from your father and already booked your passage on the ship. It sails in three days.' I was relieved. 'But you must go to collect the ticket yourself. You have to show your passport, yah?'

'How can I thank you enough for all your help?' I said bringing my palms together.

'No, no. You don't have to thank me. Dr Jivanathan's friend, my friend.'

~

On 21 August 1969, I boarded a medium-sized passenger ship belonging to the Lloyd Triestino Line bound for Durban. Over the fortnight it took me to get home, I had time enough to reflect on my overland journey.

I must have been a sucker for punishment to take on a fraught and arduous back-packing challenge. I had no previous experience of overland travel or long spells with just myself as constant companion. I had endured extremes of weather, diarrhoea, hunger, harassment by touts, rough treatment in the hands of police, injuries and relentless stretches of trekking with a backpack almost half my height and weight. All-in-all, this was a self-imposed madness of sorts.

I had certainly learnt much about risk-taking and how to survive setbacks on my own and to be attentive to my personal needs. Many a time I had to keep my cool – at least to look calm on the outside. I think I had also learnt to recognise early signs of loneliness and fear, to accept them without too much alarm until they passed. Above all, the journey presented many situations where I saw my prejudices and faulty perceptions at work. For instance, I am still haunted with guilt about how badly I misjudged the men I shared a compartment with on the train to Lucknow. It taught me to be more accommodating of people and not label them by their looks. This has helped me focus my attention on changing my ways of thinking, seeing, and acting.

~

India, my so-called motherland, was very much a letdown on this initial visit. I'd had enough of the highs and lows. I felt overwhelmed by the sheer madness of life and death jostling up close into my face without relief.

More recently I was both impressed and moved when I read of Xuanzang, a Chinese Buddhist who went on pilgrimage to India in 627 AD when overland travel would have been unimaginably hazardous. His purpose was to savour India's ancient wisdom and culture, to collect and take back to China valuable Buddhist scriptures. He experienced many hardships as he journeyed through such places (known today) as Pakistan, Nepal, and Bangladesh. But Xuanzang was never daunted, always remaining positive, always curious and interested in the people and lands that he encountered. His fascinating experiences are recounted and celebrated by Sun Shuyun in her memoir *Ten Thousand Miles Without a Cloud,* (2003). If only this book had been available to me before I had set out on my overland journey, I may have been more open to and inspired by the wonders of the history, culture, peoples, and landscape that I had encountered all along my route, but more especially in India.

I am also rather puzzled about how it could have been that as a thirty-year old visitor of Indian descent, I was totally oblivious that there had lived in this very land of India a spiritual colossus called Shakyamuni Buddha. And whose moving advice to his bereft disciples, as he lay dying, was simple and telling: 'Be a lamp unto yourself. Seek refuge in no other. Travel heedfully.' Advice I had clearly needed as a young man with much of life before me.

I feel a sense of guilt and shame in recalling how I allowed my negative mind to get the better of me. I did India a great disservice by painting her poorly, reacting too harshly to the mid-summer heat, the poverty and crush of people. No doubt I was tired and depressed and sorely regretted making the arduous overland journey on my own, inexperienced as I was. I was impatient to get home. But still……

In the years that followed, I paid three more visits to India, in better circumstances and as a much wiser and mature person. I was more accommodating and tolerant of India then, and appreciated all the precious aspects of this ancient civilization perhaps as much as Xuanzang had done centuries earlier. Even so, the continued treatment of millions of its citizens, the Dalits, as outcastes is as repugnant and painful to me as was Apartheid.

~

In opting for the long route home, I may have also hoped to delay my inevitable return. Perhaps I wanted a longer period to prepare myself, mentally, for whatever fearful surprises apartheid South Africa had in store for me. In hindsight, had the tough journey done me any good? I can't be sure. Perhaps in subtle ways I gained some insight into the historical complexities of wealth, poverty, political power, ethnic and racial animosity. South Africa, to a large measure, reflected what many other countries I travelled through had or were experiencing at the time. Conflicts, uprisings, and transformations were happening all the time in some form or the other.

The ship finally docked in Durban early on 5th September 1969. There, I told myself, that was not so bad after all. I had survived to celebrate my thirty first birthday in two weeks. I pictured my family fussing over my return with a pot of chicken biryani. And my father all emotional, 'My son, my son's come home.' I would accept a sloppy kiss on my cheek. It is the story of the relenting prodigal son finally returning home.

Having roamed the wide world and gone to India in search of my identity, I returned home feeling strongly that I was more South African than Indian. I had seen the world in many guises, in many shades, in many moods. All this, I hoped, would help me live my life as a more fully engaged and productive person under Apartheid.

Part 3

Back in Apartheid South Africa

South Africa
1969 – 1988

I sighed with relief that the journey was finally over. No more days on a rolling ship with revolting meals set before me. I shuddered in recalling my hopeless attempts to suppress surges of nausea, followed by the inevitable bitter aftertaste. I still felt shaken and unsteady and could not wait to step onto *terra firma*.

I joined the milling passengers on deck, including several anxious-looking women in saris. I overhead that these women made regular trips to India and returned with bags and bags of choicest saris, bangles, sandals, and other such items keenly sought by wealthy Indian families preparing for weddings of their loved ones. Getting past customs required guile, if not a fat wallet.

The ship passed the unmistakable Durban beach-front, an expansive stretch of golden sand and gentle surf, hemmed by a string of high-rise hotels and coconut palms. I had not enjoyed the privilege of seeing my city from the vantage point of a ship's deck before. This was so rare. I caught my breath feeling a little sentimental. I leaned over the rail and watched as the ship was escorted into the Durban Bay by a tugboat, hooting and spouting steam. We headed for Maydon Wharf.

Everyone scrambled to get off. I was keen to see who had come to receive me. Even so I disembarked with trepidation. The sky was becoming rapidly overcast. I smelt uncertainty in the air.

What was the political climate I had stepped into? Frankly, I have little recollection now fifty years later. It seems that in leaving Zambia for Britain, I had inadvertently severed myself from the traditional sources of reliable information– newspapers from home, ANC comrades and my South African friends. So here now for context, I need to trust historians like Gail Nattrass (*A Short History of South Africa*) to fill me in.

Briefly, according to this historian, the restriction and containment of non-whites had been intensified incrementally in the 1960s. The 90 days detention without trial was increased to 180 days. The Terrorism Act was enacted in 1967 with more powers to suppress opposition. The Nationalist Party, the architects of Apartheid, increased its majority to near 60% in parliament. Despondency and despair washed over the dispossessed and disenfranchised non-white majority. At the same time, the forces of dissent were forming into clandestine structures. Amidst this situation, a most dramatic and unforeseen event occurred. Prime Minister Hendrik Verwoerd, the stub-nosed godfather of Apartheid, was assassinated in the House of Assembly by a white man who the media reported was deranged. I would guess that, in the circumstances, Non-Whites across the country may have been quietly jubilant, even thanking heaven for this wondrous deed in the hope that it would be a major setback for the purveyors of Apartheid. But this was not to be. The man who stepped in as Prime Minister was none other than John Balthazar Vorster, a steely-faced, puffed-up bully. I recall his chilling emotionless face on the black and white TV screen as he delivered his threats and ultimatum in a monotonous Afrikaans drawl. In his previous role as Minister of Police, he had excelled in his capacity for single-minded viciousness. Many an opposition activist suffered horrendous torture during interrogation at John Vorster Square, in Pretoria, the dreaded headquarters of the security police (Special Branch). It was from the tenth storey of this building that thirty year old Ahmed Timol, a gifted teacher and activist, was allegedly pushed to his death in 1971 during interrogation. It defies belief that this notorious building has not yet been demolished and erased from memory. Rather, it is still in use as the Johannesburg Central Police Station.

I struggled to fit back into family and community life. I had to renegotiate my place, my roles. For a period, I lived with my family in Reservoir Hills finding my feet, while I attempted to get approval to practice as a psychologist. This meant registering with the South African Medical and Dental Council (SAMDC).

I soon discovered to my distress that the Council had never previously registered a non-white applicant – and was not inclined to change its mind. I approached Professor Ronald Albino, my former lecturer in psychology at the University of Natal. Luckily for me, he said he was an active member of the South African Psychological Association. This Association was one of a few organisations at the time open to non-white membership. Of course, I was quite confounded how this was possible in a country legally constrained by severe racial legislations. Professor Albino was more than willing to advocate on my behalf. He said that I was the very first Non-White in South Africa to have completed an internship in Clinical Psychology. Professor Albino argued my case with vigour. He sent the SAMDC a lengthy memorandum on the great need for non-white psychologists, and why I should be registered. The Council was initially adamant in its rejection, but the Professor remained steadfast and undeterred. It took him about a year to persuade this powerful institution, rigidly aligned to segregation policies, to make an exception in my case. I hold the certificate of registration in my hand now and shake my head in disbelief, in wonderment.

Professor Albino's bold and determined challenge of an apartheid institution on my behalf, impressed me deeply and qualified my perception of Whites in the country. I needed to look around, I realised, and acknowledge the many courageous democrats in the white population who opposed apartheid policies with vehemence. For a white privileged person living in apartheid South Africa, Professor Albino was remarkably brave to have stood up to racial discrimination on behalf of Non-Whites. He risked much. What he did for me was relatively insignificant compared to his appearance as an expert witness for the defence at political trials of persons charged under apartheid legislations such as the 90 days and 180 days Detention Acts.

Certificate of Registration

This is to certify that

BALASUNDRAN SUBRAMANI MUDALY

has satisfied the conditions laid down by the Council of the South African Psychological Association for admission to the register(s) of

CLINICAL PSYCHOLOGISTS

PRESIDENT

SECRETARY

DATE 25th May 1970

PLACE JOHANNESBURG

THE SOUTH AFRICAN MEDICAL AND DENTAL COUNCIL

Registration Certificate
Issued under Act No. 13 of 1928.

This is to Certify

That * BALASUNDRAN SUBRAMANI MUDALY *

* Under the provisions of Rule 5 of Government Notice No. R.1726 of 1964, as amended *

is registered as a

* PSYCHOLOGIST *

in accordance with the provisions of Section 32 of the Medical, Dental and Pharmacy Act, 1928, and is hereby authorized to practise as such within the limits of the Republic of South Africa.

W.H. Bernard
Registrar

Pretoria,
eptember, 1971

Professor Albino died in 2009 aged 93. In honouring his memory, I am reminded of the title of a movie *A Few Good Men* where integrity and honesty are abiding themes. There have been many other courageous Whites in the long and concerted struggles in South Africa against unjust laws, including people from distinguished Afrikaaner families. They suffered and sacrificed almost all, without flinching. Prominent among these were Advocate Bram Fisher and Rev Beyers Naude who were ostracised by their community and relentlessly persecuted by the security police. Bram Fischer, in fact, died of cancer while serving a life sentence. I pay homage to the many white South Africans who stood and fought side-by-side with Non-Whites in the long road to freedom. What a travesty it would be if I created the impression (or believed) the story of my life and that of South Africa was simply one of white oppression of Non-Whites. I believe that it is important to see the complexity in the South African nation in shades of grey than simply as black and white.

~

I came to realise soon enough that my hard-won certificate from the SAMDC was of little value. It did not catapult me into a fulfilling career as a psychologist. I was rather naive in believing there would be openings for me in state institutions such as hospitals, clinics, schools, or universities. Then too, family and friends actively involved in community life advised me that private practice was not a realistic or viable option because the non-white populations were largely impoverished and disadvantaged, with little capacity to pay for my service. Nor would they have much understanding of psychological services as distinct from psychiatry and mental illness, and the associated fear and stigma. In any event, I needed to appreciate, they said, that much of the emotional distress experienced by our people was, directly and indirectly, due to social and political factors – the trauma of oppression and discrimination flowing from apartheid legislations. Having chosen to return to South Africa, this was the bitter reality I was compelled to accept.

The consequence was that, in a sense, I had to walk the streets looking for work, putting out feelers here and there. As the days went by, I found myself becoming confused and uncertain about the real worth of my psychological training and qualifications. I felt a boost to my ego whenever I heard myself say, when asked: 'Oh, I'm a *Clinical Psychologist.*' I would feel somewhat puffed up in thereafter explaining what a clinical psychologist was. I would create the impression that this profession was aligned to medicine, hence carrying the same privileged status. I would dread the question that would invariably follow, prompted by genuine concern. 'But you don't have a job, yah?' My ears would heat up. I would want to shout 'You blaming me? It's not my fault I'm unemployed.' But I did not. I kept my composure, swallowing the salty taste of shame. It puzzles me now, why I had not attempted to return to teaching, as I'd done in Zambia.

Many a day I would be out, door-knocking, and cold canvassing. Concerned friends, neighbours and cousins aided me with potential leads. As a result, I phoned Lawrence Schlemmer, another liberal-minded academic like Professor Albino, at the University of Natal. He expressed concern that a Non-White with such qualifications should be walking the streets. He urged me to get an appointment with the personnel manager at Mondi Paper Mill in Merebank, an Indian designated group-area in Durban. He would write me a letter of support.

Mondi was a project of Oppenheimer Holdings and Bowaters, both international companies of considerable wealth, reputation, and economic clout. A gigantic factory to produce newsprint was just being built, and the nuts and bolts of worker recruitment were being sorted out. Of course, as expected Merebank had a majority Indian population. I am unsure if it was for this reason that the company decided to select, train and employ mostly Indians as machine operators and related technical staff.

It must have been my lucky day when I called on the personnel manager with the letter of introduction from Lawrence Schlemmer. At the time, the project team, including personnel staff, operated from temporary offices in Jacobs. I learnt that the Mondi factory itself was expected to be ready in a few months.

Yes, he said, the company would have use for me for at least a year. That was music to my ears. I was tempted to jump up and hug the man, except for a fear of breaching some racial law or other. It was my very first break in a while. I was employed as an assistant recruitment and training officer under Mike Bebb, a thick-set amiable white person in his early forties. He and I formed a training team (together with two Indian secretarial staff) under the Personnel Department. Under supervision, I designed a training manual for machine operators and other technical staff, participated in the recruitment of such staff and assisted in their training. As expected, I had to initially learn a great deal myself about newsprint and its production.

I was introduced to the other project staff, all English-speaking Whites. Mine was the only face of colour – except for the *tea-girls* and the *messenger boy* (adult black South Africans in lowly jobs were referred to as girls and boys.) The Whites, without exception, welcomed me seemingly without prejudice. It was almost as if the siloed world of Mondi was exempt from racial constraints and apartheid legislation. I was almost lulled into letting my guard down. On my very first day, I reported for work early feeling thrilled I had secured employment respectful of my status – a highly qualified Non-White, widely-travelled and experienced in the ways of the world beyond Apartheid. The personnel manager intercepted me as I arrived with an odd smile. He called me into his office and closed the door behind him. What is this, I wondered.

'See Bala, it's not of my making.' He shuffled on his feet, tugged at his auburn moustache, and shoved both hands deep into his trouser pockets. I waited in apprehension. 'It's this way. We must abide by the law. Not easy you know, for some of us.'

The bugger has changed his mind, I thought. I tensed with alarm and anger.

'Sorry, but we hadn't planned to employ a Non-White so soon. We've provided washrooms for whites only. Not to worry. I've arranged for you to use the toilet around the corner in the next building,' he said, as if were doing me a special favour. 'Belongs to OTH Beiers. Lots of black workers there.'

That did it for me. I had been brought down with a humiliating thud. But there was no going back. I needed this job as there was no other option. Served me right for thinking otherwise. This is South Africa, okay? Accept it.

Over the next three months, I had to contend with this humiliation each time I had need to use the toilet. Whenever you need to go, you need to go. I would hold it as long as possible, then hasten down a flight of wooden stairs and along a dingy back alley. The lavatory was confronting – a much-used, urine drenched hovel located at the rear of OTH Beiers, a putrid-smelling wool scouring factory.

~

In the time I worked at Mondi, I continued to live with my family in the all-Indian suburb of Reservoir Hill.

The charged political atmosphere was difficult to ignore. I breathed oppression. I felt a kind of vague anxiety all the time which sapped my energy, much like when acrid and stifling smoke from nearby cane fields drifted our way. Each day dawned rife with news of further police powers, more raids, shootings and detentions, and rumours of clandestine resistance. The Daily News and Mercury were sold out immediately they hit the streets. Pervasive fear flourished side-by-side with calls for active defiance. I found myself caught up in the fever of the times, stirred up, an urge to do something, to get involved.

~

In October 1971, the Natal Indian Congress (NIC) was revived. This was largely through the initiative of Mewa Ramgobin and his wife Ela Gandhi.

Ela was the granddaughter of Mahatma Gandhi who was instrumental in forming the original NIC in 1894 to mobilise opposition to the Colonial Government's discriminating practices against Indian traders. But in the years preceding its revival, it had largely become defunct. It seemed to me the revival was timely because ordinary Indians felt an urgent need for a relatively safe avenue to channel their frustrations and political aspirations, and to agitate for change. However, the revival met with some criticism. It was a retrograde step, some said, in that it may be seen especially by disenfranchised black and coloured populations as the revival of an ethnic and racially exclusive organisation. Yet others argued that the revived NIC was simply a pragmatic interim structure operating under the radar of the security police.

Soon NIC branches were established across all Indian areas. I put up my hand to help set up the Reservoir Hills Branch and became an active committee member. Many lively public meetings were held. Apart from Fatima Meer, I seem to recall the emboldened leaders were men. Some were skilled in public speaking and others struggled to rally the crowd.

In retrospect, the person worthy of special mention is the late George Sewpersadh, a humble and unassuming man, who was thrust into the leadership of the revived NIC. George struck me as an unlikely leader. Gaunt-faced, with a Gandhi-style moustache, wispy thinning hair, over-grown and unruly. His thread-bare coat was always threatening to fall off his shoulders. He spoke with a lisp and his sentences tended to fragment. I felt he needed a good traditional wife to take care of him – but sadly he never married. George was a person of much courage, sincerity, and generosity. He did not falter in the face of repeated arrests, bannings and imprisonment. His legal practice suffered. George certainly embodied the spiritual essence of service (*satyagraha*).

The political climate was heating up. I felt exhilarated and in the thick of things. The importance of being part of a campaign team, helping prepare and equip venues for public meetings, standing in the picket line at a political rally or doorknocking and handing out fliers. It was all low-level daring and risk taking. But being in the public eye was a boost to my ego. I had now become a *political activist*.

Apart from organising public meetings and political rallies, we contrived other creative and clandestine ways of raising the political awareness of relatively passive Indians. One political stunt a few of us mounted proved to be dramatically effective. In fact, it was outrageous enough to get the attention of the evening Daily News and the Leader, an Indian weekly. We borrowed a coffin from a member of the NIC, Harris Peters, who was a prosperous undertaker at the time. This we draped in black cloth and pinned on it, in bold print, the message: STOP VORSTER BURYING FREEDOM. The coffin was then transported in the dead of night and positioned on an advantageous spot on the nature strip on Mountbatten Drive, the busy main road through Reservoir Hills to Westville, Pinetown and Chesterville. The precise spot chosen was in front of the Divine Life Society where the nature strip was broad, freshly mowed and sloped to the road. So located, the coffin was highly visible to passing traffic. Countless buses ploughed this route at all hours of the day and night. A few of us culprits and activists rode the buses a few times to gauge the impact the stunt had on passengers. We felt extremely pleased with our handiwork.

One thing led to another. Soon I found myself active on a few political fronts, including the Durban Housing Action

Committee (DHAC) and South African Students Organisation (SASO). DHAC was set up in the 60s by Pravin Gordhan and other activists from the Indian community. Its primary aim was to mobilise the community to oppose segregated sub-standard housing, resist rent increases affecting low-income groups, stop evictions and challenge the larger impact of the Group Areas Act. DHAC forged alliances with ratepayers and housing action groups from the Coloured community such as in Sydenham and Newland East. Hence, I also found opportunities to engage with politically minded coloured people – but also, for the first time, to visit the homes of some of the activists and gain a sense of their living circumstances.

Involvement in the NIC and DHAC resulted in new friendships and new networks. One of my most enduring friendships arose from a chance meeting at an NIC forum in Asherville. This was with Zak and Anu Yacoob. This close friendship has now lasted sixty years. Zak, who was blind since infancy, qualified and practised as a barrister during the turbulent and trying years in South Africa. He was included in a few notable defence counsels in high profile political trials. Zak completed his distinguished legal career as a judge in the Constitutional Court.

As a friend, Zak has always been a regular bloke. The following anecdote will illustrate what I mean. Zak, Anu and I once went camping in the Drakensberg Mountains a couple of hours from Durban. The campsite we used, under huge conifers, was a segregated one. Early the day after we pitched camp, Zak and I went on a long walk. The air was refreshing even though the summer light was turning into a hazy shimmer. Large black birds, possibly crows, drifted lazily high up, their caws quite audible. Zak got into his usual jaunty stride, holding onto my left elbow as we proceeded, careful to keep to the edge of the sealed road and facing oncoming traffic. There was no cover from the already fierce sun. By midday we began to swelter.

As we turned back, Zak came up with one of his so-called brilliant ideas. 'Why don't we stop for a drink at that place you saw earlier?' He beamed at the very thought, shaking his head decidedly and pursing his lips.

'Hmm, why not,' I said recalling we had passed a sign to the Drakensberg Mountain Hotel not too far from the camping ground. We trudged on and on, energised by the vision of something cool and refreshing awaiting us. Of course, we ought to have known better. No sooner had we mounted a few creaking wooden steps, when a burly white man appeared on the veranda from inside of the hotel. We were given short shrift. 'You buggers blind or something? Read that sign?'

What a joke. So thoroughly seduced by the mental picture of a cold glass of beer, that I had not noticed the board with those obnoxious two words *Whites Only*. Deflated, and not wishing to create a scene, we turned tail and descended the stairs.

'Psst bru, you want a dop (drink)? Eh?' It was a skinny dark Indian in a white shirt and black pants who stuck his head around the side of the building, careful not to be seen. I hesitated, glancing over my shoulder to make sure the hotel proprietor had disappeared. Of course, Zak had no idea who had spoken to us. He pinched my upper arm whispering 'Who's that, eh? Who's that?' Then eager not to miss out on the offer, quickly responded 'Thanks bru, you fix it for us, eh? Chop, chop.'

'Okay, come this way,' said the voice. 'You NIC fellas from Durban, eh? Yah, I saw you at the meeting by Gandhi Hall.'

I said we were worried we may get him into serious trouble. He amused us with 'Bugger the white fella. Full of shit, that ou.'

This was risky business, I thought, especially for our Good Samaritan who was potentially putting his job on the line. But the thrill of the moment overrode any concern. The man beckoned again. We followed, crouching, to the back of the hotel where a few steps led to the rear door of the kitchen. And this is where we each had our double whisky on ice. On the house. 'Brilliant,' was Zak's verdict as the chill hit his throat. So it was that we conspired and beat Apartheid this once.

What with the oppressive sun above us and whisky in our belly, it stood to reason why we felt pleasantly light-headed and silly. We took leave of our generous Indian brothers in the back kitchen of the hotel and wobbled onto the road. As if luck had turned in our favour, a 'ute came by and readily stopped for us. Incapacitated by alcohol or not, we scrambled onto the open back-tray, and held on as we were tossed about – our bottoms bearing the brunt of it. The rushing breeze did its best to sober us up before we arrived at the camping ground. Anu would not have been too pleased to receive two intoxicated men. This short whisky-rewarded jaunt in the Drakensberg soon became a cherished and enduring memory!

It was pleasing to learn from the Indian waiter that he had attended NIC meetings and remembered us. Our campaigns to raise political awareness in the Indian community were obviously bearing fruit. I made sure to share this story with Ela Gandhi and Mewa Ramgobin when I next met them, after all they were the ones who had the foresight to revive the Natal Indian Congress in 1971.

Ela Gandhi & Mewa Ramgobin

As the surviving granddaughter of Mahatma Gandhi, it was Ela Gandhi who had kept alive the spirit of the Phoenix Settlement, a commune and community hub, founded by Gandhi in 1904. All through the 1960s and '70s, she with others organised various community activities at the Settlement in the hope of promoting and enhancing interracial harmony and cooperation. I have some recollection of attending two such events. One involved a field survey of people's lived experience of poverty and discrimination. This targeted black people in the informal settlement of Bhambayi in Inanda, a sprawling disarray of shacks on the hillside adjacent to the Phoenix Settlement. I was one of a mixed team of volunteers who ventured into the area negotiating open drains, sodden tracts, and mangy dogs. People readily invited us into their modest hovels, mostly kept neat and tidy, and were generally willing to share their lives, their hardships and worries.

The second project had to do with conservation farming. We were given hoes and taken through the process of preparing the soil for planting. We then planted seeds and seedlings, thoroughly watering them. The idea was that we would then go out and encourage others who had access to a small patch of unused land to grow vegetables for themselves. How practical and realistic this project proved to be I cannot tell. In any case, my association with the Phoenix Settlement was fruitful in that it offered me further opportunities for meaningful engagement with the local black community and black activists, a few of whom also belonged to a black students' organisation.

Community garden project at Phoenix Settlement (Author in the foreground holding a rake)

In recent years, the Gandhi Development Trust has organised an annual march from the Phoenix Settlement to commemorate Mahatma Gandhi's famous Salt March in India in defiance of British rule. On a visit to Durban in 2008, I participated in this annual event.

**2008 Gandhi Memorial Salt March in Durban
(Author front right with sun-visor)**

~

The South African Students Organisation (SASO) was a student body formed in 1968 to resist apartheid. Moreover, it distanced itself from the National Union of South African Students (NUSAS) which had been founded by Whites and traditionally catered for white students. SASO embraced the ideology of Black Consciousness, believing that black people could only redeem their dignity and self-confidence when they took full charge of their destiny – not simply deferring to the patronage of well-meaning Whites, Indians or Coloureds. I thought that the perspective of SASO was not dissimilar to that of the Black Power Movement of the sixties in the USA which urged black Americans to take pride in themselves and be politically self-reliant.

Despite SASO's black-power ideology, some of us were welcomed as active members. I frequented SASO's offices behind the United Congregational Church in Beatrice Street, Durban (now Charlotte Maxeke St) where I often met and fraternised with Steve Biko, Mamphela Ramphele and Barney Pitiyana, the three key leaders of SASO at the time. Strini Moodley, Saths Cooper and others became prominent much later. Both Steve Biko and Mamphela Ramphele were studying medicine at the Durban Medical School and were boarding at the Alan Taylor Residence, the hostel for non-white students, in Tara Road, Merebank. This is where I saw them in their less serious moments with the usual young people's capacity for fun, partying, and quick-witted banter. They were bright, intelligent, good-natured, and gifted. Who would have predicted then that by the late 1970s, SASO would be banned, and its leadership decimated - Steve Biko himself tortured to death by the security police? Mamphela Ramphele was banished to a remote village, and others banned or sent to prison. Apartheid brutalised and wasted many promising young lives.

Life for me in this period was both hectic and interesting. I lived at the edge. Without being politically pressured in any way, I happily identified myself with both SASO and NIC, although the latter was very much an ethno-specific organisation – for Indians only.

My fulltime work at Mondi was quite demanding but manageable. The company had moved to new modern and impressive factory premises. The training unit to which I belonged was allocated comfortable offices in a far corner of the vast factory floor. Two enormous paper-making machines took up most the floor space, each resembling a giant camel stretched out and resting on its haunches. These machines worked day and night converting pulp into gigantic rolls of newsprint. While the management was entirely English-speaking Whites, the operational and administration workforce was largely Indian. In my role as training assistant, I interacted closely with the Indians who were recruited and trained to operate the machines. They worked long hours in shifts. I soon sensed that they were becoming disgruntled about their pay and working conditions. Some confided in me as I appeared to be one of them, but in a very senior position in the company.

~

One morning, a year into my job at Mondi, I came to work as usual, parked my car outside the security fence and made my way to the gate to be let in. I sensed something untoward was afoot. The Personnel Manager was standing on the inner side of the gate. A clutch of additional security officers and two other important-looking white men stood by him. The gate remained shut. I stood on the outside perplexed and concerned.

'You're not to come in,' said the Personnel Manager in a troubled and awkward voice. 'I'm instructed to terminate your temporary employment immediately and pay you whatever is due to you.'

With that, he thrust an envelope at me through an opening in the security gate. Several of the Indian workers who had just completed their shift stood by silently witnessing my dismissal.

'But why?' I demanded recovering from my initial shock.

'Read what's in the envelope. It's all there.' With that,

he turned and walked off briskly flanked by his support. The security officers fixed me with unwavering looks which I read as: 'Scram. Get your ass out of here!'

I sat a while in my car recovering my composure, allowing the tightness in my chest to ease, and processing what had just hit me. I opened the envelope and found it contained a detailed final payment advice, a certificate of service and a short note on letterhead from the Personnel Manager indicating my temporary services were no longer needed – the word temporary highlighted. In a terse concluding paragraph, the manager expressed regret that I had involved myself in the issues of workers on the factory floor and had encouraged them to politicise their demands concerning their pay and working conditions. It required effort to suppress my anger. I had no grounds to appeal.

My father was bewildered when I returned home within two hours of leaving for work. 'What's wrong, son? Are you sick or something?' he said repeatedly until I assured him that all was well, except that there was no more work for me at Mondi since the factory was now fully staffed and operational. I would be called when I was needed again. But my explanation only served to prompt a new worry for him: what would I do now to bring home much-needed money. Just then a call on the home phone distracted him. It was for me.

'Mr Mudaly?'

'Yes.'

'Mr Bala Mudaly?' said a husky Indian sounding man.

'Yes, that's me. But who's this?'

'It's Lieutenant Nayagar. Special Branch. Man, I'm so sorry to hear you've lost your job. You weren't a troublemaker, were you? In any case, let me know if I can help in any way. I'll be in touch.'

I froze, the receiver in my hand. For a moment I was uncertain what to do. Questions whirled in my head. I had overheard the name Nayagar mentioned a few times by NIC activists. He was supposedly a high-ranking member of the dreaded security police. As mean as they come, they said. And apparently a vicious interrogator. How could he know of my job loss – and so soon? This was simply alarming. Clearly there was a veiled message in his call. But what? I felt intimidated.

~

The sudden traumatic events in my life unsettled me for days, and even disrupted my ability to sleep through the night. Concealing my troubled and anxious mood from my family was a challenge. I had to look cheerful and in control so as not to upset the tenuous atmosphere at home. My mother had been the one who held the family together, took important decisions, directed my father, and managed the household budget. With her death, my father had come to defer to my eldest sister. He was in retirement. So, my siblings and I had to meet the bills, the monthly mortgage instalment, and pay for food, clothing, transport, and other incidental expenses.

Each day I awoke with the unhappy thought that I was unemployed. I would be out and about early taking a walk or going into town on some purposeless mission. On occasion, I had run into someone who knew me. And the invariable question would follow: 'Not working again, eh? But why? Sick or something?' The questions would hang in the air expecting to be answered. I dreaded these encounters.

At the same time, I did not want to hang out at home only to be spotted by nosey neighbours. It was pointless getting the evening newspaper and scanning the *situations vacant* columns. There was nothing there for me. It was back to spreading the word around. Cold canvassing.

Yet again a helpful former university friend came to my rescue. She suggested I speak with a Mr BA Naidoo, an influential long-serving senior social worker at the Durban Indian Child Welfare Society (DICWS). BA, as he was known, received me with much interest. A short man in his late forties, formal in dress, brisk and courteous. Having heard me out, Mr Naidoo withdrew into thoughtful silence, then his eyes shone with excitement. 'Just a minute,' he said and darted out of the little office. Hope rose in me. 'Look Mr Mudaly,' he said as he opened a file when he returned, we were about to advertise a vacancy.' Would I be interested, he asked, in taking on the position of principal or superintendent at Lakehaven, a residential home for destitute children. Of course, I would, I blurted quite blindly. I was unemployed and desperate, wasn't I? I had nothing to lose.

I soon learnt this was a residential campus comprising a cluster of five orange-tiled cottages each housing about 10-15 orphaned and destitute Indian children. It provided out-of-home care, and the Principal was in loco parentis to these children – that is, legally responsible for them. Although I was both a trained and experienced teacher and psychologist, I had no experience or skills whatsoever in managing an institution for children deprived of nurturing family life and with related emotional needs. Then too I was single and hence with no parenting experience. What would

I be walking into? What would I be letting myself in for?

Despite hesitations or misgivings, I still felt persuaded to submit an expression of interest. In the meantime, I was advised to arrange a meeting with a senior cottage staff who would explain the daily functioning of the place and related challenges. I visited Lakehaven over the summer school holidays. The children, I learned, were away on holiday with host families. The place, although impressively located on a ridge, struck me as rather forlorn and windswept. Yes, my first impressions were off-putting. A senior housefather doubled-up as acting principal, met me. A middle-aged man with a sour disposition, critical of the higher authorities who managed the institution. His unsolicited blunt opinion was that a young bachelor like me would be most inappropriate and unsuited in the role of principal since the children in care included teenage girls. And housemothers were young women. Perhaps there was some merit in the man's caustic observations, I thought. This left me in a quandary. I needed a job badly but taking on a leadership role at Lakehaven seemed fraught with risks. So, what should I do – take the bull by the horns or not? I mulled over this dilemma for weeks while waiting to be formally interviewed for the job.

~

My involvement with SASO, DHAC and NIC filled my days, gave me purpose and, of course, kept me preoccupied and distracted from unemployment woes. My father, however, was constantly anxious about my safety in view of the daily newspaper coverage of police harassment, detentions, and stories of torture. Now retired, he remained interested in politics – especially in the activities and leadership of the renewed NIC. But his fervour for attending rousing political rallies was long past.

I continued to find living with family awkward and restricting. It became a little irksome explaining my movements to my father – to keep him from worrying. I was overly self-conscious and wary whenever I had friends and activists over or when using the home phone in the lounge. It seemed so public. My privacy was minimal. There was always the question from someone at home: 'Who was that?'

In the meantime, the atmosphere and political tension in the country had increased since my return from abroad. It was palpable. If anything, events, and crises followed one upon the other, the more oppressive the government, the more resistance from the community.

Reading the evening Daily News and weekend Sunday Times became a ritual for me, the key themes of the week became the fodder for fiery exchanges with my political buddies. Any potential setback for the government called for a minor celebration. We cheered silently when the economy nose-dived, and the price of gold plummeted on world markets. We were elated to learn that the freedom struggles in neighbouring Angola and Mozambique were gaining ground. On the other hand, we felt distressed and deflated on reading of activists being killed by a spate of parcel-bombs. The security police (SB), with augmented powers, had stepped up their harassment of political activists.

In the unearthly hours of 24 October 1971, all of us at home tumbled out of bed in alarm, woken by fearful banging on the front door. My father, only half-awake, was the first to respond. Holding up his loose pyjama pants at the crotch in one hand, he fumbled to unlock the door. Four of my siblings lived with my father, all younger than me. 'Who's that?' my brother called out. There was a harsh response in Afrikaans and yet more fierce thumping. Guessing it may be the police, my brother opened the door with my petrified sister and father at his side. I was a little behind, almost shielded by them. The bedrooms were to my left, down a passage. Even now it surprises me that I had the presence of mind to alert my teenage brother standing frozen at the far end of the passage – not visible to the intruders. 'Books, books,' I mouthed, gesturing frantically. It was critical that he understood my message.

A surly white man and two burly Indian men burst in, rough hands thrusting my father aside. Two black men in police uniform followed. It became immediately clear to me that this was a security police raid, now a regular occurrence across the country. But I least expected it to happen to me.

'Hey, you!' shouted the white officer in plain clothes catching sight of me gesturing. He pounced upon me like a ferocious dog. 'What you think you're doing?'

'Right, which one of you is Bala Mudaly,' said an Indian officer, reading my name off a sheet.

I cringed as I raised a hand.

'So, you the smart bugger, eh? The communist shit?'

'Old man, you and the others stand aside,' he instructed to my siblings. My teenage brother quietly entered from the kitchen and joined them. 'Don't move, you hear?'

'Kyk na hulle (watch them),' said the white officer to the black constables, 'terwyl ons die huis soek (while we search the house).'

I was forced to show them where I slept. This happened to be a make-shift study with a sleeper-couch. They searched this space like dogs after a hidden bone. Things were pulled open, turned inside out, stripped, and scattered. No corner was overlooked. They seemed to pay close attention to all publications found, at times taking photos of book titles. A folder of newspaper clippings got them particularly excited. So too, a tattered copy of *The Story of an African Farm*, with the photo of the author, Olive Schreiner, on the back cover. The rest of the house was also searched but in a cursory fashion. There were no mobile phones or computers in those days, or they would have been carted away.

I had to sign a sheet with the list of items they took with them. The contingent left as first light broke, seemingly satisfied. The sun was still a lurid smudge at the edge of the ocean far below Reservoir Hill where the Umgeni River entered the sea. The sounds of the first morning traffic could be heard. We were all too shaken to speak, instead we went about silently tidying the place. There was no question of returning to bed. My teenage brother, his face dark with distress, voiced what the rest of my family were thinking:

'I knew you'd get us all in big trouble one day.'

He had rushed back into his room immediately I gestured to him, removed two banned and incriminating books wrapped in newspaper I had concealed in his wardrobe earlier in the week, and flung them out the bedroom window. Their titles: *Autobiography of Malcom X*, and *Edward Roux's, Time Longer than Rope*.

A full frontpage headline in the *Natal Daily News* reported that scores of homes had been raided simultaneously across the country in search of politically incriminating material which threatened the security of the state and furthered the aims of communism. I was relieved that the names of activists raided were not published, since my name in the papers would have jeopardised the prospect of my being employed at Lakehaven.

I needn't have worried. In January 1972, following a rigorous interview, I was appointed Principal of Lakehaven. It was such a relief to have a job again. As far as I was aware, there were no other applicants. My father was beside himself, especially when two local Indian weeklies had front page reports of my appointment.

~

It was a full-time residential position. From all accounts, I faced a daunting task. Yet, remarkably, I lasted fifteen years, experiencing notable successes and setbacks. For all this time, I had to contend with the opposition and resentment of the senior housefather who I had met on my very first visit to Lakehaven. He never ceased to conspire to subvert my authority, to co-opt other housefathers, and snitch on me to a few members of the Board who had agendas of their own.

Although this institution, funded by the Department of Indian Affairs, was restricted under Apartheid to admit only Indian children, the fact was some children coming into care were clearly of racially mixed parentage, and a few were decidedly Black. They had characteristic peppercorn hair, although designated Indian on their birth documents. These children were embraced and cared for without prejudice or discrimination. They integrated into the life of the Institution with ease. It was a revelation that relatively few of the children were orphans in the legal sense. Most came into residential care from fractured families and impoverished circumstances. What profound learning for me!

In hindsight, it strikes me that the Lakehaven children, while deprived of wholesome family-life, had the rare opportunity, even under the constraints of Apartheid, to be nurtured by a truly non-racial team of staff and volunteers – Indians, Coloured, Blacks, and Whites. Many of the cottage assistants were black women. The ground staff were men, both Black and Indian. The cottage parents and most of the professional and office staff were Indian. They were almost all cheerful, mature, and caring, and knew the children by name.

The Whites associated with Lakehaven were a memorable few, mostly arts and craft volunteers who provided much needed continuity, and who enriched the lives of the children beyond expectation. There was a German woman, known to countless children simply as Mother Goltz, and her frail husband who, if I remember correctly, fled from their German motherland a little before Hitler's worst excesses. Mrs Goltz was an intense and troubled woman of about seventy, tall, gaunt, and distinguished, her puff of white hair always in disarray like that of Einstein. And then there was a Mrs Maingardt, an urbane elegant woman of forty with a wealthy background who seemed untainted by racism, and certainly not the liberal do-gooder kind come to patronise so-called poor unfortunate non-white kids. We employed a white social worker, Heidi Vosey-Loening, but only after receiving government approval. We had made the case that no suitable Indian person was available to fill this vacancy. Remarkably, the sky did not fall upon us with this appointment. The incumbent melded smoothly into the life of the institution.

Lakehaven staff (Author backrow far right)

Lakehaven Children's Home Durban

~

Lakehaven was built on a vast acreage, far removed from

the hassles of city life. In other words, I had the relative freedom of open spaces – a campus sitting on a ridge with hill slopes and valleys, some ten acres of sprawling bush, grassland, and giant gums. Baxter, my black spaniel, roamed the grounds with no rivals, and brought fun and joy to the kids. They called him Blackster.

My fifteen years at Lakehaven was formative. It afforded me the opportunity to grow and mature, to become increasingly certain of myself as a broad-minded, non-racial person actively engaged in the community - politically, socially, and professionally. I became steeped in the literature and enlightened philosophy of residential childcare which had emerged from Victorian-style orphanages - grim, puritanical institutions. So much so, that I enrolled with the University of Natal for a Ph.D. I would research the adverse effects on children who had languished in long-term residential care, with little or no experience of nurturing family life. The question I posed was: *will the outlook on life and sense of wellbeing of institutionalised children be significantly different to that of children who had enjoyed wholesome and undisrupted family life?*

The project took five years to complete, in which time not only had I transferred to the University of Rhodes for more appropriate supervision but was no longer working at Lakehaven. The PhD degree was awarded to me in 1985. My study largely confirmed that children subjected to prolonged institutional-style care, were less certain, less optimistic, and less realistic about their future as adults.

~

I certainly owe it to Lakehaven that I became quite well known in my immediate community. And this would largely be the reason that I was selected for the 1979 Operations Crossroad Africa Leadership program. A U.S.-based, non-profit, non-governmental organisation annually sponsored a cluster of potential leaders from African countries to travel to the USA to learn more about their special area of professional expertise. But more importantly, the program's aim was to encourage networking among the participants from the disparate countries of Africa, which may have been quite rare at the time. I felt greatly privileged. My family, friends, and the staff of Lakehaven cheered and celebrated. The contingent of over thirty Blacks I met were from several countries on the African continent. Those that I readily bonded with were, without exception, talented, personable, and seemed to know more about South Africa than I knew about their countries. While a few paraded in African kaftans, most of the men dressed in western suit and tie, while the women were radiant in their coloured African headscarves and patterned dresses. They spoke English with many varied accents. I found the English spoken by participants from Nigeria and the Francophone countries particularly beguiling. One of our hosts in America was Malcolm Boatwright, a young entertaining African American with style - the very first black American I had met. Malcolm was outraged once in our presence when he was served eggs at breakfast in a New York restaurant. He thumped the table and called out: 'I said sunny side up, didn't I? Didn't I?' The mortified waitress disappeared with his plate. A fresh serve of eggs precisely as ordered was placed before Malcolm by an apologetic manager. This was when I first learnt that an egg fried but not flipped over was referred to as *sunny side up*.

Operation Crossroads Participants (Author on the left)

My participation in Operations Crossroad Africa enhanced my awareness of the rest of Africa, its peoples, issues, and challenges. My consciousness of being more of an African than Indian was reinforced many times over. On my return to Lakehaven, I shared my experiences, especially of my visit to two residential homes for children in Pittsburgh, Pennsylvania. Several members of the Lakehaven Board seemed, however, somewhat lukewarm about my trip and its benefits. They felt my unscheduled absence from duty was unwarranted.

~

Members of the Board served in a voluntary capacity. Several of them were prominent businessmen or professionals in the Indian community, and a few were also active in cultural, religious, sporting or welfare organisations. Some became Board members to raise their profile in the community and promote their businesses. It did not surprise me that there were tensions and splits within the Board that related to differing political affiliations and agendas. I recall that the chairman of the Board at the time I commenced employment was also a senior member in the Government appointed South African Indian Council, which many considered to be a puppet body and its members no more than stooges. Others were aligned to the NIC.

Even staff seemed divided, some sympathetic to the liberation struggle against the white government, others not. Once I was accused of 'bringing politics into Lakehaven.' One housefather, in fact, waved a finger at me in a heated staff meeting. 'You're drawing the attention of the security police to Lakehaven, you know. I'm warning you. I'll report you to the Board.' It was true that on at least one occasion I had entertained a few of my SASO friends, including Steve Biko. This incident made me realise how restricted my life was living on the premises. I had to do something about it.

The opportunity, however, only presented a few years

later when I married. It happened that I grew attracted to a social work student from the University of Durban-Westerville. In her third year of study, she came to Lakehaven on an extended practical placement. We courted for a while and then married in 1978. Her large family adopted me enthusiastically. They also fully embraced Lakehaven and promoted it wherever and whenever there was opportunity.

Once married, I persuaded the Board to permit me to live in the community. We bought a modest flat in the new township of Briardale, about fifteen minutes away by car. This unit built of grey cement blocks and asbestos roof and guttering was the first and only house we owned in South Africa.

~

Over the years, I have retained fond memories of when I served as principal. This may explain why I felt so heartsore and troubled on my last visit to Lakehaven in August 2019. It was no longer the place I had known. The grounds and buildings had a tired and careworn look suggesting poor maintenance or depleted resources. The campus was now virtually sealed off by unsightly security fencing, yet another reminder of the widespread fear of crime. Lakehaven had effectively become a gated institution. Much of the land had been sold off for revenue. One cottage had burnt down a year earlier in a harrowing fire in which several children perished. I walked up to a memorial installed near the tragic site and quietly read the names of the dead. A wealthy Indian man had since sponsored a replacement cottage.

Children from the black community made up the full

complement of admissions. What did this mean? I wondered. Had child neglect in the Indian community largely disappeared as an issue in post-Apartheid South Africa, or had this simply become a larger problem in the black population? I never found a satisfactory explanation. But I was pleasantly surprised that several Indians continued to serve on the Board of Management in a volunteer capacity. Community service was still held in high esteem by Indian South Africans.

Memorial Plaque at Lakehaven

~

In 1984, the first director of DICWS and the person I had reported to as Principal, died unexpectedly. Many believed that the job had killed him, that he had become a casualty of a bitter conflict between two rival factions in Management. The Director had found himself harassed almost daily, belittled, and openly accused of incompetence by those in Management who denied they were ever party to his appointment.

Not too long after, I learned that DICWS was in severe financial crisis and drastic measures had to be taken to address it. I was, therefore, coerced to double-up as both Director and Principal. The Management believed that since Lakehaven had functioned reasonably well with me living away, it would now survive without a dedicated person in that role.

I was certainly not enraptured about taking on the Director's role. I feared it was a veritable hornets' nest. After all, my life at Lakehaven had been relatively blissful and stimulating, one that offered varied challenges as well as interactions with staff, volunteers, children, and service agencies. I would say, in effect, I'd functioned much like the Lord of a Manor.

In my new job as Director, I had to drive into the city where the Head Office was located and return in peak hour traffic. And I was confined to a four-walled office on a floor with thirty or more staff, accommodated cheek-by-jowl in poorly sound-proofed rooms. I recall having to contend with the earnest (at times distressed or agitated) voices of social workers and clients competing with the incessant ringing of countless desk-top phones.

I sat at a desk for much of the day, taking calls, shuffling paper and fielding both petty and intractable issues off-loaded onto me by a steady stream of staff and management

TAKING A NEW DIRECTION

At last, Durban Indian Child Welfare Society has a top man who is articulate and hard-working

By LEELA NAIDOO

THE hot seat of director of the Durban Indian Child Welfare Society, which has been vacant since 1976, has been filled by Bala Mudaly, the former principal of the Lakehaven Children's Home.

Mr Mudaly, a clinical psychologist, is astute, perceptive, serious, diplomatic, hardworking and, above all, has the ability to emerge unruffled from any crisis.

He readily admits that his new position is extremely demanding. He has taken over the post at a difficult time — the society has financial problems.

"But," says Mr Mudaly with one of his rare smiles, "within the three months that I have been with the society, things have eased considerably, although we still have large debts.

"We have held several meetings with our creditors and, as a result, the situation at the society seems more settled. Management does not feel hemmed in and constrained by financial hassles and planning has become more progressive.

"If things carry on moving in this direction, we will be well out of the rut and planning very creatively and constructively by the New Year."

Mr Mudaly says financial problems have always been associated with welfare and a number of factors led to the society's predicament.

A solution will be for the society to raise its own funds.

"To do this," says Mr Mudaly, "we have to create an awareness in the community that we are a community-based organisation.

"People seem to have lost sight of this over the years.

"Maybe we are at fault because we have been getting money from other sources and people have not been kept informed.

"Our image has not been good with the community as it believes we are 100 percent Government-subsidised.

"We are now letting the people know we are a community-based organisation and if the community does not help us to help them, then they are going to be the poorer for it.

Bala Mudaly — new head of the Durban Indian Child Welfare Society

"This is the message we are trying to put across at all levels."

The society is gradually to change the nature of its services, he says. It will become less concerned with individual, clinical cases and more involved in promotive and preventive work in the community.

Mr Mudaly hopes that by this means, the society's role will become clearer to the community.

Role

"Through this awareness, we are hoping to get the community's financial support and to let them know that we are not fund-raising from a highly professional and detached way, but that we belong to them and want to be involved with them."

Asked about his functions as director, Mr Mudaly replies that he has yet to define his role.

He feels he would rather sit in on discussions — especially those that involve the professional staff — so he can help the staff to define their goals more clearly.

He is also to examine the functions of the local committees. These played a very important and dynamic role in the community but have now lost impetus.

Discussions have been held to find ways of injecting new life into the committees and to identify the kind of support they need so they can resume a meaningful role.

How will the political dispensation affect welfare?

Mr Mudaly says there is much uncertainty.

The society has become increasingly dependent on the State for financial support, which is given with certain conditions, he says.

If the society were to become fully dependent on the State, it would lose its character and initiative.

"Our vision has always been that the welfare movement be one movement across racial and political barriers, but the present political dispensation counters this," Mr Mudaly says.

"At the moment we don't know the Government's plans or the blueprints for the concept of 'Own Affairs'."

The society is not party to any particular political view, he says.

Need

However, the society's staff and management members are from all walks of life and hold different political views. When they get the opportunity, they express their views and identify themselves with certain events or movements, he says.

Is there a need for the Child Welfare Society?

Mr Mudaly says many people feel there shouldn't be such a service.

He believes: "As long as the present political, economical and social conditions prevail, the need for child welfare will always be there."

members. The latter would often insist on 'having a word' with me even when told I was engaged on other pressing matters. My new role wore me down.

The ghost of the previous Director sat by me. He was the one I had reported to weekly on Lakehaven matters. I remembered him as lanky and dark-complexioned, always in suit and tie, with neatly set wavy hair parted at the centre. An urbane man. He was often wistful, yet only too eager to entertain a social phone call from family or friends – even if this interrupted a serious discussion with a Board Member. On occasions, it would be the President of the organisation, a large puffed-looking man. The President would be scowling while the Director continued jovial, and light-hearted, seemingly oblivious of the fuming President right there in front of him. I was aware that each had a dim view of the other.

He would often confide in me about being abused and harassed by some Board members. He would slap his forehead. 'See what I've done to myself, Bala! Why did I ever leave my solid lecturing position at Springfield (a teacher training college)? Why? You tell me. There I was respected and liked. Gave it all up in a moment of madness - just to be called Dee-rector, eh? He would pronounce the title with much affectation. 'Now, I'm in deep shit and see no way out.' His pain was palpable. But I could not provide comfort. How ironical then that my brief stint as Director also ended abruptly and in disconcerting circumstances.

In April 1986, less than two years into the role of Director, I was given my marching orders. It was alleged that I had contributed to acrimony and discord in Management by playing one faction against the other. At the very same time, it was rumoured in the community that, on my watch, a vast sum of money had gone unaccounted for at Lakehaven, which created the impression in the community that I had something to do with it. This story almost killed my father. My reputation was being well and truly sullied. Fortunately, the Management promptly inserted a public notice in the local papers refuting this as unfounded rumour. It explained that my departure had nothing to do with financial mismanagement.

Even so, this episode unsettled me, and was very distressing for my family and friends. After all, I had occupied a high-profile public office in an esteemed community organisation.

Friends, relatives, and a few officials of the NIC and others active in the Indian community called on me at home to express their support and commiserate with me. But my feeling of pain and humiliation persisted. I felt diminished and vulnerable, and wanted to disappear from public gaze. Some of these activists and well-wishers also took it upon themselves to meet with officials of the welfare agency in the hope of having me reinstated as Director, but they were unsuccessful. The issue caused disagreements and tensions within the NIC itself, simply because Board members who had axed me were also NIC members.

~

I remained politically active over the years that I was employed at Mondi, Lakehaven and DICWS. In some ways, this involvement provided welcome relief to the pressures and tensions at work. Being an activist also helped me maintain social connections so vital to my wellbeing. More importantly, it infused purpose and meaning into my life.

Welfare group urged to reinstate director

By Yogin Devan

THE Durban Indian Child and Family Welfare Society has been urged to reinstate former director, Dr Bala Mudaly.

The call came from the Concerned Community Persons' Group (CCPG), which was formed to look into the matter of his resignation.

After meetings with the president of the society, Dr Khorshed Ginwala; Vassie Nair, chairman of the society's staffing committee; members of the executive of the society; Dr Mudaly and other concerned persons, the CCPG found there were differences of opinion about why he had left the society. Although the executive committee said it had intended to dismiss Dr Mudaly when it planned to restructure the society. Mr Nair was of the view that Dr Mudaly's response to the Lakehaven Inquiry and his abrasive attitude to some management committee members were among the main reasons for the executive committee's unhappiness with him.

Mr Nair believed the decision to dismiss Dr Mudaly was "morally indefensible" and he had resigned from all standing committees in protest.

The CCPG found there was conflict between Dr Mudaly and some management committee members but he had not mishandled funds at the Lakehaven Home. It had asked the society's board of management to clear Dr Mudaly's name and to look into the relationship between the society's professionals and volunteers.

I recall participating in two momentous political events which further energised and politicised me. These events still resonate in my memory.

Early in 1983, my wife and I joined a contingent of mostly NIC members, to demonstrate in front of the Durban City Hall where the State President, Hon P.W.Botha, was to speak on further apartheid policies. Our placards demanded an end to Apartheid and for the release of political prisoners. It was late afternoon. Workers were streaming out from the high-rise office buildings heading home. A large supportive crowd of onlookers gathered around us shouting encouragement and raising clenched fists. The peak-hour traffic came to a standstill. Drivers hooted to indicate support or abuse. We became the focus of frenzied media keen to get a scoop for the late evening news. I felt elated by my bravado, yet very anxious of potential consequences. I stuck close to my wife.

NIC demonstration at Durban City Hall

Suddenly, as anticipated, police sirens came blasting from all sides. Police vans and Saracen Tanks surrounded the area. Onlookers scattered. A squad of rough and determined police officers descended upon us with guns and truncheons drawn. Our carefully crafted placards were ripped off our hands and we were bundled unceremoniously into the backs of police vans, where we held on for dear life as the vans sped through the busy afternoon traffic. As there were no seats or handrails in these fully enclosed police vans, we found ourselves being tossed about like unsecured trash. I was shit scared, and so were the others. This was altogether a totally new experience.

In about twenty minutes, we were deposited at the central police station and herded into a large room, some thirty of us. We were shouted at and coerced into queues. Fingerprints and mug shots were taken, and various documents completed.

We milled about in the room or stood in groups uncertainty written all over our tense faces. We were each permitted, as detainees, to phone our next of kin and to contact a lawyer. However, to our relief, lawyers were already at hand, senior stalwarts of the NIC such as Thumba Pillay, George Sewpersad and Rabbi Bhagwan. They seemed to know the senior officers of the Special Branch and did not letup haggling over the charges, negotiating a way out for us. After what seemed like hours of anxious waiting and hunger pangs, we were all abruptly released on bail. Nevertheless, this event made international news. We were lauded and feted for our bold but very risky stance at a time when the security police were on edge and on high alert on account of a spate of bombing of public buildings. It was rumoured that the African National Congress in exile was pursuing a new initiative to make the country ungovernable.

All oppressed people and opposition forces were urged to rally together, to form a common front.

I was most amazed when a little-known churchman answered the rallying call. Allan Boesak, a Cape Coloured and a cleric from the Dutch Reformed Church struck me as a bold and charismatic leader. He articulated a need for a united front of churches and other organisations to confront Apartheid. Once the notion of a united front took hold, it fired the imagination of activists across the country. I too was carried away by the national fervour. How could I not participate?

On 22 August 1983, about a thousand delegates representing over five hundred organisations including churches, trade unions, community, youth, women, and political groupings met at the Rocklands Stadium in Mitchells Plain, Cape Town to launch the United Democratic Front (UDF), a broad-based non-racial resistance movement - and I was there in the thick of it!

Formation of the UDF

The details of my participation escape me now: How was

my trip to Cape Town paid for? Where and with whom did I stay? Was I a mere spectator at the event or had I an active role? Whatever the circumstances, it was my great good fortune to attend and be inspired by this my very first full-on non-racial political event against the juggernaut of Apartheid.

I still feel a lift in my gut when I recall that experience. The auditorium, draped in colourful banners and slogans, reverberated with the excitement and expectation of a thousand delegates. The rousing applause. The camaraderie. The earnest and animated debates late into the night. I can still hear the silver-tongued Allan Boesak moving the crowd to new heights of passion. A fresh surge of political energy and hope was infused by the formation of the UDF which propelled the political struggle forward.

It amazes me, even now, that the government and the security police allowed the UDF to be born at all. Of course, it was only given a short leash. In 1986 it was banned from receiving foreign funds, and soon thereafter its activities severely curtailed. The government accused the UDF of being a front organisation of the ANC. Its leaders found themselves at the mercy of the country's harsh security legislation. Some were banned and others sent to prison.

Across the nation, it was a time of heightened political strife, with crisis after crisis. I recall that the country was under a State of Emergency with the security forces hyper-vigilant and trigger happy. Activists, including myself, were deeply engaged at the time in clandestine activities and under-the-radar campaigning. ANC cadres were being systematically and repeatedly attacked in neighbouring countries like Botswana. We all had to be scrupulous and conduct ourselves with utmost care so as not to put ourselves at needless risk or expose other activists through some careless talk or act. Once, our flat in Briardale was used as a 'safe house' from where to monitor the progress of a secret mission – so secret that even I did not know its substance and goal. A closely-knit group of activists turned up, all Indians, to take regular calls on our home phone from points on the route from Durban to the ultimate destination of the mission. Mobile phones were unheard of. Neither did we know if there existed such a thing as phone-tapping.

~

All this heightened political drama was certainly a distraction for me from the nagging reality that yet again I was unemployed. No amount of political activism would buy me bread and milk or pay my water bill.

It was door-knocking time again. After weeks of trying, I had to accept that it was unlikely another suitable job would turn up. My employment history was no longer marketable nor was my age – I was now nearing fifty. I checked my bank balance repeatedly. It dipped and dipped like the level in a major dam during protracted drought. In desperation, I thought I should at least try to see if a private psychology practice was now viable. I rented a small office in a building on Grey Street near the Greyville Racecourse (opposite Shan Jehan Cinema) and furnished it with what I could afford. I worried over how very sparse it looked with only a student desk, two chairs and a two-shelf bookcase, almost bare. My business card and flyers indicated that I would be offering psychological services to children and consultancy to parents and teachers. Indians, of course. I did my rounds of GPs and schools. Then I sat and waited and waited. For a while, not even a curious fly chose to enter.

Despite my hard stint in promoting the service, I did not receive enough referrals to make the business pay for itself. Only a few parents turned up with their anxious-faced fidgety children. But then they pleaded financial hardship and requested a discounted fee. My limited savings became dangerously depleted.

Strangely though, some people assumed I had struck gold. Pravin, whom I had known at university, was one of them. He breezed in one day, unannounced, looking flashy in a pin-striped suit and tie, cufflinks, a gold slit and an enormous ring. He lugged a bloated satchel, unzipped like the pants of an obese man. 'You're doing well for yourself, Bala. First Indian psychologist in business and all that.' He was certain, he added, that I could afford (and needed) a good insurance policy to cover my life and my practice, and he had the right products for me. His face, however, fell after I explained my dire situation. 'Unbelievable,' he said fiddling with his cufflinks. 'That's tough.' With that he took off saying he was running late for his next call. His conspicuous material success ruffled me. I wished he had not visited. But later that day I received an unexpected call from him and an offer that virtually floored me. 'Come, join my brokerage. A smart guy like you would make pots of money. Psychology should help you learn the tricks of the insurance trade in next to no time.' I was not amused. But Pravin wearing a mask of concern (more suited to undertakers) turned up a few more times pestering me with his smooth talk.

When I fell into arrears with my office rent, I gave in. I quit my failed private practice venture and soon started peddling life and funeral policies. But I was a lousy salesman! I had psychology but not the heart. At the weekly Monday morning meetings, each agent stood up and spoke of his activities and success. Pravin oozed with compliments. One agent claimed he had sold five policies in a day to black teachers who he swayed easily by his insurance talk. He was pleased to add that he managed to wangle himself into a school in the black township of Lamontville, with the help of an office worker who he had induced with a generous incentive. His colleagues applauded him with enthusiasm. When it came to my turn to give account, all I had to share was: 'Oh, I got my widow sister interested in a funeral policy. She's seriously considering it.' As I sat down, a flush of humiliation washed over me. Pravin tut-tutted. 'I suggest you ask one of the others here if you could go with them to pick up their skills. I see you need to try a little harder.'

I said nothing. Hell, what I needed was a complete makeover, a new beginning. I got home hoping to unburden my woes but found my wife on the phone. She merely raised her eyebrows and continued chatting. Baxter, spread-eagled on the couch and out for the count, jumped up and bolted upstairs. I withdrew to the kitchen, sat sipping gin and tonic, and stewed in my misery.

'What was that all about?' I asked when she drifted into the kitchen wearing a preoccupied look. No response. She set the kitchen table for dinner. 'Sounded like you were unburdening yourself to your sisters in Australia.' After more silence, my wife said: 'I told them about your situation. Feeling stuck and frustrated without a decent job and all that.'

'You shouldn't have,' I said petulantly.

'See, I was right. I told them that you'd not be even remotely interested in their suggestion.'

Although curious, I did not feel like jumping up all excited to know.

But my wife could not hold it in for too long. Just as we got into bed, she divulged that her two sisters, who had settled in Australia years earlier with their husbands, had urged that we too consider joining them. Migrate. The emotional leverage they used with effect was that their elderly parents would receive excellent medical care in Australia. They would love it there. But they would not be granted resident visas as long as they could be adequately cared for in South Africa by remaining adult children. Meaning my wife and her brother Jason.

'We're already working on sponsoring Jason and his family. So, you'd be the remaining hurdle. We could easily sponsor you and Bala. No problems. And with Bala's qualifications and yours, it would be plain sailing. Think about it. Okay? Pleesee!'

We agonised over the problem. Should we stay, or should we go. It was fraught with consequences. We consulted my family and our close friends. It was certainly, an attractive option, I thought, given my wasted life. Yet painful misgivings plagued me. I would be leaving my family in the lurch once again. They would not take it well, especially my father. And what about that letter I had written to Lionel, many years ago? All that fretting and wringing of hands, anguished soul-searching and trying to persuade myself that South Africa needed me as much as I needed to be back home – for good.

Standing up to Apartheid. Joining others on the ramparts. Was it all so much fairy floss? Do I simply abandon my involvement altogether? Dump my comrades? Quit my role? Activists who escaped on a one-way ticket to greener pastures were considered to have chickened out. He's joined the *chicken run* they'd probably say behind my back. But still....

Our predicament was, however, appreciated with great magnanimity by family, friends, and our activist comrades alike.

'We know, Bala, you're hurting,' they said. 'Going exactly nowhere in your career. I guess, you must wake up each morning fearing a bleak future. That's simply awful.'

~

As an act of supreme generosity, people from our various networks pooled together and organised a surprise farewell party for us - a magnificent function. A couple of bosom pals spun a clever ruse about taking us out for dinner. Why are we pulling up here? I wondered. I see no restaurants. My wife gave me a puzzled what's up look. Intrigued, we played along. We followed our friends up a flight of stairs and down a hallway, arriving at a closed double-door. A gentle knock and it was flung open revealing an expansive hall dimly lit. Loud cheering, a standing ovation, and bright lights! I caught my breath as my eyes scanned the faces of clusters of people at tables smiling our way. 'Oh my God, oh my God,' uttered my wife as she rushed from table-to-table hugging neighbours, family, work mates, friends and activists. Over a hundred and fifty guests were present. We were overwhelmed. I apologised and became teary as we were feted and farewelled.

Farewell Party – Author explaining reasons for leaving.

Thirty years on, I occasionally pour over the bumper-sized *bon voyage* card presented to us on that memorable evening with messages from each and everyone. I count the names of the many who have since died.

We felt the pain of finality in turning away from a richly cherished and meaningful life in Durban. Baxter, our first and only pet dog, was too old to accompany us to Australia. Euthanizing him was most traumatic. I held him down with a gentle hand while the vet injected him. He had resisted when I had dragged him from the back seat of my car. He probably knew instinctively that this was it. As the sedative took effect, Baxter went limp. I felt the throbbing warmth of life drain away.

Separating from my father was equally distressing. Since he had quit living at the family home in Reservoir Hills, following an acrimonious falling-out with the wife of his youngest son, my father had drifted. Much like a homeless person, he had moved from one daughter's house to another, and in turn to our place – always with a little soft duffel bag in hand. At some point, he had adopted us and our home in Briardale as his emotional base. But we packed up, locked the doors, and left for good. In effect, this move had made my father homeless for a second time. He had no choice in the matter but to accept the traumatic loss with a brave face, but he never quite recovered from his sense of profound loss and abandonment.

Author on left with his father and wife / Author feeding Baxter

No doubt those close to us would certainly have suffered the finality of our departure, turning away in sorrow as our plane taxied and took to the sky, soon no more than a vanishing speck in a vast emptiness.

Part 4
Becoming Australian

First Hurdles

We arrived in Melbourne in June 1988. It was mid-winter. The clothes put out to dry turned into sheets of ice. The seeping cold was a shock to my system. My wife's family took us under their wing and showed us the way things were done here, especially how to job hunt and how to buy a house. In fact, we lived with my sister-in-law for just on three months.

My wife had little difficulty getting her professional training and experience in social work vetted and approved by a Commonwealth Government accreditation agency. Soon thereafter, she was employed at the prestigious Royal Children's Hospital in the city in the Child Abuse Unit.

I did not fare that well. In the first instance, I thought I would try high school teaching, having done so years earlier in Zambia. However, while my certificates were approved, I was told that I would have to start at a junior grade level with a lowly salary. This I felt was an affront to my age, so I asked around and hunted for positions where psychology training was an essential requirement. I learnt that most vacancies in this profession only considered members of the

Australian Psychological Society. I promptly became a member. The Society advised me that I could be employed in a government funded institution like a hospital as an entry level psychologist under supervision. However, to be a clinical psychologist I would need to undertake a period of study and sit an exam.

Three months went by and I was still not employed. Firstly, there were not too many vacancies I could apply for. Secondly, none of my applications were successful. Sitting and waiting was getting to me. In this situation, I began having doubts about having migrated. My moodiness was becoming noticeable. People expressed concern. 'Do something, anything,' they urged. 'Just sitting at home, is no good.' My wife thrust a copy of the weekly Leader Newspaper on the table where I sat. 'Here, read the job vacancy page.' 'Why? What's there?' I said not feeling up to it. 'Just look at the ads, will you,' she said, and walked away.

All I saw was advert after advert calling for cleaners. House cleaners, office cleaners, hospital cleaners and so on. What do I know about cleaning? I thought. The following day, rather reluctantly, I phoned a few places. Sorry but you have no experience, was the refrain. However, a lady at Como House suggested I come for an interview. My sister-in-law was delighted. 'Oh my god, that's wonderful. You know, Como House is a heritage listed Victorian manor. Stunning gardens. You'll feel distinguished cleaning a place like that.' 'You must be joking,' I said hoping my annoyance would not show.

'You'll probably have to put on a tuxedo,' added her husband. 'Bala, the Como Cleaner.'

Como Heritage House Melbourne

First and Only Employment

Fortunately, it did not come to that. I was rescued by a job offer from Springvale Community Health Service (SCHS), only twenty minutes by train from where we lived. The Health Centre was relatively new and had no more than five staff. I was to complete the multi-skilled team of health workers as the psychologist. It was the only job offer I received and the only job I have held in Australia for thirty years until I retired in December 2018 at the age of 80.

My first task at SCHS was to establish a dedicated service for disaffected young people, which included a drop-in centre. The community in Springvale at the time comprised a substantial population of recent refugees from countries of conflict such as Vietnam, Cambodia, Bosnia, Chile, and Argentina. The Enterprise Hostel in Springvale was a government processing and settlement centre for new refugee arrivals. (In later years there were also refugees from Iran, Afghanistan, Iraq, Sri Lanka, Burma, and Syria).

It was such a thrill to head a group of young, vibrant youth workers. I learnt much from them and felt young myself. Who would tell from the photo that at fifty, I was at least twenty years older than others in the team?

The first youth services team at SCHS (Author on the left at the back)

I did not, however, retire from SCHS in 2018 but rather from Monash Health, a mammoth health network of hospitals and community-based clinics, with a staff of over seven thousand. The government called its policy of integrating relatively small health facilities like SCHS into a mega health service, *economies of scale*. So, in the years before retirement, I worked at Monash Health Community in Dandenong, a twin city of Melbourne. My last manager was an ex-South African white woman of Jewish background. We had a good working relationship and sometimes shared safe (not politically sensitive) stories about holidays in South Africa. However, I was always conscious of the irony of our shared racial history. She would have belonged to a white privileged world where I was a Non-White. Wherever I go, it seems I'm pursued by my colour-conscious history.

~

For months after our arrival in Australia, my wife and I were acutely aware of being surrounded by Whites all the time. It was a little unnerving. There were white faces in the streets near home, at the shopping mall we frequented, and on trains and buses. I suspect I may have broken into a broad smile whenever a rare dark face was spotted. But once I began work, I met people of many cultural backgrounds in all shades of colour. People who had suffered horrendous political persecution, refugees from war-ravaged countries like Cambodia, Vietnam, Zimbabwe, Congo, Iraq and Lebanon, and from Latin American countries like Chile. I felt humbled listening to their stories and their struggle in adjusting to Australia, a very alien world.

We often read or heard about so-called *Australian values*. Was this a newer version of the outmoded White Australia policy I wondered, with concern and discomfort. But it was countered by the realisation that we lived and moved daily among Australians experiencing mostly genuine warmth and goodwill.

Our First and only Home

We still marvel at how we came to buy a house in an all-white street in Oakleigh in 1988. The house was owned by an Australian couple with British ancestry.

While house hunting one Sunday, we drove into Ford Street hoping to look over a house advertised for sale in the Sunday Age newspaper. We parked on the street and stood scanning the noticeboard, then took in the property. The house was a 1950s weatherboard, in a reasonable condition – at least on the outside. Nothing fancy. A jacaranda tree with an expansive canopy graced the front garden. Sitting underneath it on a well-tendered lawn was a wheelbarrow converted to a flowerbox, now overflowing with pink and purple petunias in full bloom. A single white butterfly flitted about. Along the perimeters of the garden were upright wooden trellises which supported sweet peas, in a riot of colours. What an impressive show on a bright summer's day!

'You interested in our house?' It was an elderly woman who appeared from the side of the building, with a green watering can. She was a small energetic woman with an apron over a loose floral dress, floppy hat, runners, and garden gloves. She smiled and the creases of her aged face reflected her delight.

'Sorry,' I said, feeling a little flustered.' No, no, just looking. Hope it's okay?'

'Will be in the papers next Saturday.'

'Oh, thanks,' added my wife. 'That explains it.'
The lady put down her can and removed her hat revealing a dishevelled white fluff.

She wiped her brow on the sleeve of her overalls. 'Predict a scorcher today,' she said taking a step towards us, a knee-height picket fence separating us.

'Where you from – India? All us folk in this street were born Aussies. Mostly built our own houses.'

A warm breeze stirred in the jacaranda.

'When'll your house be open for inspection?' I queried.

'Oh, you could come in now if you wish. Meet Mal my husband. He'll be keen to show you the place.'

I glanced at my wife to see if she was as taken aback as I was with the spontaneous invitation.

'Thanks, but we don't wish to intrude on your privacy. Especially on a Sunday,' said my wife.

'No, No, No worries. Give me a sec while I open the gate. Come in and I'll get something to cool you down. Mind the sun. Simply bad, you know.'

The house felt much cooler than outside. With windows shuttered and curtains drawn, the dim lighting seemed to add to the cooling effect.

An elderly man with a smooth cheerful face and a comfortable paunch waddled into the living room, bare feet, singlet and black track pants. His thinning hair was plastered back, adding to his broad forehead.

'Hello, hello and who have we here, Marge?'

'Folks looking for a house. Show them around, dear.'

Marge apologised for not introducing herself earlier. We told them our names and a little of who we were. While Marge got us drinks, Mal painted us a picture of his life story which it appeared was tied up intimately with this house and his long marriage to Marge. He pointed to photos on the shelf above the fireplace saying his two daughters were born here and had grown into adults and had since set themselves up in life. No grandchildren yet. 'One can't have everything in life,' he said with a wistful gaze.

In half an hour, we felt strangely at home, as if we belonged to this house. Marge and Mal had so warmed to us, that they seemed quite in earnest to entrust their house to us, the place in which they had invested almost their entire adult lives.

They pointed out things they would leave behind for the

new owners, items they would not need or accommodate in their one-room unit at Happy Valley Retirement Village. The items included a wall unit with a selection of drink glasses, a kitchen table and chairs, garden furniture, and two well-used cane chairs installed side-by-side in the fernery, with a panoramic view of a thriving back garden. Marge explained they would especially miss the chairs because this was where they'd sat with their breakfast, lunch and dinners all through many, many summers. 'But not to worry', she said with a laugh. They would not be leaving behind their memories for the next occupants. That would be giving away far too much.

~

So it was that we came to live in Ford Street, Oakleigh, thirty years ago. The house was withdrawn from auction and sold to us at a bargain basement price. When told of our lucky purchase, my wife's sister gasped in disbelief.

'Your colour didn't matter to them? Really? That's simply amazing.'

'And, you know what,' said my wife 'we are invited to a farewell party arranged by their close neighbours.'

'How good is that?' I added. 'We'll get to know our neighbours even before moving in.'

We kept in touch with Mal and Marge until they died. In the words of Bruce Chatwin: *They knew where they were going, smiling at death in the shade of a ghost-gum (*Songlines*).*

Orientation to Indigenous Peoples

In our first few years in Melbourne, we rarely ever saw or interacted with Indigenous people, the original black inhabitants of Australia. The relatively small population of

Indigenous families in the State of Victoria were, it seems, scattered in clusters in the outskirts of Melbourne CBD. Occasionally, we would see a few adults lounging on benches near the Flinders Street train station in the city. A few Indigenous liaison workers were recruited by Monash Health, my employer, in the years before my retirement in 2018. They were located both at the hospital sites and at Monash Health Community where I worked. I got to know them as work colleagues but rarely had the opportunity to engage them in any serious conversation about the nature of their work or their background. Perhaps I took my cue from others around me. I sensed a respectful wariness among the general staff not to encroach on sensitive political matters in casual encounters with these workers.

Initially I was not sure how to refer to Indigenous people since such terms as Aborigines, Blacks, blackfella, First Australians, or First Nations people were also used. But I was soon advised that the safest and most respectful term was First Nations people, although the term *Indigenous peoples* was widely evident. I was rather puzzled to read, that while the term *Black or black people* had gained currency in democratic South Africa, local Indigenous peoples frowned upon it. They considered being labelled *black* was outmoded and highly offensive (*Common Ground*). First Nations people seem comfortable to speak of themselves as *us mob* or *us blackfellas*.

There was always something in the media about the historical violence, dispossession, discrimination, and indignities suffered by Indigenous populations. I was acutely aware that we had escaped almost similar circumstances in South Africa under Apartheid. Yet here we were now very much part of the privileged majority population. Whereas the health and material circumstances of most First Nations peoples remain dire.

The least I could do, I thought, was to get to know the sorry history of the indigenous peoples and actively commit myself to campaigns that promoted their aspirations and wellbeing.

~

The rehabilitation of the Maralinga nuclear test sites was one such high profile campaigns. In the 1950s, the British Government had detonated six atomic bombs in an area of scrubland in South Australia which local Indigenous people later named Maralinga or the 'fields of thunder.' It was said that in the years that followed many local people died of radiation poisoning, and children were born with birth defects.

In September 1990, the Community Psychologists Interest Group of the Australian Psychological Society, which I'd joined a year earlier, organised a workshop to explore the interrelated themes of environmental abuse, nuclear proliferation, uranium mining and Indigenous dispossession. The workshop was rather original and unique. It was held over eight days. Thirty of us travelled from Melbourne to Maralinga and back, 4500 kilometres. Some seminars took place on the coach and others at overnight campsites around a campfire. Topics that related to indigenous issues were facilitated by Tracey Bunda, an Indigenous person and, currently, Professor of Aborigine and Torres Straits Islander Studies at Queensland University, Australia.

Author chatting with Professor Tracey Bunda

When we arrived in Maralinga, a legal advisor of the local Indigenous community arranged for us to meet with a group of Maralinga Tjarutja elders, to hear first-hand their painful experiences and historical concerns.

Apparently, the community had not been told or consulted about the decision to use the site for atomic bomb testing. And after the testing was over, the site was largely left heavily contaminated and unsecured. It took years of protests and representations by the local Indigenous community before some effort was made by the British Government to clean up the place. Even so, there seems to be no guarantee that the radiation from the soil had been eliminated.

The encounter proved to be profound and moving. We sat on the ground with the elders in a bush clearing. I was conscious of the wind in the trees, the heat of the day, the distant laughter of children and the discomfort of sitting on a carpet of twigs and dried grass.

Meeting with Tjarutja elders.

Author (far left) chatting with an elder.

Two elders, Mervin and Hughey, introduced themselves as the spokesmen. We did likewise. The proceedings in English were low key and informal. Mervin and Hughey spoke in an eloquent and dignified manner, with broad expressive hand gestures and long pregnant pauses.

I was appalled to learn, among other things, that some

Indigenous people had continued to live in the test area quite unaware of the dangers. Those that survived had their hair turn prematurely grey.

We departed from the meeting subdued and humbled. On the journey we also passed by Roxby Downs and Woomera and learnt about uranium mining in the vicinity and about the Woomera Rocket Range. We resolved, as Community Psychologists, to commit to active participation in campaigns promoting reparation and reconciliation.

~

Signs of First Nations people's historical presence and passing were to be found in many places in Melbourne. But awareness only came with an abiding and respectful interest in authentic Indigenous history – not just 'whitefella' history.

Whenever we had family and friends visiting from overseas, we would take them to visit the William Ricketts Sanctuary in the Dandenong Ranges. The Sanctuary was a forested area overseen by Parks Victoria where one would view the sculptures of the late artist William Ricketts depicting Indigenous peoples and their affinity to culture and the natural world.

A William Ricketts Sculpture

The sculptures were scattered among mountain ash and tree ferns, and within rocky grottos. The Sanctuary was designed to have a spiritual appeal for visitors, triggering reflection and contemplation. However, it did not take me long to realise that some local First Nations people felt strongly that William Ricketts had a patronising or paternalistic attitude, and that his sculptures depicted Indigenous peoples as primitive and, unlike modern man, still firmly embedded in the natural world of flora and fauna.

They felt much used by Ricketts for his narcissistic indulgence. This critique certainly gave me a deeper insight into the nature of colonial exploitation from the perspective of Indigenous people.

The Aboriginal Heritage Walk is a feature of the Royal Botanic Garden. It is led by an Indigenous elder. When my wife and I did this walk, we learnt a great deal about Indigenous connections to plants as medicine, food and as tools.

'You're always speaking about wanting to know more about First Nations people,' said our neighbour one day. 'Central Australia is the place for you, mate - the heart and soul of this ancient country. Melbourne tells you nothing.' So, I read up whatever I could find on *Uluru* (Ayers Rock) and the *Red Centre* as it is called because of the burnished red landscape. Soon my wife and I were there in person witnessing a spectacular sunrise and absorbing the stunning and breathtaking landscape.

Sunrise over Uluru

We felt spiritual awe as we walked at a meditative pace around mighty Uluru which rose like a mythical ochre-red whale from the depth of an ocean of red-clay dust. Climbing the Rock, we were told, was an act of sacrilege. So, we did the next best thing – touch it for a sense of connection.

Spiritual feel of Uluru – the rock of ages

We joined an all-Indigenous tour company for a brief experience of local culture and customs, and to learn first-hand from Indigenous folks their perceptions of past, present and future.

Indigenous cultural dance (Author second from left)

Author throwing a boomerang

Indigenous tour guides (Author on far right)

Before returning to Melbourne, we spent a day in the town of Alice Springs. Here we had a distressing glimpse into the dispossession, impoverishment and urban degradation wrought on the First Nations community.

As new migrants to Australia, we felt this trip to Central Australia was an invaluable orientation on the history, politics, and social circumstances of First Nations people – a learning which we have been consolidating ever since.

For example, there are two roads not too far from where we live – Boundary Road and East Boundary Road. I was aghast to be told only recently that these roads were relics of a racist past. They represented the former town boundaries which Indigenous people were not permitted to cross over at certain times.

More recently in 2018, I returned to Central Australia to absorb the majesty and grandeur of the MacDonnell Ranges. The Arrernte people are the traditional custodians of the vast area not too far from Alice Springs. I learned that the famous Indigenous artist, Albert Namatjira, was inspired by these mountains and the surroundings. I marvelled at the ghost gums depicted in his paintings still standing tall in the grounds of the Hermannsburg Mission nearby, now a heritage site.

Trekking in the MacDonnell Ranges was a rare and unforgettable experience.

Author camping and trekking

Later, I wrote a poem to capture my insight into the affinity of Indigenous peoples to country.

A Kind of Blindness
You there,
See
This here burnt fractured land
Is *Country*
Ancient beyond time.
See how
Ghost gums stand darkly still
Against a star sprinkled sky,
Ochre-red gorges
In deep, deep mourning.
Creeks and riverbeds dry
Show scars of floods past.
Where burnished spinifex clumps
Keep watch
Over us Mob,
Invisible to you,
At the waterhole.
You wayward hiker
Stomping regardless

In reading the regular Koori Mail, the fortnightly national Indigenous newspaper and watching the national Indigenous TV, I'm inspired by the aspirations and achievements of First Nations communities in areas such as education, sports, writing and publication, arts and politics. And all this in the face of tremendous odds.

I do not know what awareness and opinion the Indigenous communities here have of the historical struggle for freedom in South African culminating in a post-Apartheid democracy. However, it amazed me to learn that the British army had recruited and deployed Indigenous trackers in the Anglo-Boer War.

In April 1994, when South Africa held its historic first democratic elections, Australia was one of many countries to contribute volunteers to the United Nations Election Observer Mission. The team included Mai Katona, an esteemed First Nations person.

Mai points to a photo of her in South Africa in 1994

~

Australian Red Cross Volunteer

It wasn't very long before we realised that Australia was a country of devastating fires, droughts and floods. The 2009 Black Saturday wildfires was our first frightening experience. For days preceding Saturday 7 February, the temperature hovered around 45 degrees. Melbourne was blanketed in an ominous heat haze. And a warm wind picked up and swirled menacingly. By midday on Saturday the predictions of impending disaster saturated the air waves. We made a hasty decision to go the movies, to seek the safety and cool sanctuary of Hoyts Chadstone. Emerging from the cinema a few hours later, we were confronted with stories of death and widespread destruction. We learned with distress that beautiful Marysville, one of our favourite holiday destinations two hours north of Melbourne, was almost completely incinerated by the firestorm.

Hundreds of people responded to the Red Cross call for volunteers to help out in various ways in the worst affected areas. I, too, answered the call. This was the beginning of my ten-year stint with the Red Cross as an Emergency Services Volunteer. In the years following the Black Saturday bushfires, I've been deployed many times following other disasters, including the cataclysmic Victorian floods of 2010, the Bourke Street tragedy in January 2017, and the Mallacoota fires of January 2020. More recently my wife and I assisted the Food Bank to distribute food hampers to people compelled to quarantine because of the Covid pandemic.

For most Australians, volunteering is a national virtue, an essential aspect of being truly Australian. Hopefully, my contribution to the worthy efforts of the Red Cross has made me more of an *Aussie*.

A Red Cross Emergency Team. Author on left.

Author deployed to Mallacoota by helicopter.

~

ANC Support Group

With a home to call our own, surrounded by friendly neighbours, and secure in employment, you would say we were well set to transform into good loyal Australians, minus the Aussie twang. However, it did not turn out quite that way. With uncluttered time on my hands and few domestic worries, long suppressed regrets and feelings of loss began to surface. Most of all, I missed the life of a political activist, the dread, the adrenaline rush, and the heightened sense of purpose. Once more unto the breach, dear friends, as Shakespeare's Henry V had urged.

One day, at the dentist waiting my turn, I paged fitfully through a copy of the previous week's Leader newspaper. Hello, what is this? A photo and an article on the ANC. In the blurb, a Mr Naidu thanked donors for the success of a recent fundraising drive organised by the Melbourne Support Group of the African National Congress. How astonishing, I thought, an ANC Support Group in Melbourne! Immediately I got home, I scrambled to contact this Mr Naidu. It was the very antidote we need, I said to my wife.

'Yes, I've noticed you've not been sleeping well lately.'

Homesickness and political alienation had got to me like Melbourne's winter chill. I could tell that my moodiness was affecting others near me.

Soon we were attending Support Group meetings in members' homes across Melbourne and assisting with fund raising events and socialising with like-minded people. Migrants and refugees from South Africa, representative of all four races, were scattered in suburbs all over Melbourne. Yet it puzzled us why, apart from two black South Africans, only Indian South Africans were active in the ANC Support Group.

Then there came the momentous news that Mandela was to be released. Glued to the TV with breathless anticipation, I gasped as Mandela and Winnie finally appeared, hand-in-hand, walking into the sunlight of Cape Town amidst a jubilant throng. The world watched with us. Mandela beamed, his face graceful and radiant. Tall and lanky, somewhat gaunt, and just a little unsteady on his feet from the ravages of age and long imprisonment. I realised with surprise that I had no idea of what he looked like. When he was sent to prison for life, the government had made it a criminal offence to speak of him, to mention his name, or to publish or circulate his image in South Africa, the intention being to obliterate Mandela from our collective memory.

Soon after his release, Mandela flew into Melbourne to thank Australians personally for their gallant and unwavering anti-apartheid campaigns – especially the boycott of the South African national cricket team over the years when he was languishing in prison. We joined an enthusiastic crowd at the airport on 25 October 1990. We pushed our way forward breaching the police cordon and thrust out our hands as Mandela and his welcoming hosts came by. Ours was just two among a forest of others eager for a historic handshake.

Later that day we attended a gala public welcome at the Melbourne City Hall. We found ourselves in the thick of a packed and excited audience. Mandela was ushered in. For a moment there was absolute stillness as everyone savoured the significance of the event. Then the silence was shattered by a pandemonium of clapping, cheering, stomping, and rallying calls of Mandela! Mandela! Mandela! All too soon the Mandela Magic was over, and we were left with no more than the afterglow.

Mandela Welcome - Melbourne City Hall

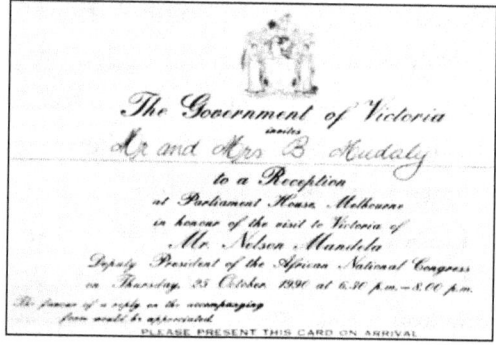

Invitation to Mandela Reception

Prime Minister Bob Hawk Hosts Mandela

Australians almost universally appreciated Mandela's visit to honour them for their concerted opposition to Apartheid. I read the lead articles in the Melbourne Age and watched reports on TV. Similar sentiments were expressed.

However, lost in all the euphoria was the unhappy voice of the indigenous peoples, the downtrodden black people of Australia. Their feelings about Mandela and the Australian Government were reflected in the response of Michael Mansell, a Tasmanian Indigenous leader, activist, and lawyer. Mansell acknowledged Mandela's greatness but regretted he did not seek permission from Indigenous peoples to visit, nor did Mandela insist on meeting with them. I cannot recall if any First Nations leaders were invited to the City Hall welcome.

Apparently, Mandela, once a persecuted black man himself, later explained to journalists that he did not wish to interfere in Australia's internal affairs. I feel saddened that the First Nations people were seemingly snubbed by a black political icon. I am left wondering if Mandela, like Gandhi, in deferring to his hosts, compromised his principles on political and social justice. I guess, as humans, we all suffer blind spots.

~

For a short while after Mandela's visit, the ANC support Group continued to remain active. We were buoyed by visits from other distinguished ANC members serving in the first democratic government in vital roles. The Deputy President of the ANC, Walter Sisulu, and his wife Albertina arrived in August 1991.

Walter Sisulu and Albertina were humble, quietly spoken people, wise elders with no affectations. In the conversation, they showed keen interest in us as members of the ANC Support Group. 'We're so happy you all did your bit for a free South Africa.' They were respectful and understanding of why we had emigrated. Walter Sisulu's parting words come to mind. 'South Africa needs people like you. Committed. I pray you'll both be home soon.' They have now both passed on. And we remain migrants to Australia, in self-imposed exile.

The visit of the Deputy President was followed by Max Sisulu and Ketso Gordhan on an economic mission. Later there was a visit from Pravin Gordhan, the Minister of Finance at the time.

**Albertina & Walter Sisulu
(Author standing at the back)**

Ketso Gordhan & Max Sisulu Melbourne
(Author on the right)

The ANC Support Group in Australia disbanded soon after South Africa held its very first democratic elections in 1994. It had served its purpose. What now, I wondered. Where and in which direction do I channel my activism?

Amnesty International Australia

It is a mystery how I first stumbled upon Amnesty International (AI). Back in Durban, I was ignorant of its existence, even though it was recognised and acclaimed the world over for its human rights campaigns. My long-standing interest in human rights soon found a natural home in the Australian chapter (AIA).

Now my involvement, as a seasoned AIA activist, has been many and varied. Campaigning on behalf of 'prisoners of conscience', writing countless *Urgent Action* letters, signing petitions, and mounting displays in libraries to publicise the work of Amnesty. Many a time I have stood with others on the steps of State Parliament in Spring Street with a placard promoting campaigns such as banning the death penalty, and advancing local aboriginal social, political and human rights. At other times, I have joined AIA marches through Melbourne CBD – once to highlight the plight of asylum seekers and refugees in off-shore detention centres.

The great irony, however, is that Amnesty International, on principle, never recognised Nelson Mandela as a prisoner of conscience. It did not campaign for his release from Robben Island, where he was incarcerated for twenty-seven years. This was because the ANC under Nelson Mandela had initiated an armed resistance against apartheid.

In 2007 I was recognised for my contribution to human rights by being presented with the annual Claire Wositzky award by the Victorian Branch of Amnesty International Australia.

Amnesty fundraising events

Journal

Amnesty hero

After decades of commitment to human rights, Bala Mudaly, a member and convenor of South Eastern Group of Amnesty International, has been recognised for his tireless efforts. Diana Wells reports.

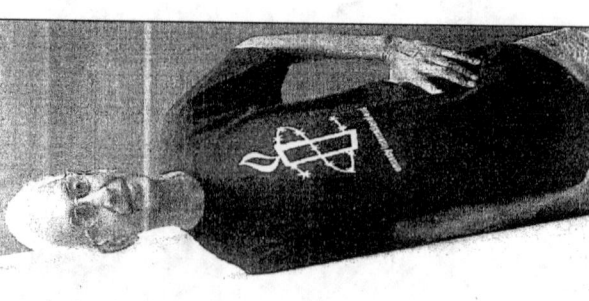

BALA Mudaly wears several hats, and they all have the threads of common decency deeply woven into them.

He has been a member of the South Eastern Group of Amnesty International for the past six years, but has fought for human rights since the 1960s in his birthplace of Durban, in Southern Africa's east coast.

Since coming to Australia 19 years ago, he has continued to lobby Australian and overseas governments on human rights issues, and was recently presented with the Claire Wrositzky award by the Victorian branch of Amnesty International.

Wrositzky was instrumental in setting up the Victorian arm of Amnesty International Australia in 1962.

Bala was 50 years old when he came to Australia with his wife, Neerosh in 1988.

It was just two years before South Africa's then newly elected president F. W. de Clerk freed Nelson Mandela, leader of the African National Congress and leading anti-Apartheid campaigner, after 27 years in jail.

He was still in South Africa when his colleague Steve Biko, founder of the Black Consciousness movement, died in police custody in 1977.

Officially, apartheid existed in South Africa from 1948 to 1991 — until the release of Nelson Mandela, but racial discrimination had existed there from British colonial times.

Bala has experienced first-hand the oppression of black Africans.

He protested with student movements and the African National Congress against "discriminatory laws that allocated the most desirable land to the white population".

He and his family endured late "night raids by the security police" and were evicted from their family home in the 1960s as the then South African Group Areas Legislation displaced all people who were not of the white ruling class — except Japanese people who were classified "honorary whites".

These displaced Africans were left with no property and no livelihood.

But, he says, he endured less than many others.

He was involved in national student movements, opposition movements and non-government organisations, experiencing first-hand the security apparatus of the time.

South Africa was "essentially a police state," he says.

Life is very different for Bala and his wife here in Melbourne's south-eastern suburbs, yet as part of his Amnesty work, he still writes letters to governments on behalf of prisoners of conscience and to raise human rights issues.

Bala is employed as a psychologist and counsellor for Southern Health and supports many people who come from areas of conflict and persecution, including refugees and asylum seekers from East Timor, Cambodia, Vietnam, Bosnia, Iran, Iraq, Horn of Africa, Sudan and Somalia.

"People don't realise the stories behind these people who come from other countries where they have endured some form of persecution or conflict," Bala says.

"They come here with little English, perhaps little qualifications, and wait sometimes a long time to secure work and a work permit.

"They have come from traumatic lifestyles — they may have escaped refugee camps, they may have had family members disappear, been victims of political strife or have been child soldiers — there are just so many reasons why they are here and they need a lot of help."

Why did Bala and Neerosh decide to leave South Africa, when seemingly there was light at the end of the dark and oppressive apartheid tunnel?

"There was no work for me there, and my wife's family were here in Melbourne," Bala says.

Today Bala is involved in several recent Amnesty International campaigns, including stopping violence against women, Osiru, opposing the death penalty, and in the release of Australian David Hicks from Guantanamo.

Bala hopes people will take time to "think about those who are oppressed and without human rights and will support the work of Amnesty International".

"There are many levels that people can get involved in," he says.

"Amnesty International has many projects that address human rights abuses.

"I realise I can only do so much — we need people to join in our right to preserve dignity for all humans."

Amnesty International is a democratic self-governing movement where major policy decisions are taken by an international council made up of representatives from all national sections.

To join the South Eastern Group of Amnesty, call Sue on 0404 850 820 or Bala 9569 7802 (ah) or Amnesty International's main office on 94120700. The group meets on the third Tuesday each month in Mount Waverley at 8pm.

For more details, visit www.amnesty.org

Feeling Australian

I was recently quizzed by my Australian neighbour if I now felt like an *Aussie*. In thirty years of living in Melbourne, I had not given it a thought. The question got me wondering and reflecting. To be honest, I am not sure.

Of course, I was now more aware of such thorny national issues as refugee policy, Indigenous rights, climate change and so on. I also note my distress at learning about the terrible history on which modern Australia is founded, especially the callous treatment of so-called convicts dumped here in great numbers by colonial Britain, the persecution and near extermination of Indigenous peoples and the painful saga of the forceable removal of Indigenous children from their parents (*the stolen generation*).

I seem to have acquired an appreciation of Australian landscape and literature. I would delight in spotting a kangaroo all alert on an open field. The raucous laughter of a kookaburra is always hilarious. The sound of bellbirds stops me in my track as I scan the trees nearby for their elusive presence. And, of course, I am wholly sympathetic to Ned Kelly, the aggrieved Irish settler, standing up for his rights. It appals me that he was simply regarded a bushranger and a highway robber and executed at the Melbourne Goal.

My partiality is perhaps best revealed when I am watching a rugby or cricket international between South Africa and Australia. I would be crestfallen if South Africa were thrashed, but silently overjoyed if Australia was given a thumping. That speaks a ton, doesn't it? Yet, when I am on an extended holiday in Durban, I would tire soon enough and long for *home*. The very moment I land in Melbourne, however, I cringe at the wretched weather, and yearn for balmy Durban. While I have yet to unpack what politicians here mean when they speak of *Australian culture and values*, I have learnt to say *traffic lights* instead of robot, *BBQ* in place of braai, to call my best friend *mate,* and happily use acronyms by the dozen.

To the extent to which all these aspects impinge upon my consciousness, I am truly Australian. And what is more, I now travel Qantas on an Australian passport.

Part 5
Visits to South Africa as an Outsider

Visits to South Africa as an Outsider

Since migrating to Australia in 1988, I have visited South Africa a few times. Three such occasions were necessitated by the death of my eldest sister, my father and a favourite niece who died in a motor vehicle accident with her little daughter.

When possible, I would plan and prepare ahead to make each trip a fresh learning experience. I would decide on places to visit, things to do and questions to ask, all intended to help me appreciate how South Africa was moving along as a free, non-racial, and independent democracy. So it was that on my visit in 2018, I listened to the lived-experience of friends and family, all Indians, scattered across the country, noticing the houses and neighbourhoods where they lived, their employment situation, lifestyles, their worries and hopes – and more importantly their interactions with other communities of colour. I scanned newspapers and TV channels for news and current issues. I roamed bookshops to get a sense of the books being written, and of their authors. My visits to the Apartheid Museum, Liliesleaf Farm, and to Groutville, the home of the late Albert Luthuli, a former President of the ANC, were journeys of discovery into a collective historical past.

For all my pre-planning, I found it rather difficult to initiate meaningful encounters with Blacks, Coloured or Whites. Of course, I had a few brief chance exchanges with Blacks – a bank teller, three domestic workers, an Uber driver, and a couple of hotel staff. But several of them were refugees from Zimbabwe or elsewhere in Africa. On one rare occasion, I got to sit and talk informally with five black professional Child Care Workers around a table. They worked on an outreach project called *Isibindi* aimed at providing creative nurturing skills to childcare workers in the black community. The project was the initiative of the National Association of Child Care Workers (NACCW). I left this discussion feeling uplifted and a little hopeful. But overall, I had the sense that things were sliding backwards in South Africa, in many areas of political, economic and community life.

Siloed living according to colour had become ever more entrenched and accepted. Most Indians I spoke with simply shrugged their shoulders. Perhaps parallel living was the accepted new norm. At least this was how it appeared to my casual eye. Could it be that beneath the surface, cross-racial and cultural collaboration and integration were taking place?

The very first visit my wife and I made to South Africa after migrating, was to reconnect with friends and family, but also to see the country as foreign holidaymakers. I recall we went on a memorable organised group tour to Khayelitsha, a sprawling impoverished, crime ridden black Township near Cape Town. Excursions into black townships were a new promotional initiative of tour companies. It gave non-blacks the opportunity to have a glimpse of the awful living circumstances of the majority black population. I thought it a cheap thrill for tourists to be taken, under cover of security, into a no-go zone, to step into an alien and fraught world. Of course, there was also an element of voyeurism involved. As tourists we paid, it seemed, to gape at the degradation wrought upon a disenfranchised majority by Apartheid.

The group were also taken to a local beer hall to sample a popular local brew. Curious street urchins looked on as we alighted from the kombi and were herded to a wood and iron shed the size of half a standard single-car garage. This was the poor man's pub. The only item of furniture here was a u-shaped wooden bench seating about ten customers. We joined a drunken lot of working-class black men, shabby and unkempt. They received us with amused nods of welcome. But anyone reading our faces and body language could easily tell the measure of our discomfort. The sight of dazed and groggy black men combined with the pungent, sickly smell of fermented sorghum was just too much. But we did not wish to offend. Like sheep we did what was expected of us here. A five-litre metal container filled to overflowing with frothing discoloured beer was passed around, person to person. Then it was my turn. I received the cold and wet tin, sipped half-a-mouthful, and handed it to my wife. She pursed her lips and sipped, trying her best not to grimace or throw up. Many glazed and approving eyes were on us. A white tourist, however, gave it a miss, whispering 'Don't want to catch Aids.' She voiced the very fear I had. Thankfully, I survived to tell the story.

An overnight stop at New Brighton African Township in

Port Elizabeth was our second astonishing experience. Our train journey from Cape Town to Port Elizabeth was interesting as this was a first for us. On the way, we were drawn to the varied landscape of farms, forests, and quaint towns along this coastal route. Equally, we enjoyed the cosy comfort of our compartment, and chit-chat with passengers, who were mostly well-dressed blacks. In post-apartheid South Africa, most non-blacks were still wary of train travel. Perhaps this explained why my family and friends frowned at us for 'taking unnecessary risks.'

On arriving at Port Elizabeth Central Station in the late afternoon, our beaming hosts, Ruth and Zola Valakasi came rushing over to greet us. There was much laughter and hugs while our luggage was snatched from our hands. 'Yah, you've come, eh? That's good, that's good.' Zola couldn't resist talking.' This way, please. Winnie's with the kombi. You've heard of Winnie our baby, ne? She's good. Helps us a lot. You'll like. Yaah.'

Not expecting such a welcome, I was knocked off my feet with the warmth and attention. My wife attached herself to Ruth while Zola and I weaved through a throng of disembarked passengers making for the exit, the trolley with our two suitcases deftly pushed along by Zola. Although we had not known Winnie, she jumped out from the driver's seat and embraced us, her dreadlocks, stretch jeans and *takkies* (runners) proclaiming youthful wellbeing.

Ruth, now in her 50s, was solid, tall, and matronly, with her frizzy hair secured in a patterned *doek* (head scarf). She had spent a few months in Melbourne, a year earlier. A nurse with a wealth of experience working with Aids patients, Ruth had been sponsored on an educational visit to Australia to see how this illness and its spread were being managed as a public health issue. My wife had the good fortune to run into Ruth at a health forum. The excitement of meeting a fellow South African had been mutual. One thing led to another, and here we were now being hosted by Ruth and her family in New Brighton Township – an experience which may not have happened if we had not migrated. Certainly, it was an opportunity not in the realms of possibility for our South African Indian friends and family. That is how deep the chasm was between the racial groups in South Africa even after our hard-won freedom.

I looked about me with much interest as the kombi left the town and headed into the all-black township, a visible transition from affluence into drabness and congestion. Presently, we drove through a bus and taxi rank, chaotic with hurrying people, a clash of competing sounds, of clutter, and carts selling fried meat or essentials such as paraffin and mosquito coils. This was a dizzy and somewhat unsettling scene for visitors unaccustomed to witnessing the everyday reality of black lives. Even so, when my wife spotted a stall selling fresh mealies on cob, steaming in a large, improvised pot, she called out to Ruth 'Could we please stop a moment?'

'Really? You eat *umbila*?

We crossed the busy street warily and made for the cart-stall. We waited our turn and made our purchase. Surprisingly, none of the Blacks going about their business seemed to notice or react to the presence of Indians in their midst. It was a huge lesson for us.

Ruth and Zola lived in a relatively new middle-class part of the township with brick urban-style houses that were well-designed and maintained. That evening neighbours and friends turned up to celebrate our presence and socialised around a BBQ. The evening was still, warm, and surreal. Later, our hosts relished the opportunity to take us on a stroll through the immediate neighbourhood. The streets were properly sealed, the nature strips respectably tidy. The night had a lively feel – soft jive music and chatter emanated from houses, there were glimpses of people through lit up windows flitting about, a girl calling to her friend, a baby crying. A dog or two were to be seen but did not go for our heels. How strange, I thought. Adults were still lingering about in the shadows having their last puff, seemingly reluctant to turn in. A few curious neighbours in their front yards came over to be introduced. Laughs, smiles and handshakes were in generous supply.

Sadly, upon returning to Australia, we lost contact with Ruth. The rare and insightful over-night experience we enjoyed in a black home with a black family in an all-black township was never to be repeated. Such is life in South Africa.

Concluding Thoughts

Concluding Thoughts

On my visit to post-apartheid South Africa in 2018, I found that little had changed. Whites, Blacks, Indians and Coloureds, all South Africans, still lived their lives in parallel universes, mostly defined by race, colour, and wealth. Recent migrants and refugees had a difficult time fitting in or feeling welcome. The refrain of Kipling's poem still contains an element of truth:

East is East and West is West, And Never the two shall meet.

As a result of my experience and observations, I have shifted in my understanding of Mandela's *Rainbow Nation*. I now see the rainbow as a combination of merging strips, each a subtle variation, a separate hue, but adding equally to the vibrancy of the composite. Unity in diversity. The appearance of a rainbow across a stormy dark sky is often a sign of hope that the storm will soon pass. I am, however, acutely aware that the notion of a *rainbow nation* is frowned upon my many who still suffer the indignity of being at the bottom of the woodpile. What rainbow nation? they ask, when South Africa remains one of the most unequal nations on earth. It is a deception, nothing more than a feel-good mirage.

Nevertheless, I am reminded of the title of one of Athol Fugard's plays – *Blood Knot*. This seems an apt and powerful metaphor for the reality that is South Africa. It has been and will continue to be a nation of disparate peoples defining themselves by such factors as race, colour, class, and culture. Religious beliefs often mediate these factors. But here is the thing, Blacks, Whites, Coloureds, and Indians are inexorably bound together by history and destiny. Even during the bleakest period of Apartheid, under the harshest attempts at police-enforced racial separation, South Africans continued to meet and engage in clandestine transactions for mutual survival. Shared humanity had a way of asserting itself, transcending hurdles. And this is what the *Blood Knot* is all about. Cross-cultural fusion is a reality, an unstoppable process. Much of it happens without us even noticing it.

For instance, Indians have taken for granted Zulu, Afrikaans and British place names that form part of their everyday lives – Umgeni River, Bloemfontein, Durban. Then too we are naturally into having *braivleis* (BBQ), eating *boerewors*, Ouma Rusks or wearing *veldskoens*. The more I ponder it, the more I realise that the swiftly globalising world is really one enormous melting-pot. No, perhaps not so much a melting pot but, more realistically, a salad bowl. In a salad bowl, each ingredient retains its individual integrity, bonded by an irresistible dressing, to rival even the flavour of *Nandos*! And there is the much-loved bunny-chow (*bunny* for short), a South African creation, a street food once the poor man's life saver, but now celebrated and promoted by the local tourism industry as a gourmet delight of Durban. The *bunny* which is no more than a quarter loaf of fresh white bread with the soft centre dug out, the resultant cavity filled with authentic curry and re-plugged with the dugout bit of bread. To derive maximum enjoyment, the *bunny* must be eaten with messy fingers – to be licked clean later. A chunk of bread with any other filling cannot claim to be the authentic thing.

In an odd way, the humble *bunny* encapsulates for me the very essence of an Indian South African - a fusion of all things South African. Its history, landscape, peoples, and cultures, yet retaining an Indianness at the core.

The late Johnny Clegg, social anthropologist singer-songwriter, was courageous in bucking the system that zealously fragmented peoples' lives. He strove to unite race, colour and culture through protest song and dance. He came to be known as the 'White Black Man.' On the other hand, Peter Abrahams, the distinguished Coloured writer, realised that living in an oppressive racist state stifled creativity. He had to break free. '*Perhaps life had a meaning that transcended race and colour,*' reflected Abrahams. '*If it had, I could not find it in South Africa. I had to write, to tell freedom, and for this I needed to be personally free ….*' (Peter Abrahams: *Tell Freedom*, 1954). He exiled himself to Trinidad in 1956 and made it his home until his death in 2017.

Es'kia Mphahlele (*Afrika My Music*, 1984), the doyen of African Literature, reflects on his own period of self-imposed exile, his longing for the land of his ancestors, his return to South Africa after twenty years absence, and living again the humiliations of a *non-white* under Apartheid. '*Each one of us has finally his or her reason for going into exile or being forced into it by circumstances to which he or she shapes a unique response. Likewise, the decision to stay out or re-enter.*'

Thirty years on, I am resigned to the fact that there is no turning back. Should we return to South Africa, we would certainly not be returning to the world we had left behind. The best I can do now is entertain occasional moments of nostalgia, wonder (and foolishly speculate) what life would have been like had I remained. Here unfortunately, my crystal ball is quite murky.

Australia has been the vantage point from which I have surveyed my life, indulging in elusive memories of South Africa. It is almost as if, while long settled and secure in a marriage, I pursue fanciful thoughts of my first love.

Even so, South Africa still matters deeply to me. I continue to invest emotionally in the land of my birth, although I cannot avert my eyes from the fact that the country remains mired in inequality and racism. Corruption, crime, poverty, and poor service delivery have become endemic. Like feral dogs, these problems prowl at the very doorstep of the impoverished masses, hemming them in. What could they do but wring their hands in despair and become cynical? Or vent their pent-up anger in wild street protests, which often culminate in the burning and looting of meagre community resources such as schools, clinics, and libraries.

How fortunate then that I enjoy the benefit of distance. I can adopt a pragmatic and philosophical view of South Africa past, present and its possible future. I see the country against the backdrop of other countries in Africa, Asia and Latin America experiencing almost similar challenges and upheavals, where people strive and suffer, enjoying interludes of respite and joy. I tell myself that even a first world country like Australia is unable to free itself entirely of racism and religious intolerance; that even here there is a widening chasm between the poor and the rich. And here too there's corruption in high places.

I come now to accept the world for how it is – fraught, complex, full of contradictions and uncertainties. Yet even when the clouds are dark and foreboding, I know from long experience there is an abiding sky above, eternal and forever azure. This is how it has always been and will likely be into the distant future. The world is as it is - just so. People of goodwill and democratic institutions (if not corrupted) will always strive to make the lived world a better place, to alleviate inherent human suffering and enhance peoples' capacity to endure with courage, hope and wisdom.

To conclude, then, I pay homage to Cato Manor, the place of my birth and my humble beginnings, to my family and the Indian community - the formative influences on my identity.

The rest of my life has been lived elsewhere. I embraced motion, became a traveller, embarked on a lifelong road trip. I have journeyed long, travelled far and, in the process, faced many inconvenient truths about myself. Over time, the road I chose crossed the paths of people of many lands – people of varied colour, culture, race, and ideology. My horizon extended, my consciousness expanded, my sense of self suffered ceaseless sea change as I crossed racial divides. I mellowed.

I feel I have arrived at a sort of resting place for now. The ultimate journey's end could be just over the horizon. Who can tell for sure? And yet....and yet a voice tells me that I am not quite done, that my life remains a work in progress. Like Tennyson's *Ulysses* I seem to be unwilling to accept the constraints of old age. The quests never end. How to strike a balance between heaven and earth; how to remain grounded while enabling one's imagination to soar; how to cultivate a universal worldview while confronting the challenges of the here and now; and, how to remain focused on the inner journey while distracted by the external transient landscape.

'We shall not cease from exploration, and the end of all our exploring will be to arrive where we started and know the place for the first time.' (TS Eliot, 1941).

Such is my reality. Both stillness and flow. My way of being.

Family in 1953 (Author back right)

References

Abrahams, P. (1954) *Tell Freedom*. London: Faber & Faber.

Achebe, C. (1958) *Things Fall Apart*. London: Heinemann.

Angelou, M. (1986) *All God's Children Need Traveling Shoes*. New York: Random House.

Bosman, C.B. (1981) *Mafeking Road & Other Stories*. Cape Town: Human & Rousseau.

Carey, H. (2016) *Ubuntu: My Life in Other People*. Leicester: Matador.

Chah, A. (1985) A Still Forest Pool. Wheaton, USA: Theosophical Publishing House.

Common Ground: *Aboriginal and Torres Strait Islander Peoples, Indigenous, Aboriginal, Aborigine, Blackfella, First Nations or First Australians. What's the appropriate term?* www.commonground.org.au

Chatwin, B. (1987) *Songlines*. North Plymouth: Franklin Press.

Cleaver, E. (1968) *Soul on Ice*. New York: Ramparts Press.

Diop, C. (1950) *Africa My Africa*. Online: Folukeafrica.com.

Eliot, T.S. (1941) *Four Quartets*. Online: philoctetes.org

Fitzpatrick, P. (1984) *Jock of the Bushveld*. Johannesburg: Ad Jonker.

Fugard, A. (1980) *Tsotsi*. Melbourne: Text.

Govender, R. (1996) *At the Edge & Other Cato Manor Stories*. Pretoria: Manx.

Haley, A. & Malcolm, X. (1965) *The Autobiography of Malcolm X*. New York: Grove Press.

Ijimere, O. (1966) *Everyman.* (English Trans: by Ulli Beier). London: Heinemann Educational Books.

Jones, M. (1953) *The Therapeutic Community: A New Treatment Method in Psychiatry.* New York: Basic Books.

Kipling, R. (1889) *The Ballad of East and West.* Online: www.kiplingsociety.co.uk.

Kornfield, J. & Breiter, P. (1985) *A Still Forest Pool: The Insight Meditation of Achaan Chah.* Wheaton: Theosophical Publishing House.

Manganyi, N.C. (2019) Being Black in the World. Johannesburg: Wits University Press.

Mangona, S. (1998). *Mother to Mother.* Cape Town: David Phillip.

Miller, P. (2007) *The Memoir Book.* Crow's Nest: Allen & Unwin.

Mishra, P. (2004) *An End of Suffering.* New York: Picador.

Mphahlele, E. (1984). Africa My Music. Johannesburg: Ravan Press.

Murakami, H. (2008) *What I Talk About When I Talk About Running.* London: Harvill Secker.

Nattrass, G. (2017) *A Short History of South Africa.* Johannesburg: Jonathan Ball.

Paton, A. (1948) *Cry, the Beloved Country.* London: Vintage.

Proust, M. (1996) *In Search of Lost Time, Volume VI.* London: Vintage.

Roux, E. (1948) *Time Longer Than Rope.* Wisconsin: University of Wisconsin.

Shakespeare, W. *Julius Caesar.* Online: www.pdfdrive.com

Schreiner, O. (2008) *The Story of an African Farm.* South Africa: Penguin.

Simmons, P. (2000) *Learning to Fall.* New York: Bantam.

Shuyun, S. (2003) Ten Thousand Miles Without a Cloud. London: Harper Collins.

South African History Online. sahistory.org.za.

Tennyson, A. (1854) Charge of the Light Brigade. In: *Tennyson, Collected Poetry* (2014). London: Broadview Press.

Yeats, W.B. (1921) Easter 1916. In: W.B. Yeats, *Selected Poems* (1991). London: Penguin Books

Acronyms

AI – Amnesty International
AIA – Amnesty International Australia
ANC – African National Congress
AYS – Arya Yuvak Sabha (???)
BPS – British Psychological Society
DHAC – Durban Housing Action Committee
DICWS – Durban Indian Child Welfare Society
ECT – Electro Convulsive Therapy
NACCW – National Association of Child Care Workers
NIC – Natal Indian Congress
NUSAS – National Union of South African Students
SAMDC – South African Medical & Dental Council
SASO – South African Students Organisation
SB – Special Branch/Security Branch
SHCS – Springvale Community Health Service
SRC – Students Representative Council
UDF – United Democratic Front

Chronology

Under a South African Sky (1938 – 1963)
- 1938　　　　Born
- 1947 to 1954　Primary School
- 1955 to 1958　High School
- 1959 to 1963　University

Breaking Through the Apartheid Barrier
- Zambia (January 1964 – December 1967)
- Britain (February 1968 – 1 June 1969)

Back in Apartheid South Africa (1969 – 1988)
- Return　　　　　Sept 1969
- Mondi　　　　　1970 -1971
- Lakehaven　　　1972 -1984
- Welfare Agency　1984 – 1986
- Migrate　　　　June 1988

Australia (1988 onwards)

Acknowledgements

This memoir had a long incubation. And many people helped ensure its birth. Foremost to thank is my wife who gave me space to persevere without being intrusive, yet was always ready to assist when asked.

From the outset I counted on my good friends Greg Tantala, Marcus Heath, and Gary Dellora to read sections of early embryonic drafts and give me their frank and invaluable impressions. Sylvia Karakaltsas was ready to chat with me over coffee and give me useful advice, drawing on her own writing and publishing experience. Thank you Sylvia for reading the final draft from cover to cover with a discerning eye.

I was extraordinarily lucky to have had ongoing feedback from three writers' groups: Caulfield Writers' Group, Monash Writers Group, and the Phoenix Park Writers' Group. The opportunity to present pages of my drafts and have them closely vetted, helped me hone my memoir writing skills, to keep in mind the reader. My sincere thanks to members of all three groups.

Naturally, I had to revise the manuscript (MS) many times over as it underwent levels of editing. I express thanks to Annie of AJ Collins Editing for securing three Beta Readers to read and indicate if the preliminary draft had potential literary merit. I extend my appreciation to Patti Miller, a doyen on life writing genre, and her team for editing a subsequent version of the MS and guiding me on how it may be brought to publishable standard.

I am immensely grateful to Omar Badsha. Hazel Carey, Betty Govinden, Uma Dhupelia-Mesthrie and Ashwin Desai, accomplished South African writers and academics, who willingly read the MS and were generous in their encouragement, suggestions, and support. This was the litmus test I much needed to persevere to the final lap.

I am enormously beholden to Robert New for educating me on such technical aspects as layout and formatting, cover design, and transforming a MS into what looked like a book.

Finally, I express my most sincere gratitude to Professor Johnathan Jansen of Stellenbosch University for writing the Foreword to my memoir. An act of much generosity.

My apologies to whoever I may have overlooked in this acknowledgement. Your support would certainly have contributed in good measure to the final product.

Appendix:
Shaping of Identity – Other Influences.

Landscapes, Memory and Me

Any landscape is a condition of the spirit:
Henri Frederic Amiel

The first few years of life in Australia was painful. My wife and I felt quite homesick. On our long Sunday drives to get a feel of Melbourne and beyond, I would catch myself saying things like: 'Oh, doesn't this remind you of the 'Valley of a Thousand Hills'? or 'This is so much like the market gardens along the Umgeni River in Springfield.' It took many years before I grew to love the wildness of the Australian bush. I, too, would be appalled when recurring summer wildfires laid waste vast swathes of natural forest of gum, wattle, mountain ash and eucalyptus. I, too, would feel the grief when my eyes fell upon miles and miles of stripped and blackened trees standing gaunt across the horizon. But I guess I would be considered un-Australian to nurse a single lantana bush in my garden when this shrub, so prolific in Durban, was classified as 'one of the worst invasive weeds in Australia.' When my lantana bush bursts into bright orange-yellow flowers in summer, I would invariably be transported back to the landscape of my childhood years which so shaped my identity.

'Okay class paint anything you wish today,' announced the teacher to my delight. It was the weekly art class again at my primary school in Cato Manor. Seldom were we given a free hand. I loved painting outdoor sceneries, and my choice now was the Durban Bluff. When fishing at the Durban Docks, my father had pointed it out to me. It was as close and as large as a Union Castle passenger-ship I had seen at Maydon Wharf. The Bluff was a prominent jutting land mass, a ridge that embraced and sheltered the Durban Bay from the threatening storms of the Indian Ocean. It stretched out like a sunning crocodile. From Cato Manor, we would normally go into the city by an Indian owned bus, and then walk for about forty minutes to get to Maydon Wharf. And if we wished to get across the bay to the Bluff itself, we would have to do so by ferry. The image of the bay hemmed by the Bluff was considered striking and unique, and hence attracted the attention of notable artists.

The Durban Bluff

Gilbert Sir was our art teacher. He would wear a double-breasted suit, tightly buttoned. He was a tall, urbane man with thinning hair neatly plastered back, and a face that readily creased into a broad smile. He praised my watercolour landscape of the Bluff and submitted it for the Annual Natal Indian Schools Art Exhibition sponsored by the Department of Education. I could not conceal my pride, more so when on a school excursion to the exhibition, I spotted my painting displayed prominently on a wall with other submissions. Mine had a blue sticker at the bottom right with the words 'Highly Commended' - fourth prize in the Junior category.

There were many other such images familiar to me in my childhood and youth that still linger in my memory – including some reminders of emotion-charged events. Take for instance, the fenced field next to where we lived in Cato Manor. Dimly through the winter mist, I would often see cows grazing on dew-drenched grass. Once my sister, Kamala, and I crawled under the barbed wire fence to collect fresh cow-dung, easily spotted by the smelly steam rising from the squishy blobs. We would hand the heavy bucket of pickings to my mother who'd be keeping a wary eye on the other side of the fence. Later we would see her smearing the stuff over a dusty patch of earth in the backyard to firm it up. I distinctly recall, too, a contraption of bamboo poles on this field, complete with rope and bucket. Many a time my sister and I would stand at the fence intrigued by how the farmer lowered the bucket into a well and drew water and emptied it into a network of shallow make-shift channels in his field of mealie crops and pumpkin. Father called the contraption a *shaduf* – which I learnt years later originated in ancient Egypt.

These recollections of landscapes were the very stuff in which I swam, like fish fully immersed in and sustained by the ocean. I consider *landscape* to be in the fullest cultural sense embracing places, traditions and ordinary activities of family and community. Landscape nurtured in me a sense of belonging and influenced how I thought of who I was. Consciousness is said to be embedded in context. As Philip Simmons (*Learning to Fall,* 2000) says: '*the world moves through us as we move through the world.*' Yes, I did not exist in a vacuum but thrived in a dynamic and rich environment, a blend of constructed neighbourhoods and natural landscape. Cato Manor (on the fringes of the city of Durban) for me was a vibrant, flourishing community. I lived and journeyed through this landscape of colour, movement, sound, smell and so much more. Tropical Durban was mostly warm. Not many of us owned cars or even bicycles, hence people were always out and about walking everywhere. Old men would be seen toiling in their modest vegetable gardens, women hanging out washing on make-shift clothes lines - bright patterned saris and skirts, people exchanging news with curious neighbours over their common boundary fences, children engaged in excited street play (hop-scotch, marbles, or gully-thunda – an improvised village cricket), itinerant vendors peddling clothes or kitchenware from house to house and, of course, dogs of all shapes, colours and sizes indulging their barking skills all day and night. Any moving shape or shadow was worth a barking frenzy. On weekends there was bound to be traditional music emanating from someone's backyard – shrill singing accompanied by the tabla and harmonium. Ah, that could be a wedding or a religious event, I would speculate.

Much cooking occurred on woodfires, the enticing aroma of curries, especially chicken curry, drifting on the evening breeze. Since the community was closely knit, we were often invited to participate in the festivities. At dawn on Sundays, when most people were still asleep, I would hear the plaintive cry of a peacock rising heavenwards. I would have an immediate picture of the white-washed Cato

Manor temple on a hilltop across Second River where several peacocks roamed in a shaded mango grove.

Somehow it did not seem to matter much then that Cato Manor was impoverished, constrained by years of white imposed racial segregation. It was the encapsulated world of my childhood and youth. The only world I knew then, a world of senses which seeped into my consciousness transforming me in subtle ways, turning me into the man I have become. It took me a long while to understand, to realise that there was another world just over the horizon.

Certainly, my immediate family-life contributed much to my identity, influencing my values, habits of mind, looks and preferences. To this day, I fancy cooking curries the way my mother did. I can still conjure up the image of her deftly removing from the oven of her sturdy black coal stove a fresh-baked oval-shaped bread. The distinct yeasty aroma was irresistible.

Now almost eighty years on, I realise that the dividing line between reality and memory, between memory and imagination may be rather tenuous. As I write, the textured tapestry of the 1940s and '50s Cato Manor unfold in my mind's eye.

I spot a stork or two dropping, long legs extended, onto a patch of fresh-ploughed field. One moves its neck snake-like and strikes, catching a cricket. Its companion stands still on one leg like a Masai herdsman. It was common knowledge that these precious white birds migrated each summer all the way from Holland where they built their nests of straw near chimney pots. I have not seen a single stork since those early years. There were also the brown long tailed birds (we called slazis) which often beat us to a ripened pawpaw, creating gaping holes. This silly bird, so engrossed making a meal of the fruit, would often be oblivious of us wicked boys creeping up with catapults. What a 'pot shot' it made! The myna birds, I recall, were prolific and noisy. It did not please me that they were called *Indian* mynas since it seemed to demean the image of the Indian.

Slender pawpaw trees grew in most back gardens. Indian South Africans loved growing fruit trees anywhere on their modest allotments – front, back or sides of their houses. It was almost second nature for us to know the more common fruit trees by name: mango, guava, avocado, lemon, banana. Jackfruit trees were huge, and so were the fruit whose outer casing reminded me of an armadillo carapace. There was a jackfruit tree at my maternal grandparents' house in Aryan Road. Once, when I was there on a sleep-over, I was jolted in mid-sleep by a crashing sound in the backyard, like a large sack of potatoes falling off a vegetable delivery van. The mighty fall would split open the casing to reveal a feast of yellow fleshy segments. The sweetish smell of an overripe jackfruit was overpowering. Eating it was messy with our hands soon covered with a resin-like substance, which we would remove with cooking oil. It is most likely that most of the fruit here originated in India.

'What's so special about your fruit,' a fellow Australian neighbour once asked, 'I've bought and eaten local and imported avocados, paw paws, guavas and mangos often, and they've tasted just fine.' I protested with vehemence. 'No, no. Believe me. The fruits grown in Durban are totally different and much tastier.' Of course, my friend simply humoured me. 'Yeh, yeh, too right.' He would probably never claim to have seen or heard of mutton goolas (Natal Plum) – a dense shrub with vicious thorns that produced glorious reddish pink fruit. For some reason, the ripest fruit would be enticingly out of reach, ensconced in the thorny dark and glossy foliage. You would almost hear it teasing, 'Come get me - if you can.'

Summers were always hot and sticky. Very tropical. As a teenager, I always worried my armpits smelt. Of an afternoon at school or at a soccer match, I would glance repeatedly at the darkening sky, growing ever more anxious of being caught in a lightning storm as I ran home This wasn't needless fretting, but fear born of a traumatic experience. I recall once, when I would have been about twelve, running home *shit-scared* (as the expression goes), all the way from the football field next to the Cato Manor cemetery as lightening cracked its vicious whip all about me. I cried and whimpered 'Arjuna, Arjuna, Arjuna,' pleading to the Indian god of thunder to be merciful and spare me. My mother, wide-eyed, opened the front door against the determined wind. I fell into her embrace drenched and numb with terror.

After a brief storm, the world would appear steamy and refreshed. The afternoon sun would reassert itself. Rain birds (swallows) would be out in force crisscrossing the sky deftly devouring *eisels* (flying ants) in mid-air, as wave after wave of these insects flapped their wings in a desperate attempt to escape the onslaught. They had shed their wings and fallen to the ground hoping to scurry into a dark place, but only to be devoured by waiting predators like frogs and lizards.

The names of many common flowering plants and

shrubs of my early years are etched in my memory, infused with the all too familiar landscapes of home. On my way to the bus stop or school, I would spot clumps of colourful flowering trees and bushes - poinsettia, pride of India, hibiscus, and bougainvillea with their flower-spangled arms reaching over fences. Vacant lots and untended back yards would be thick with bush, briars and creepers all gone wild and carefree. The purple blue morning glory would cover bush and shrubs with indiscriminate glee. Just about visible under this cover, would be the fleshy leaves of sisal with spikes at the pointy ends, and dusky broad-leafed bush tobacco. I also came to recognize the *kaffir boom,* a tree native to this area. It had a sparse leaf-cover but made up with bunches of attractive small trumpet-shaped orange-red flowers. I had seen cows rub themselves against the trunk of the kaffir boom as the bark was coarser than elephant hide.

People were generally a little wary of the elegant oleander shrub with pink and white flowers. Children were warned that these were haunted trees. I had seen many at the Cato Manor cemetery and crematorium, where my mother years later would be buried (and soon forgotten by family, including me). Perhaps the oleander flourish here because of the deep red earth fertilized by the countless burials of garden-loving, *green-fingered* Indians. I later learnt that all parts of the tree were toxic, and people ingesting the leaves or flowers were known to become deranged. Yet resourceful wayward boys discovered that the branches of the oleander provided the sturdiest Y-shaped handles for catapults.

The syringa was quite common. Always seen laden with perfumed bloom or full of yellow berries bunched like grapes. The bitter leaves were considered by my family to have medicinal properties. I have a vivid picture of grandmother repeatedly smearing a yellow wet paste of syringa leaves and turmeric on the entire body of Uncle Sunny (my mother's younger brother) when, soon after returning from war in Egypt, he came down with a most virulent form of measles. We cried believing he would soon die as doctors couldn't do much for him. But in a fortnight of treatment with grandmother's powerful potion, my uncle began to stir. The turmeric and syringa paste fell off his body like parchment, revealing healthy healing skin. Uncle lived a long life but turned out to be the most surly and mean-spirited person I had ever known. Could it have been the unavoidable side-effect of grandmother's miracle paste?

Greater Durban is mostly a landscape of hills and river valleys. But in the Cato Manor of my childhood, there were also treacherous gravel roads hemmed by drains and *dongas* (gullies formed by heavy rain). I recall occasions of disastrous floods when even minor streams came down in spate washing away people, houses, pets, and gardens. When the water flowed over the concrete bridge across the Cato Manor River, boys would play *dare* by wading through shin-deep water, dangling school shoes in their hands. Auntie, my mother's sister, would have me firmly by the hand as we stood on a ridge overlooking the bridge. 'Arreh,' she would exclaim with fingers on her lip, 'look at the boys. They've no sense doing a risky thing like that.'

The Cato Manor River skirted Bellair Road, the main road for traffic from town. Rickety buses owned by relatively wealthy Indian entrepreneurs, plied this road. The buses were painted in garish primary colours, and had flamboyant names embossed on the sides and rear. One such inspired name was *Kunthi's Dream* (Kunthi I'd guess was the name of the bus owner's wife or daughter, or less likely the mother, and even less likely a favourite grandmother).

The hurtling buses and cars would make a momentary squelching noise as they sped by the all-and-sundry CN Rana's Shop, reducing to pulp and string the sisal leaves strewn on the road on purpose by the ingenious workers of the store. Once shredded and dry, the lengths of sisal fibre were collected and used as rope to tie up small bundles of firewood for sale.

Pedestrians on the way to CN Rana's were wary when walking this stretch of Bellair Road. Many a time, from my grandparents' wood and iron house I'd see people screaming and scattering. I would laugh thinking it rather funny, but my irate Grandfather pinched my ear one day. 'It's funny, eh? Wait till a bee stings you, my boy. Now go inside before I whack you.' Only later was I told bees nested in the cliff-face along Bellair Road. In periodic fits of rage, they would attack innocent passers-by. Thereafter, whenever my eyes strayed to the cliff-face, I would imagine spotting swarms taking off to wage war on people - especially market gardeners for indiscriminate clearing and burning of their habitats of wildflower.

Burning rubbish and garden clearings were quite common. Patches of mealie stalks were to be seen long after harvest time paper-dry and spent, waiting to be cut down and disposed of. I can remember plumes of grey acrid smoke rising into the late autumn sky, swaying, and drifting in the gentle breeze.

At about the age of ten, I moved with my family to a house of our own nearby in Mayville. Ronnie Govender's sketch map in his book *At the Edge and other Cato Manor Stories* (1996), shows Mayville as just a newer part of Cato Manor. A brisk walk of about fifty minutes would get my father from our new house in Mayville to the previous rented one in Cato Manor. But the landscape in which I now moved and breathed seemed subtly different. Of course, I was a little older and more aware of my surroundings and allowed to venture out and explore with minimal supervision. When sent to buy the daily loaf of Baker's bread and a bottle of Clover Dairy milk, proved the ideal opportunity to wander. 'Why so late again, eh?' my mother would admonish. 'Just to Udyian's so long time, eh? Wait till your father comes home.'

Often, when seated at the table in the dining room doing homework, I would allow my eyes to stray through the open door, to scan the already familiar landscape in the near distance: Bellair Road with frantic traffic going both ways, and Mayville Theatre, where I had seen many a cowboy movie immediately after school, unbeknown to my parents. Eightpence, was what I would pay to enter. The land behind the cinema rose to a respectable hill covered in grass and thicket. That is where we would go on our secret picnics, two or three special classmates and I. We would pool what little pocket money we had to buy half a loaf of brown (whole meal) bread, a tin of Glenrych pilchards in tomato sauce, and an onion. What a memorable picnic feast that made. My fingers would smell of tinned fish and onions long after I returned home – which was always a give-away worry.

We lived on the slopes of a hill in Mayville, crowded with ramshackle houses of Indian families. It descended into a valley along which ran Standard Road, following the course of a shallow sickly stream. My house sat in the middle of a grid of roads forming a rectangle – Standard Road at the bottom, Jansen's Avenue on the top, and Rathlin and Droma Roads on either side. A network of other roads stretched out on all sides from these four roads. Familiar landmarks that dotted across the network became signposts by which we navigated or gave others direction much like how songs embedded with markers of landscape served the indigenous peoples in the Australian outback. This was our grounded territory, our internalised landscape which defined the immediate lives of the people of Cato Manor.

When Indian families were evicted from Cato Manor to make way for Whites under Apartheid, this familiar cultural landscape was systematically obliterated. Families and immediate neighbours were scattered, shunted to undeveloped fringes of Durban. My family settled in Reservoir Hills, hilly rock-strewn and mostly yellow clay. It sat above the Umgeni River which flowed across a fertile valley, Springfield Flats. This river entered the sea at Blue Lagoon, a popular fishing spot, and not too far from where the frantic sardine shoals beached themselves annually. Poorer Indians developed thriving market gardens along the riverbanks. A cluster of shacks sprang up nearby with the euphemistic name Tin Town which was subject to regular flooding whenever the Umgeni River broke its banks.

I got to know new Indian neighbourhoods along the Umgeni River such as Sea Cow Lake, Newlands and Parlock. It was surprising how rapidly these areas acquired an intangible Indianness about them, almost as if the distinct smell of curry clung to the landscape.

The designated areas for black South Africans in this part of Durban such as Clermont and KwaMashu were far removed and largely remote and invisible from where Indians lived.

All this once seemingly solid terrain is now transformed – parts quite unrecognisable to me. The reality is that landscapes are not static. They are ever changing, becoming something else. And simultaneously re-imagined. Every moment in Cato Manor, it seems, was for me a passage of no return. Erased by time, relentless forces of change, politics, poverty, and population growth. It exists now only as a mindscape relegated to memory and captured in the imagined hand-sketched map of Ronnie Govender.

But there is one landmark of my childhood that has endured looming large above the waters of the bay – the Durban Bluff. It was certainly there when I returned by sea on 5 September 1969 from India after a few years of self-imposed absence abroad. I could not rejoice then in seeing it once more, brooding under a dark overcast sky. Far from rejoicing, I felt a foreboding not knowing what fearful challenges Apartheid had in store for me.

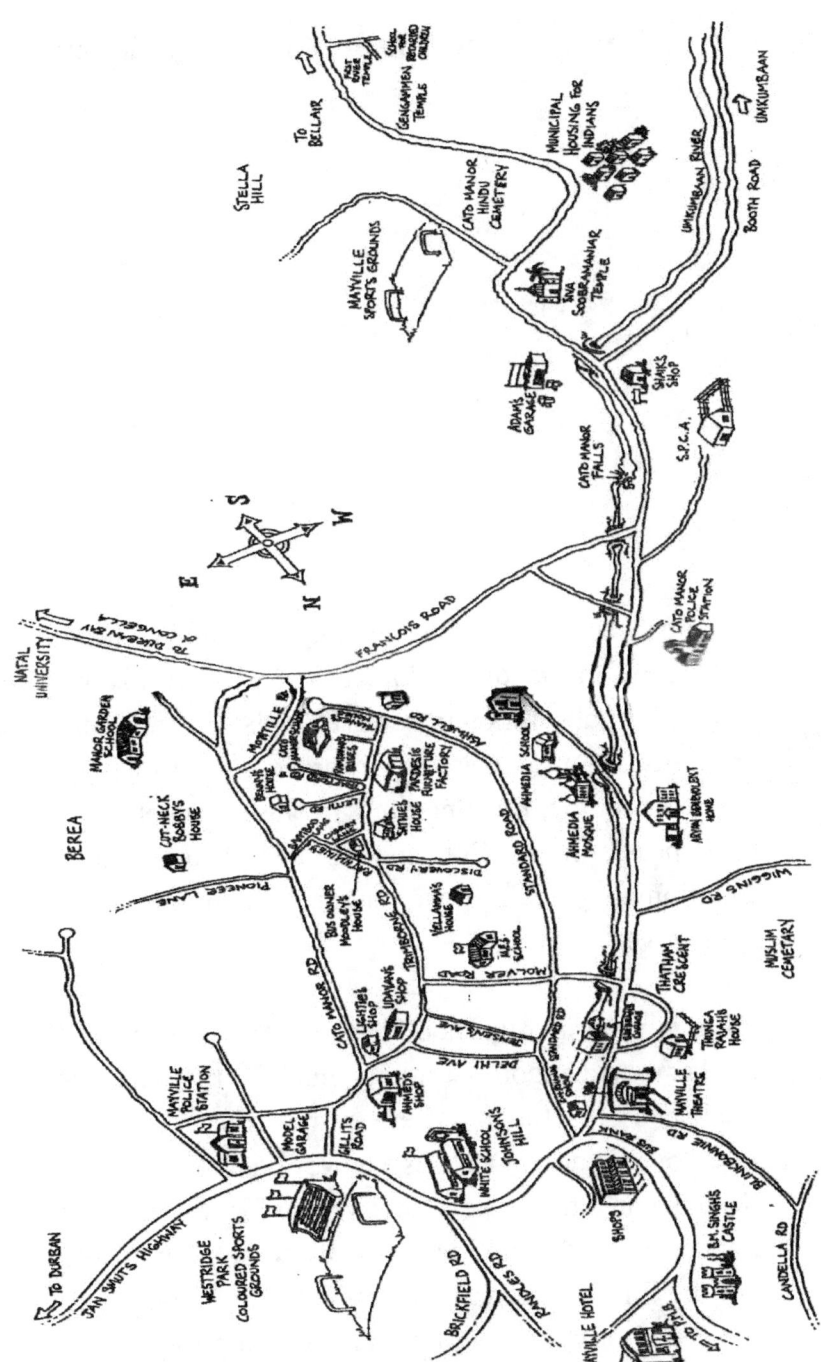

Ronnie Govinder's Map of Cato Manor

A Life Lived in South African Books and Writing

As much as my evolving identity was embedded in and shaped by the landscape of my early years, my growing interest and absorption in books also played a formative role in nurturing my expanding awareness of myself and the world about me. Reading drew me into alternative realities and possibilities. Got me thinking, comparing, and questioning. Feeding my imagination, introducing me to time travel.

~

During my primary school years (1946-54), the only story books we had at home were my mother's two Tamil readers published in India. They were slim volumes with discoloured pages. One was a book of devotional songs, and the other an introductory Tamil reader for children. This was not unusual at the time as few in my community would have had the financial means to invest in books. In any case, I had not even heard of such places as bookshops or libraries.

I was quite surprised to learn one day that there was a

public library in Durban. We were on a class outing to the Durban Museum when the library was pointed out to us. It was located on a floor below the Museum, both housed in the old and distinguished Victorian-era City Hall. But this library was for the exclusive use of Europeans. A 'Whites Only' sign at the entrance warned us to take note. By now, most of us kids were quite accustomed to seeing such signs and understood their meaning.

Around 1950, the all-white Durban City Council, under pressure from non-white ratepayers, established the segregated Brook Street Library for non-whites in the town centre close to busy markets and bustling bus ranks. A longish unused railway shed, not too far from the Berea Station, was converted to serve this purpose. It would take me about forty minutes to get to the library by bus from Cato Manor where we lived.

I was about thirteen years old when my father enrolled me as a member, but only after I had pestered my mother for weeks. I felt overjoyed and special while holding my borrower's card, knowing that none in my family seemed interested in reading, apart from the daily evening paper. I cannot recall any of my neighbours or school friends borrowing books either. I visited the library on Saturday mornings after my father and I had done the shopping. I would make sure to carry my library book in my hand for everyone to see. My pride as a reader knew no bounds.

Although I continued to be an avid reader into my youth, I have little recollection of what captured my fancy at that time – romance, boys' adventures, crime? I do, however, recall becoming immersed in comics especially Superman, Batman & Robin, American war comics obsessing about the yellow peril (China) and, much later, Classic Comics which featured stories of novelists like Mark Twain, Charles Dickens, and Jules Verne. These I bought by penny-pinching whenever I was sent to the corner Tea Room for bread, milk, and newspapers.

Late into my high school years, I stumbled upon English stories set in South Africa, distinguishing these from foreign ones such as Shakespeare, Dickens and the like introduced to us in school.

Some books from my youth and early adulthood have left lasting impressions, books that would likely have fed my imagination and influenced how I saw the world.

A few discoloured and tattered books still sit snugly on the top-most shelf in my study in Melbourne as clues to my early reading choices. My attachment to them is pure sentiment. These books have travelled with me whenever my family moved. Eventually they *migrated* with me to Australia.

To start with, there are two books once considered classics in South Africa. Whether they still hold this venerated appeal, I have no idea.

The first is Percy Fitzpatrick's *Jock of the Bushveld* published in 1907. It is a story of a bull terrier and his owner, a transport rider in the early gold rush days in South Africa. I recall, as a teenager still in shorts, finding a quiet corner of the house to hide from family and, undisturbed, pour over the gripping adventures of Jock, a bold and plucky little dog, his coat the colour of burnished gold. Over the course of the story, Jock survived several dangerous encounters. However, his luck ran out one evening when he was set upon by marauding dogs as he stood his ground protecting his master's chicken coop.

I was simply distraught when the novel ended with Jock being found fatally wounded. The image conjured up in my mind was too painful and traumatic. Jock died cradled in his master's arms as the first miraculous life-affirming sunlight broke over the *veld*, the expansive grassland of the high country. And such finality in the concluding sentence. *Jock had done his duty.* I sobbed, too distressed (and naive) to accept the reality of death. Why, oh why did Jock have to die? The world was a most cruel place if goodness could perish in this way. I sulked over many days to the puzzled concern of my mother.

The last pencil sketch in the book was of Jock trotting happily along a dirt track, into the soft glow of an autumn sunset.

~

The second book is Herman Charles Bosman's collection *Mafeking Road and Other Stories* (1981*)*. The stories of Bosman captivated me after I attended a stage reading. The reader was Patrick Mynhardt, an accomplished actor, who had mastered Bosman's stories. He was large and sturdy, wore a beard, and had a bemused face with a perpetual twinkle in his eyes. This was how Mynhardt chose to portray the narrator of Bosman's stories, Oom Schalk Lourens, a wily rustic character who had a sharp eye and a wry ironic insight into his community. Mynhardt's voice was a sonorous rumble like distant thunder.

Of course, I assumed that the persona of the actor on stage was one and the same as the narrator created by Bosman. A bearded, wise old Dutch farmer sitting on a stool at a cosy fireplace in the kitchen, smoking a pipe and weaving all these whimsical stories in his head to amuse and confound his listeners.

The backdrop of *Mafeking Road* is the remote Groot Marico, a rural Afrikaner village (dorp) in the northern bushlands of the Transvaal, where marauding wild animals were still to be found. It was a time when the Boers were warring with both the British (Roineks) and local indigenous stribes referred to as *Kaffirs* at that time. Horses and carts were the means of transport. The Boer community were mostly illiterate, poor, god-fearing racists. Hence, for me Bosman painted a picture of a world both intriguing and very foreign, much like the setting of fairy tales. Stories that unfolded with a dream-like quality and often quite funny. Oom Schalk Lourens entertained his listeners in foolish, weird, or eccentric tales, making them sound convincing, true to rural life. Like fables, these stories conveyed a moral.

As a young avid reader, it did not seem to matter to me that the stories were about Afrikaners, white people who disliked us. This thought may have come to me much later. But the truth is that even to this day I enjoy Bosman's writing as literature that is authentic and original, of a bygone era. And they are not unlike the stories of early Australian writers such as Henry Lawson and Banjo Paterson.

My political awakening happened gradually as I moved from high school years (1955-58) into university life. I discovered and became drawn to books, fiction, and non-fiction, with themes of race, colour, and political oppression. By now I was becoming aware of the political and racial tensions all around me, the hardships suffered by the oppressed in South Africa, and personally felt the bitter taste of abuse. I began to be angered and roused by daily harsh actions of the all-white government and the police. It soon dawned upon me that I was not just an Indian but part of a larger non-white population. I had no choice but to attend a non-white university. There was a subtle shift in the books I began reading.

One of the books from this era that is still in my collection is *Olive Schreiner's Story of an African Farm* (2008). The backdrop was a rugged, wind-swept part of South Africa called the Eastern Cape. The story took place in colonial times during the reign of Queen Victoria. A sparse and unrelenting rural landscape accentuated the prevailing themes of impoverishment, racial discrimination, and exploitation of women. Olive Schreiner was a free spirit and a suffragette. A woman ahead of her time.

This autobiographical novel, first published in 1883, was an easy read. However, I am almost certain that the subtleties of the themes would have eluded me as a non-white teenager growing up under Apartheid. What resonated and has remained with me all these years are a few fragmentary images. One was of the protagonist, Waldo, worn out by age, loneliness, and poverty squatting on his haunches in the warmth of the morning sun, his arms folded and resting on his knees. He was so motionless that a chicken, pecking at the dry earth, pecked at his boots without the least fear. They knew better. Waldo, the stoic man had finally departed, leaving behind an unfulfilled life of desolation and pain. Here again, the finality of death was what haunted me long after I had shut the book. The irony, however, was that in identifying with Waldo and his stoic suffering, I had really thought I was investing my compassion on an oppressed and dispossessed black man – or at least a person of mixed parentage (Coloured). Now belatedly, I have discovered that Waldo was in fact of German descent.

I am not exactly sure how I stumbled upon Peter Abraham, a gifted South African writer of coloured background. It could have been in my high school years when I perhaps became a more discerning user of the Brook Street Library, and when I was becoming increasingly aware of the politics of the time. It is likely, too, that the tantalizing titles of Abraham's books caught my attention: *Tell Freedom, Return to Goli, Dark Testament, Mine Boy, A Wreath to Udomo, The Path of Thunder, Wild Conquest*.

Reading *Mine Boy* (1954) opened my eyes, in a disturbing and telling way, to the plight and suffering of ordinary, impoverished Blacks. It affected me more profoundly than when I had seen black people harassed by police not too far from the Brook Street Library. Abraham's relatively short simply written novel speaks of the exploited and soulless life of a black migrant worker who leaves his family behind in some distant rural village to work in the gold mines on the Witwatersrand. He suffers great indignity living in a congested filthy dormitory with countless other black men, his bed as his only personal space.

I realise now that Peter Abraham was the very first non-white writer to come my way, and his books were profoundly absorbing. It was not like I could simply close *Mine Boy* with its emotional impact dissipating as I moved onto another good book.

Alan Paton's *Cry the Beloved Country*, published in 1948, became an internationally acclaimed classic. The theme of the novel was the corrosive tensions existing between rural and urban lives, effectively between black and white communities in South Africa. This was a time when the unwelcome impact of a white-driven moneyed economy caused traditional rural family life to unravel. Young disaffected black men resorted to crime as the surest way to get their share of conspicuous material wealth. Paton's story explored the profound and painful repercussions when a black youth from a strong Christian background murdered a young white man whose parents too were ardent Christians. It was not just any white man, but a passionate liberal who was on a mission to fight for the social betterment of Blacks. Nowadays, Blacks would feel strongly against this theme as being no more than blatant old-fashioned white Christian patronage – the view that the interests of poor Blacks could best be represented by *liberal* Whites. In the story the murderer was repentant, seeking forgiveness, and was redeemed.

I recall the evocative landscape with which the novel opens, deliberately casting into relief the appalling crime. We read passages of the book in high school, and I recall how Paton used lyrical writing to accentuate the pathos of the story.

Paton was often in the news and I attended political meetings where he spoke as the founder and leader of the South African Liberal Party. He was a short stocky man, with a strong jaw line and a fierce clipped manner of speaking. He would stare at the audience with his piercing eyes from over his glasses that hung low on his nose. He may have been himself a passionate Christian.

Fifty years on, in 1998, Sindiwe Magona, an

accomplished black female writer, had her novel *Mother to Mother* published. Ever since, it has been a prescribed reader in high schools. I came upon it when I visited South Africa in 2018. What amazed me was how closely Magona's story and theme resembled Alan Paton's book. Here, a black mother discovers her son has joined a mob of black youth who set upon a young unsuspecting white girl, a foreign student, when she strayed into their township to drop off a fellow black student. She was bludgeoned to death in a frenzy of anti-white rage. The distraught mother of the boy reached out to the traumatized mother of the murdered girl pleading for her to understand how generations of living under colonial-era discrimination followed by Apartheid had fractured black family life and had virtually eroded the capacity of parents to rear and nurture children. Consequently, boys in the black ghettos had become brutalized, developing a vengeful hatred of Whites. While the mother of the boy pleaded to high heaven for her son's forgiveness, she resigned herself to the reality of crime and punishment. Her sorrow for the mother of the murdered girl ran deep, yet not even an ocean of grieving could set things right. I had the sense that the gods were either not listening or felt powerless in the face of man's inherent inhumanity to man. The stuff of an ancient Greek tragedy.

My interest in theatre initially arose from my 3-year study of speech and drama at Natal University. This opened my eyes to how alive theatre was at the time, especially protest theatre, a vogue in the sixties and seventies. Here the focus was themes of political and social inequities under Apartheid. This was experimental theatre – at times quite amateurish and didactic – with little evidence of the subtleties of stage craft. I kept an eye on what was being staged, where, who the producer was and the performers. And I attempted to attend as many performances as possible. My interest in protest–theatre related to my involvement at the time in struggle-politics. For a time, an added incentive was a commission I had from the Graphic (Indian) weekly to write short theatre reviews. I was usually given two free tickets to shows. Transport to the venues in the city and back home at night was a perennial challenge.

~

The playwright, Athol Fugard, together with his two leading black male actors, Winston Ntshona and John Kani, became all too familiar. Although they based themselves mostly at the now famous Market Theatre in Johannesburg, their shows invariably staged in Durban as well. These three, in their self-effacing humble appearance, were to me so much alike. They were near middle-age, short and stocky, and every bit working class. Their plays confronted issues of social inequality and racial oppression as experienced by the dispossessed masses. They were mostly staged in fringe venues accessible to non-whites. However, the performances were equally well supported and acclaimed by affluent and educated liberal Whites and the English-language press. Of course, the shows also received close attention from the security police.

The titles of three of Fugard's plays are etched in my mind as they depicted in vivid images and anguished voices the fractured lives of impoverished and dispossessed people in South Africa under Apartheid. Themes of compassion and humanity are central in *Sizwe Banzi is Dead, Blood Knot, and Boesman and Lena*. I regret not possessing copies of these plays.

I also recall seeing the movie *Tsotsi* based on Fugards's 2006 novel of the same name. Yet again the agonizing theme differed only slightly from that of Paton and Mangona in their novels. 'See,' Fugard seems to be saying, 'the pernicious harm Apartheid has wrought upon black youth, turning them into vicious mindless thugs who spare no one, not even their own kind.'

Besides these authors, I also became familiar with works of South African Indian playwrights Kessi Govender, Ronnie Govender and Strini Moodley. Kessie founded the Stable Theatre in Durban where he staged protest plays such as *Working-class Hero* and *the Shack*. Ronnie's plays had a more satirical edge to them. As I recall, the plays were commentaries on the political machinations, affiliations, and tensions in the Indian community. The audience at these performances was predominantly Indian. For me, his collection of short stories (*At the Edge and Other Cato Manor Stories,* 1996) had a greater appeal. They related to a life familiar to me and as lived by Indians in Cato Manor in the fifties, before they were uprooted under the Group Areas Act. The stories brought alive the world I'd known intimately. As a young boy, Cato Manor was my home ground. *At the Edge* has been performed on stage at several international theatre festivals to much acclaim.

However, Strini Moodley was relatively more confrontational as he actively adopted theatre to advance the ideology of Black Consciousness, very current at the time. I have a vivid mental picture of him on stage – tall, dark, and strident. He would be joined in his plays by notable others such as Asha Rambally, Saths Cooper and Sam Moodley. It is a pity I can't seem to recall the titles of plays they wrote, adapted or improvised. They also engaged in protest verse and narrative monologues which encouraged the audience to be resolute in resisting oppression and being self-reliant as Blacks. Community theatre in its essence. The exhortations would be explicit, defiant, and uncompromising, even though the players were aware of the likely presence of security police in the audience taking note of every gesture and utterance. Strini was charged and sentenced for treason and served five years on Robben Island as a political prisoner with Mandela and other struggle stalwarts.

I'd got to know Strini quite well as he was my contemporary, and our paths often crossed –notably because I was also at the time taken up with the Black Consciousness inspired South African Students Association (SASO) led by Steve Biko. Further, Strini's father was my boss when I was employed at Lakenhaven Children's Home.

Many books were banned under apartheid. The government's censorship board was overzealous in readily labelling what it disliked as communist propaganda and a threat to the state. At one time I heard that the classic children's novel *Black Beauty* by Anna Sewell was banned because of the word black in the title.

I recall the mixed feelings of fear and daring when I read and passed on banned books. I soon became skilled in furtive whispering and clandestine sharing of politically charged literature such as: *Soul on Ice* by Eldridge Cleaver (1968); The *Autobiography of Malcolm X* (1965); *The Fire Next Time* by James Baldwin (1963); *Mao's Red Book* (1964); *Time Longer than Rope* by Edward Roux (1948). On occasions, I stumbled upon copies of *Sechaba*, the magazine of the armed wing of the African National Congress in exile (published across the South African border). I knew that I would receive a very harsh sentence for possessing or transmitting so-called seditious literature. But this did not seem to deter me. Once when the security police raided my family home, it was my brother who had the presence of mind to throw two of my banned books out the bedroom window.

In the mid-1950s and into the '60s there was a renaissance of young black writer-journalists. I found them by way of the *Drum Magazine* and the related literary journal *The Classic*. I became intoxicated with such names as Can Themba, Nat Nakasa, Todd Matshikiza, Lewis Nkosi, Bloke Modisane and Casey Motsisi – the so-called 'Drum Boys.' They were talented in the use of English. It seems it was a time of rapid change, turmoil, and uncertainty – and excitement. They lived at the edge, drinking, womanizing, taking enormous risks in venturing out to report on crime, poverty, police brutality and so on, as if they had an instinctive sense that the charmed lives they led would not last. In my collection of valued pamphlets, magazines, and newspaper clippings of that heady period, I find just a single copy of *The Classic*. Within a decade, *Drum* lost its steam (after having become the most read magazine in Africa), the cream of the journalists and photographers had scattered. Nat Nakasa exiled himself to the USA, only to find isolation and the loss of home unbearable. He committed suicide by jumping from a high-rise apartment in New York in 1965 at the age of 28. He had been the first editor of *The Classic* magazine.

The Heinemann African Writers Series burst upon the literary world in 1962 with Chinua Achebe as the founding editor. Within a few years, there were almost a hundred titles published of quality and original African writing. Some of the South African writers on this list were Dennis Brutus, Alex La Guma, Nelson Mandela and Can Temba. The distinct orange and white cover with black print caught my attention like a magnet whenever I visited the library or grazed in a bookshop. Of course, the very first book I read in this series was Achebe's now classic *Things Fall Apart* (1958).

My deep interest in South African literature has continued to this day. If anything, I feel I have become more discerning and selective of what I read. I am conscious of the limited hours remaining in my twilight years. However, Damon Galgut continues to be one of my favourite novelists.

Sadly, here in Australia I feel cut-off and isolated from the on-the-ground vibrancy of the literary buzz in South Africa. At the same time, I am quite uninformed of the lay readership in South Africa who may be reminiscing about the writing world that I had lived through. Would there be many who continue to marvel at all the inspirational writers who had gone before, celebrate the literature that captured life as it was then, particularly for the oppressed and dispossessed masses? Or was this interest relegated to academia?

I concede, too, I retain in my mind little of the substance of that literature. There is a subdued thrill in recognizing and roll-calling the names of these writers even as they inevitably vanish into the gloom of dusk. I wish I had the time and energy to revisit this literature if only to remind me of the crazy impassioned world in which they lived, loved, and captured in such imaginative writing. But that's no more than wishful sentiment. Even the thoughts I record here and share with you have a dubious and limited shelf life. All is of equal value - all grist to the mill. As Marcel Proust, a renowned French writer of the nineteenth century, muses: 'No doubt my books too, like my fleshy being, would in the end one day die....... A self in me deplores the loss of these treasures, (but) then I perceive that memory, as it withdraws from me, carries away with it this self too.' (*In Search of Lost Time,* 1996)

~

Looking back now there is no doubt in my mind that books and reading enabled me to learn about South Africans who existed beyond my narrow ethnic horizon, to know them as people not unlike me and my family. They, too, in various ways experienced a mix of joys and struggle, loss and perhaps lasting pain. And there was endurance, too, through sheer courage. This I found uplifting. In such moments, I felt one with them, forgetting barriers of race, colour, or creed. My pukka *Indianness* may have begun dissolving then, in favour of a *South Africanness*.

~

The opportunity to read widely also raised my political awareness, accentuated my sense of disadvantage, and got me thinking about what would make for a better country, and ways in which disaffected people could aspire to transcend barriers imposed by racial prejudice and Apartheid.

About the Author

Bala Mudaly is an Indian South African, born in Durban in 1938. Chronic job insecurity and political harassment compelled him to migrate to Australia in 1988 with his wife.

He retired as a clinical psychologist from Monash Health in Melbourne in Dec 2018 at the age of 80.

His debut collection of poems and short stories set in Australia, *Colours of Hope and Despair*, was self-published in 2018 and is available on Kindle. He has also had a short story, *Self-Inflected Pain of the Writer's Kind*, published in the Victorian Writer, a quarterly writers' magazine. The author contributes short pieces to a fortnightly online publication of UKZN in Durban, the Creative Network Magazine. As an amateur writer, he has workshopped almost all his creative writings in a Writers Group sponsored by the City of Monash public library service. His memoir, *Colour-Coated Identity*, is his most ambitious creative non-fiction project.

Currently, the author is working on a novel with the tentative title: *Imperfect Lives*. Its theme is the challenges of friendships and family relationships in post-apartheid South Africa beyond the constraints of race and colour.

Contact Bala at: bala.mudaly@gmail.com

www.ingramcontent.com/pod-product-compliance
Lightning Source LLC
Chambersburg PA
CBHW050304010526
44107CB00055B/2104